China's Agrarian Transition

Challenges Facing
Chinese Political Development
Series Editor: Sujian Guo, Ph.D.
San Francisco State University

In an attempt to reflect the rapidly changing political environment of the People's Republic of China, editor Sujian Guo has assembled a book series to present specialized areas of research in current Chinese political studies. Incorporating theoretical, empirical, and policy research on contemporary Chinese politics both domestically and internationally, this series contemplates the Chinese past, present, and future by utilizing interdisciplinary perspectives to approach issues related to Chinese politics, economy, culture, social development, reform, the military, legal system, and foreign relations. Aimed at bringing a greater understanding of the current Chinese political climate to Western audiences, this series is focused on the emerging voices of Chinese scholars and their perspectives on the ever-changing Chinese diaspora.

Recent titles in the series are:

China's Agrarian Transition

Peasants, Property, and Politics

René Trappel

LEXINGTON BOOKS
Lanham • Boulder • New York • London

Published by Lexington Books
An imprint of The Rowman & Littlefield Publishing Group, Inc.
4501 Forbes Boulevard, Suite 200, Lanham, Maryland 20706
www.rowman.com

Unit A, Whitacre Mews, 26-34 Stannary Street, London SE11 4AB

British Library Cataloguing in Publication Information Available

Library of Congress Cataloging-in-Publication Data

Trappel, René, author.
China's agrarian transition : peasants, property, and politics / René Trappel.
pages cm. — (Challenges facing Chinese political development)
Includes bibliographical references and index.
ISBN 978-0-7391-9936-7 (hardcover : alk. paper) — ISBN 978-0-7391-9937-4 (ebook)
1. Agriculture and state—China. 2. Land reform—China. 3. Land tenure—China. 4. Capitalism—China. I. Title.
HD2098.T75 2016
338.10951—dc23
2015031659

Printed in the United States of America

Contents

Measures and Transliterations

Mu   1/15 of a hectare or 1/6 of an acre

RMB   Renminbi, Chinese currency (1 RMB = 0.13€ in May 2013)

Jin   1 catty, 0.5 kg

Huanggu Standard rice variety used to calculate land compensation and land rental prices.

The Hanyu Pinyin system is used to transliterate Chinese characters. All quotes provided have been translated into English. Transcriptions of the interviews in Chinese are available for reference. For ambiguous or relevant terms and statements, the English translation and Pinyin have been provided.

Preface

In early 2008, I found myself wandering around in Qionglai, a city near Chengdu, talking to villagers and cadres about the importance of land, the difficulties of farming, and a new local project that promised villagers social insurance in exchange for their land usage rights. This was the first time I heard about "land transfer" (*tudi liuzhuan*) and that it had become a major trend. Intrigued but without time to do more interviews, I put the topic aside for a while. Later that year, I started a new position at the Chair of East Asian Politics at the University of Duisburg-Essen in a research project dealing with strategic agency of leading local cadres in the countryside. During our first fieldwork a new government program, "Building of a New Socialist Countryside," was taking off in rural China and almost everyone we met wanted to talk about the transformation of agriculture and land transfer, which sounded like a complete departure from long-standing structures in the countryside. This was when the idea of my dissertation and, consequently, this book was born.

Writing this book has been a great journey—at times an excursion to some of the most interesting parts of rural China, occasionally an odyssey through theories and deadlines but mostly a very humbling and fascinating experience. This project would not have been possible without support from the German Research Foundation (DFG) and the German Federal Ministry of Education, who funded my position at the Chair of East Asian Politics and the research trips to China, for which I am very thankful.

My interest in the Chinese countryside was sparked when I took part in a student research project in the Cold Mountains (*Liangshan*) in Sichuan. This project was organized by Prof. Thomas Heberer, to whom I am forever in debt for the things he has taught me about China and life in general. As my PhD supervisor, he provided me with loyal support, freedom to pursue my interests, and guidance whenever needed. Our joint fieldwork in Sichuan, Shandong, and Guizhou has been an outstanding experience for me.

I also thank my co-supervisor, professor Gunter Schubert, for the opportunity to begin my work on rural China at his Chair in Tübingen and for his thoughtful feedback over the years; Dr. Peter Paulenz, Dr. Jürgen Steiger, and Eva-Maria Werner at the Deutsche Gesellschaft für Internationale Zusammenarbeit (GIZ, formerly GTZ) for the opportunity to take part in the Great Western Development Conferences, for the funding of my trips to Qinghai and Qionglai and for their interest in me and my work; as well as the numerous helping hands during our fieldwork that ensured everything went as smoothly as possible. In particular, I would like to thank Dr. Liu Duo for his persistence in the interviews and our discussions. Without the help and friendship of our partners at the China Center for Comparative Politics and Economics in Beijing, especially Chen Xuelian, Dr. Yang Xuedong, and Dr. He Zengke, the research for this project would not have been possible.

Furthermore, I am greatly indebted to Prof. Christian Göbel and Prof. Björn Alpermann for their very helpful comments and suggestions on parts of the draft, sometimes on rather short notice, to Prof. John Donaldson, who is right about so much and gave invaluable feedback on early chapters of this book, to Dr. John Davenport for his hospitality and for the introduction to Qinghai, and to the members of the research network "Governance in China," who read and discussed several chapters during our annual network meetings.

At the INEAST, I would like to thank Harald Krähe for the excellent maps he prepared, Le Weijing and Patrick Prädikow for their assistance with the interviews and research materials, the DFG Research Training Group for its financial support and the "home office," and Cornelia Feldmann for more than a decade of moral and organizational support. Sharing the experience of writing a thesis with Susanne Löhr, Dr. Armin Müller, Dr. Kai Schulze, and the rest of the Research Training Group provided relief, inspiration, and support, often when needed most. I also thank everyone at Lexington—and especially Brian Hill—for their help in getting this book published.

I am especially indebted to Assoc. Prof. Linda Schmitt, my aunt, for going through the manuscript with the supportive eyes of a native speaker interested in language and to my uncle Stefan Schmitt for the many ways he helped in matters big and small. Finally, I am at a loss to find the words to express my gratitude to Maya, Jakob, and Merle, who suffered under the stress and uncertainties of this project at least as much as I did.

Abbreviations

AL   Agriculture Law

CPC   Communist Party of China

HI   Historical Institutionalism

HRS   Household Responsibility System

LAL   Land Administration Law

LCRL Law on the Contracting of Rural Land

OLVC Organic Law of the Village Committees

XNCJS "Building a New Socialist Countryside" (*Shehui zhuyi xin nongcun jianshe*)

ONE

Introduction

For the third time in less than a century, agriculture in China is experiencing tremendous structural changes. After the collectivization movement in the mid-1950s and the de-collectivization in the early 1980s, commercial and industrial agrarian production structures are now mushrooming everywhere in the countryside. Villages close to urban centers and regions with small amounts of farmland per family are spearheading a transition from small- and sub-scale peasant farming to commercial operations of scale.[1] New types of agrarian producers are appearing on stage, from small but specialized entrepreneurial farmers to new types of cooperatives and big agro-industrial conglomerates. As different as they may be in their internal structures, their motivation to engage in farming is the same: profit. Rural China, it appears, is experiencing an *agrarian transition*. In the words of Byres (1996, 27), these are structural transformations characterized by "those changes in the countryside of a poor country necessary to the overall development of capitalism and its ultimate dominance." This implies that in the long-run most non-monetary exchanges and services, a cornerstone of both traditional agrarian societies and the variant of socialist agriculture promoted at the beginning of the reforms in the 1980s, are being replaced by transactions quantified in monetary terms. Food is produced for sale and not primarily for direct consumption.

The magnitude of the current changes in China should not be underestimated. Yet, these developments in Chinese agriculture have received considerably less scholarly attention than the return to smallholder farming in the early 1980s. It is, after all, often a very quiet process of individual adjustment that takes place at the household level. While there are many conflicts in rural China, especially at the fringes of urban areas where the expansion of booming cities frequently clashes with the inter-

1

ests of villagers, the contemporary transformation of production structures does not feature prominently in these conflicts. Moving out of agriculture and making room for new producers instead includes both the
notion of a painful economic necessity and the promise of better welfare
for rural households struggling to secure their livelihoods.

This transformation of Chinese agriculture is taking place in spite of
the absence of a free market for farmland and with the fragments of a
socialist property regime. Instead of going through a privatization of
land as had occurred in the former socialist countries in Eastern Europe
and even in its regional neighbors Vietnam and Cambodia, China started
its transition with its own variant of collective ownership for farmland
still in place. The Chinese leadership decided in the early 1980s to distribute usage rights for plots of the collective farmland to villagers. These
usage rights, however, came with certain conditions that were detailed in
contracts. The resulting system, frequently called the *Household Responsibility System* (HRS), was the starting point of smallholder farming in
China and continues to exist to the present day. While it guarantees villagers long-term access to farmland, it severely limits their ability to trade
land or to use it as collateral for much-needed capital, nor can villagers
use the land for anything but farming-related activities. How could commercial agriculture emerge and thrive given these institutional constraints?

This book investigates the role of socialist property institutions in the
most recent transformation of Chinese agriculture. It tells the story of the
rise of new priorities within a changing political system, the role of socialist legacies for the economy, and in particular focuses on the reactions of
major actors in agriculture to the transformation of their political and
economic environment. The findings presented here suggest that the current agrarian transition in China is taking place not despite socialist property institutions but rather is enabled by them.

The sheer size of China and its great internal differences in economic
development and agricultural structure pose difficulties for all studies
based on investigative research. As a member of a collaborative research
project, I took part in three field trips to Shandong, Sichuan, and Guizhou
Provinces between 2008 and 2010.[2] The trips, twice to Laixi, a county-
level city in Shandong and Anju, a district under the jurisdiction of Suining City in Sichuan, as well as to Xifeng and Meitan County in Guizhou,
generated enormous amounts of data through interviews and the collection of relevant documents. Scholars at universities and party schools in
Beijing, Qingdao, Jinan, Chengdu, and Guiyang provided additional valuable information. Still, primarily using data from only four different
county-level locations of the over 4,000 total in China, this book certainly
cannot make any qualified statements on statistical trends of the Chinese
agrarian transition. The intention is a different one. With this book, I aim
to provide an integrated model of the transformation of Chinese agricul-

ture based on empirical findings for further discussion and testing. It should be noted that the main empirical data comes from locations that tend to have progressed more in their agrarian transition than other locations in China.

The case and topic were chosen keeping in mind the sensitivities in some policy fields in China. Agrarian transition does not belong to the more restricted sectors of the Chinese political system. In fact, governments on all levels as well as the national and local media and even the farmers themselves report with great pride on the achievements in this field and the steps it took to get there. Most of the relevant policies have been well-documented, leaving behind a giant paper trail of great value for any researcher.

The following sections of this introduction will discuss the concept of agrarian transition and the current scholarly debate on the framing of the Chinese transition. The introduction will conclude with a brief summary of the contents and structure of this book.

AGRARIAN TRANSITION AND
THE COMMODIFICATION OF FARMLAND

Transformations such as the one now taking place in China have long been at the focus of scholars influenced by the teachings of Marx and his political economy. This theoretic perspective distinguishes between different *paths of transition* from pre-capitalist to capitalist production—depending upon the unique configuration of a nation's political, economic and social system and the actions of core actors in the process (Byres 1996).

This book conceptualizes agrarian transition in a similar manner. In particular, the works of Robert Brenner (1985a) and Karl Polanyi (1997) inform its understanding of the transition process. Both of these scholars have based their framework upon the historic developments in England leading up to the emergence of the first capitalistic agriculture there. Brenner and Polanyi highlight the importance of a forced integration of peasants into competitive markets as a crucial first step. In consequence, peasants had to give up or reduce all agrarian activities that did not create a monetary surplus. Changes in the property system provided a solution for those farming households for which market risk had turned into market failure—it allowed for the transfer of the land to another producer. Finally, the involvement of the state (or ruling class) was necessary to create these competitive markets in the first place and to ease the access of capitalist farmers to the means of production.

The work of both authors does not stop there and especially Polanyi links agrarian capitalism to the emergence of capitalism in general and industrialization. These latter aspects of their respective theories are of lesser concern for this book. More relevant is their search for the preconditions of an agrarian transition. Polanyi points us to the importance of "fictitious" commodities in capitalism. These commodities—land, labor, and capital—are not produced in a material sense, yet they are the pillars of a capitalist society. Brenner, in turn, points to the leasehold system in England with a similar argument. The introduction of this system turned land into a more flexible asset for production and opened up the opportunity for capitalist investors to engage in agriculture, for the first time being able to access the means of production via capital only. Polanyi has called this process *commodification*.

In regard to one important aspect, however, the works of Brenner and Polanyi fall short. Their classification of the role of the state and its agents does not take into account the pro-active role these actors have taken in more recent transitions. The importance of state actors becomes especially evident in countries at the brink of an agrarian transition, in which they fail to play such a supportive role. Katherine Verdery, for example, describes how the dysfunctional nature of the Romanian political system facilitates the end of smallholder farming but at the same time also delays the transformation toward alternative and commercial structures in Transylvania (Verdery 2003). The title of her book, *Vanishing Hectare*, refers to a situation in which land is taken out of production because political and economic conditions turn all types of farming activities into a very risky and financially unattractive endeavor.

Recent contributions within the framework of *agrarian change* in the *Journal of Peasant Studies* and the *Journal of Agrarian Change* provide a more sophisticated characterization of the role of local and national states in agrarian transitions in modern nation-states. Borras Jr., for example, stresses:

> Taking politics seriously in rural development theory and practice offers a more dynamic, not static view of agrarian change. It is constant political struggles between different social classes and groups within the state and in society that largely determine the nature, scope, pace and direction of agrarian change (Borras Jr. 2009, 19).

In this book, politics are added as a third major contributing factor to agrarian transitions, in addition to property institutions and peasant differentiation as outlined by Brenner and Polanyi above.

The *commodification of farmland* is at the core object of the empirical interest of this book. This process has links to all other important aspects of agrarian transitions. Commodification offers an institutionalized way out of agriculture to smallholders who are struggling with or do not want to make a living in farming. It is based upon the existing property institutions and can take place only if the necessary legal institutions are in place. The nature of these legal institutions, as is the main assumption of this book, will have a great effect upon the nature of the commodification process and its beneficiaries. National and local states may restrict, delay, or promote the commodification in line with their general development agenda. Finally, the conditions of the commodification of land will make investment in agriculture more attractive for some investors than for others. The new structure of a commercial agriculture thereby becomes a function of this commodification of land. The main research question of this book, which is how the continued existence of collective land usage rights has affected the agrarian transition in China, plays out to a large degree in the commodification process.

Drawing on insights from *historical institutionalism*, I argue that the effects of the institutions governing the commodification of farmland could only be properly analyzed if the political, social, and historical context of these institutions is taken into account. The research design of this study is therefore based upon the *process tracing framework* as outlined by George and Bennett (2005). Both of these concepts are introduced in more detail in chapter 2.

FRAMING THE CHINESE AGRARIAN TRANSITION

China's agrarian transition is a highly contested topic. Although there is some difference within the empirical data presented in the literature, the true amount of disagreement becomes evident in the divergent perspectives on the role of smallholders and collective land. The following review of the existing debate attempts to map its important rifts. Organized in four sub-sections, it will discuss general accounts of the transition, the debate on how to frame the connection between land and people, the commodification of collective land, and the role of state interference for the future of agriculture.

A New Type of Agriculture

While there are few studies on the current transformation in Western academic literature, there are noteworthy exceptions. Among the first empirical investigations are two articles by Forrest Qian Zhang and John Donaldson, published in *The China Journal* (2008) and *Politics & Society* (2010). The articles are mainly based on fieldwork conducted in Shandong and Yunnan Province. Both portray the metamorphosis of the Chinese peasant and intensively theorize on the impact of land usage rights on the nature of the Chinese agrarian transition. Given the proximity of the topic and locations used for empirical data gathering, they offer a great opportunity for comparison.[3]

The article from 2008 argues that Deng Xiaoping's "two great leaps," outlined already in 1990, provided a "guiding vision for the central government's agricultural policies" (Zhang and Donaldson 2008, 29).

While the first leap was the HRS reform, the second is the scaling-up of production within the collective economy (Zhang and Donaldson 2008, 28). They refer to a central document from 2008 outlining the characteristics for this modernized agriculture. It should be "commercialized (*shangpin hua*), specialized (*zhuanye hua*), scaled up (*guimo hua*), standardized (*biaozhun hua*) and internationalized (*guoji hua*)" (Zhang and Donaldson 2008, 29). The primary tool for this should be *nongye chanyehua*, which they translate as *vertical integration* (ibid.).[4] Dragonhead enterprises are characterized as a centerpiece of vertical integration. These companies are described as a special category of agricultural conglomerates of a certain size (allowing for operations of scale), created to promote the industrialization of agriculture. They receive financial and political support by governments on various levels (Lingohr-Wolf 2011; see also Waldron, Brown, and Longworth 2006). Zhang and Donaldson cite a survey which mentions that already in 2004 114,000 Dragonheads existed, as compared to the 27,000 in 2000. The same survey stated that in 2004 about 84.5 million rural households were working for these companies (Zhang and Donaldson 2008, 30).

In the remaining part of the article the two authors look at the ongoing differentiation of peasants into five new categories, each describing a different kind of market integration of agrarian producers (Zhang and Donaldson 2008, 32). The first category consists of commercial farmers, who engage in agricultural production on their collective land primarily for profit (and not to satisfy their subsistence needs). Contract farmers form the second category. These farmers have procurement contracts with companies who also provide technical support. Zhang and Donaldson characterize the position of the farmers in this arrangement as one of dependence upon the company. The third category is that of the "semi-proletarian farm worker with Chinese characteristics." Here the enterprise rents land from the village collective. In order to ease the villagers into agreeing to these rental arrangements, the company offers to hire the former peasants as workers. The fourth category is that of semi-proletarian farm workers. In this form, the peasants have become employees of agricultural companies but continue to have land usage rights in their home villages. In this last category, peasants are only employees on a wage basis—without any land usage rights of their own.

The authors argue that the formation of these new arrangements in agrarian production in China is strongly linked to land usage rights. In the current design of land usage rights, they see an effective protective barrier for villagers against enclosure by agribusiness and therefore strongly oppose any drive to privatize farmland (Zhang and Donaldson 2008, 32). In fact, the protection of the land usage rights is so comprehensive that, according to their empirical data, companies interested in investing in new agricultural bases have had to rent previously unused wasteland in order to be able to start or expand their business (Zhang and Donaldson 2008, 44–45).

Their main argument in relation to agrarian capitalism is that its breakthrough in China came with the development of factor markets, especially with markets for land and labor (Zhang and Donaldson 2010, 463). According to the two authors, land rental markets have "developed rapidly" since the mid-1990s (Zhang and Donaldson 2010, 464). Most interesting for this book is their discussion of the HRS and the land usage rights. Zhang and Donaldson highlight the importance of the HRS in mediating the confrontation between capitalism and agriculture in rural China: "the institution that determines the distribution of land rights—in rural China's case, collective ownership and individualized use rights—constrains the form and extent of capitalism's penetration into agriculture, as well as the proletarianization of direct producers" and "[t]he entitlement-based land rights, on one hand, allow subsistence peasants to reject commoditization and resist capitalism; on the other hand, these rights also provide a base for commercial farmers—and contract farmers to a much less degree—to continue independent household production" (Zhang and Donaldson 2010, 481).

The work of Zhang and Donaldson is an important contribution to the discussion on the agrarian transition in China. Despite the value of these two articles, several issues remain. First, the sole concentration on the differentiation of the peasantry neglects to a certain degree the importance of newly emerging forms of primary agrarian production. For example, cooperatives are not adequately considered. Yet so-called specialized cooperatives (*zhuanye hezuoshe*) and its sub-type, the land transfer cooperatives (*tudi liuzhuan hezuoshe*), have become increasingly popular in rural China, as will be shown in later sections of this book. Second, their description of the land rental appears to be an unsatisfying simplification of the actual process. Land rental between a whole village and a company, the only rental practice described in their two articles, is just one variant among many. And even in this variant, a job guarantee to the land usage rights holders is not always a given. The structure of the rental market and its influence on the shape of China's new agriculture does not feature prominently in either article. Their argument of an early development of vibrant land rental markets in the mid-1990s should also be viewed with some skepticism. This author argues that instances of land rental arrangements beyond family, friends and relatives remained an exception, even for a long time into the new century. In fact, this is an important question for the discussion of the Chinese agrarian transition: why did land rentals only become popular at such a late point in time?

Zhang and Donaldson come forward with another interesting argument. Although privatization of land might offer a road to quicker mechanization of agricultural production, only the capitalist producer would realize these benefits and not the peasant. Even in its current fragmented

state of production the output of grain per unit of land is already close to
the output achieved in developed countries. If mechanization would increase, however, villagers could be displaced and land productivity may
decline "as a result of declining land-use intensity under mechanized
farming" (Zhang and Donaldson 2008, 45). This line of argumentation is
problematic on two accounts. First, even if it would be the case that
small-scale farming has similar levels of productivity, this argument ig-
nores the strategies smallholders chose in order to remain competitive.
To compete with operations of scale, they do not take into account their
labor costs—and hence become painfully frugal. More than a century ago
Karl Kautsky already pointed out the vicious nature of this development
(Banaji 1976, 26–28). Second, the argument of Zhang and Donaldson assumes that most if not all peasant producers want to continue farming as
long as possible. Although this may be true for a subset of the rural
population, many members of the younger generation do not see their
future in small-scale farming.

The biggest difference between the work of Zhang and Donaldson
and this book is the characterization of the HRS. At no point in their
analysis the issues villagers themselves have with the HRS were mentioned. In contrast, this book argues that for many rural households in
China land has become an obligation more than an asset, a trajectory
similar to the one discussed in Verdery (2004). Farming small plots without adequate skills and inputs has lost a lot of its financial attractiveness
for Chinese villagers, especially in the well-connected parts of rural China. It seems that only in the more remote and poorer areas or in locations
with some kind of specialized and profitable agriculture the main workforce still engages in smallholder farming. In rural regions close to urban
centers and those with a low per capita distribution of farmland, most
owners of land usage rights struggle with this asset and how to benefit
from it. This aspect may perhaps not feature prominently in their articles
because land rental or the transfer and consolidation of farmland is not a
central aspect of their analysis. For example, the position of farmers in
these rental markets is not discussed at all. Finally, the local state and its
role in the transformation of agriculture is completely left out in their
discussion. While the authors refer to some important national policy
guidelines, they do not take into account the role of provincial, county,
and township officials in shaping this new rural reality. Leading local
cadres, as this book aims to show, do play an important role in the creation and vitality of the market for land usage rights.

Despite these points, Zhang and Donaldson are the first to truly capture the fundamental change happening in the Chinese countryside today. They clearly see the current differentiation of the peasantry as a new
stage in Chinese agriculture. Their typology is a valuable tool for empirical testing. In particular, the category of contracted farming is getting

more and more attention in the current debate (Huang, Yuan, and Peng 2012; Zhang 2012).

A very different picture of the Chinese agrarian transition is provided by Philip Huang (2011). Huang argues that China may achieve vertical integration for its agriculture—which for him represents a link between the producer and the processing, marketing, and procurement of agricultural goods—without horizontal integration into commercial capitalist companies. He links a perceived revival of smallholder farming to changing patterns in Chinese food consumption. Only smallholder farming would be able to produce the supply to match the increased demand in meat and vegetables in China. Given the present system of land usage rights, according to Huang, "small-scale family farming is here to stay for quite some time, despite the entry of big business into the food industry, on account of the distinctive Chinese institutional environment and also the multiple economies related to small farming when it comes to livestock-poultry-fish raising and vegetables-fruits horticulture" (Huang 2011, 126). China now has to decide how to integrate these smallholders into the market and faces two very different options. One method of vertical integration would be Dragonhead enterprises, which Huang argues would be the clear preference of state agents. The alternative would be to integrate these producers into cooperative structures, an option he strongly prefers. In regard to the role of the land usage rights, he cites the work of Zhang and Donaldson (Huang 2011, 125) and agrees with their understanding of the protective functions these land usage rights provide for primary producers.

Throughout the entire article Huang never really discusses his assumption that smallholders will remain the main organizational form of agrarian production for an indefinite time to come. The link between the consumption patterns and the organization of agriculture is not convincing, nor is it even in line with data he himself presents. For him, peasant differentiation, the centerpiece of the Zhang and Donaldson articles, is never really considered in its implications (e.g., the emergence of new forms of agrarian production). Even his main empirical source, a single statistical report of the Chinese Ministry of Agriculture from 2008, suggests that commercial operations of scale are on the rise in China. The role of land usage rights for peasants is described in a perhaps overly optimistic way—including the argument of land as a substitute for a social security system (Huang 2011, 111). Little of his findings are in line with the empirical data collected for this book.

A core part of the agrarian transition in China is the idea of *nongye chanyehua*. Susanne Lingohr-Wolf (2011, 27–51) carefully analyzes Chinese literature discussing the usage of this term and its development up to the year 2005. Early on, agricultural industrialization was described in Chinese literature with the following sentence: "The market is the guide [*shichang wei daoxiang*], rural households are the foundation [*nonghu wei jichu*] and "dragon head" enterprises are the backing [*"longtou" qiye wei yituo*]" (Lingohr-Wolf 2011, 29). In this new agriculture, "integration" (*yitihua*) has become a central element which refers to structural reforms that are supposed to strengthen the link between production, processing and marketing of agricultural products. Other goals include "specialization" (*zhuanyehua*) and "intensification" (*jiyuehua*). She finds that the central argument for agricultural industrialization is to increase rural incomes.

Framing Land and People

Theories of agrarian transition emphasize the differentiation of the peasantry as an important part of the process. As seen above, a core aspect of this differentiation concerns the relationship between primary producers and agricultural land. In China, the link between these two has become the topic of heated debates and considerable scholarly output. In a wonderful article Sally Sargeson (2012) took a closer look at the framing of peasants in relation to the recent commodification of collective land among Chinese intellectuals, academics, and officials. It is argued here that her portrait of the various images of the peasantry in the context of land grab could also be brought to great use in structuring the arguments of the relationship between the peasantry, land, and agriculture in China. She identified three distinct frames for the representation of peasants: villains, victims, and aspiring proprietors.

Villains sabotage the modernization of the countryside. They collude with corrupt officials and developers and use every possible means to extract as many resources as possible from society. These resources are usually wasted on alcohol, gambling, and other unproductive uses. Victims are losing out to the interests of local state officials and their allies. The interest of the latter in creating an industrialized agriculture endangers both land and lifestyle of smallholders. Aspiring proprietors, in turn, are rational utility maximizers who want to bring their land to the most profitable use but are prevented from doing so by legal limitations and state interference. They cling to their land because they are exercising their property rights, not because they depend on farming for their survival. A closer look on each of the three frames follows. If not noted otherwise, the characterization is based on Sargeson (2012).

The "villains" have neither the resources nor the will to transform themselves into modern producers. In this view, peasants are out of tune with the current economic development in China. Their fields, therefore, should give way to economically more efficient, non-smallholding (and in many cases non-agricultural) use of the land. The present dual land system should continue to exist, only the "monitoring and supervision of local officials" (Sargeson 2012, 767) needs to be improved. Villagers should become part of a "state managed workfare program" and move to concentrated housing projects in order to become urbanites (Sargeson 2012, 767–68). Rural development is understood here as a "civilizing project" (Harrell 1996) in which the periphery should be catching up with the presumably more developed center. Related to this are calls to raise the "quality" (*suzhi*) of the peasantry (Kipnis 2006; Murphy 2004) and to manage their financial affairs on their behalf—until they are able to do so themselves. For example, compensation from land deals, according to these authors, should be directly invested in social insurance schemes and not handed out to the villagers. A speech by the head of the Chinese Development Bank, Zheng Hui, is a good example of this way of thinking (Wang 2011). Zheng Hui proposes a number of institutional changes in order to ease the transfer of land. Ultimately he suggests that:

> Peasants need to leave behind the land, need to leave behind their peasant status and become employees of big farms. 800 million peasants must change their way of life and their mode of production. The "one family, one household" mode of small farming economy does not allow agrarian modernization.

Contrary to this line of argumentation is the second frame. Sargeson notes "[m]ost authors deploying a victim frame argue that villagers' potential to contribute to the country's modernization has been suppressed by the state's negation of their collective ownership of land" (Sargeson 2012, 769). Many scholars in this line of thinking argue that the basis of agriculture is and continues to be smallholding (see, for example, Huang 2011). According to Sargeson, this frame is based on a "neo-collectivist" vision of agriculture and "also speaks to widely held nationalist and socialist anxieties about the country's capacity to forge a uniquely Chinese alternative to both statist strategies and 'Western' neo-liberal models of accumulation" (Sargeson 2012, 769). For many scholars with this orientation, collective land usage rights of the villagers represent a form of "social protection" (Wen 2006) or "unemployment insurance" (Wang and Zhong 2008). In China, the "New Rural Reconstruction" movement may be the primary voice for this position. Alexander Day calls this movement a "major intervention by intellectuals and rural activists, who argue that this rural crisis cannot be understood simply as a problem of rural economies and agricultural production but as a social crisis that calls for the reconstruction of rural social life, [. . .] best grasped as a Polanyian social protective movement in reaction to the marketization of society and the perceived lack of an urban solution" (Day 2008, 50). Wen Tiejun, a prominent member of this group, anticipates a lack of housing and work opportunities for the former peasants and now superfluous workers in the cities and the subsequently enormous costs for social security, which the state would not be able to afford (Day 2008, 55). For this group, rural reconstruction can only be achieved through a mixture of initializing cooperatives and community development. As a final consequence,

Wen Tiejun argues that economic efficiency is less important than equality (Day 2008, 55–56). Privatizing land is seen only as a way to polarize land ownership and not as a valid path toward development. Commodification of land as an effort to create economies of scale is firmly rejected within this perspective. In many ways, this stand mirrors similar arguments by the international "Food Sovereignty" movement (McMichael 2008, 220).

The third frame takes yet another stand on how land, people, and agriculture should relate to each other in the future. According to Sargeson (2012, 772) this frame "shares Marx's condemnation of small peasant agriculture as an impediment to capital accumulation, growth of the productive forces, and formation of class consciousness; but rather than viewing land-losing villagers as clinging to the institutional foundations of a pre-modern mode of production, here they are framed as the heroic supporters of liberalism in markets, civil society, and polity, whose inclinations are suppressed by an authoritarian state and the anachronistic property institutions and rural collective organization it has foisted upon them." In this view, the collective nature of land ownership is a burden for entrepreneurial and quite capable villagers who are not interested in the state or a collective taking care of their interests for them. The notion that collective land represents some kind of social protection net for villagers is largely lost on this group. This frame also has a different perspective on the protests against land expropriations. Ray Yep (2013), for example, argues that most of the conflicts on land expropriation are not taking place in locations where villagers depend upon farmland for subsidence farming but rather in well-off locations. Yep suggests that for a considerable group of these villagers the value of farmland has changed, and under present conditions they want a bigger share of the land sale money on the real estate market—not the ability to continue farming (Yep 2013, 283). In regard to the future of agriculture, there is little alternative to larger and more commercialized farms. According to Qin Hui the only question left now is whether China will follow the American or the Prussian model of agrarian capitalism, the former being dominated by many small-to-medium farmers, the latter by big landlords and companies (Sargeson 2012, 774).

If one sees the land usage rights holders as aspiring proprietors who may use these rights as an asset for production, the security of these rights, e.g., tenure security, moves to the center of interest. In the past, local governments redistributed the land within the HRS to account for changes in household composition. This has been strongly criticized by a number of economists as endangering household investments in agriculture (Brandt et al. 2002; Brandt, Rozelle, and Turner 2004; Tao and Xu 2007) and affecting out-migration (de la Rupelle et al. 2009; Mullan, Grosjean, and Kontoleon 2011). Others have argued that reallocations were not as frequent as assumed, mostly partial in nature and perhaps have even been accepted by villagers (Kong and Unger 2013; Kung 2000; Unger 2002b). Deininger and Jin (2009) argue that while the Rural Land Contracting Law[5] has greatly improved the position of villagers against illegal land takings, it had no such effect on "illegal" reallocations of land—becoming evident by the fact that an average of 8.31 percent of all villages in their sample conducted such land reallocations between 2003 and 2005 (Deininger and Jin 2009, 30). Kong and Unger find that in their sample of villages, only 33 percent of the small groups (natural villages) reallocated the land between 1996 and 2008 (Kong and Unger 2013, 18). Earlier work by Jacoby et al (2002) suggests that tenure insecurity may indeed impact villagers' investments but that at the same time these differences in investment behavior had only a marginal effect on output value or on general welfare. For several reasons the tenure security debate may have lost some of its relevance. Kong and Unger show that in locations with high labor migration rates land reallocations were less frequent and argue that agriculture in general had lost some of its importance. They also mention that only 16 percent of the heads of the small groups in their survey expected another reallocation of land in the next ten years (Kong and Unger 2013, 18–19). This seems to be in line with the strengthening of legal rights to contracted land and the introduction of greatly improved control mechanisms, as will be documented in chapter 3.

Commodification of Farmland in China

Two very different paths toward the commodification of farmland in China have developed since the beginning of the economic reforms in the late 1970s. On the one side is its marketization via the transformation into construction land. On the other side is the development of transfer mechanisms for agricultural land usage rights, sometimes insufficiently called land rental markets, which have been created to allow for continued and improved agricultural usage of the land. In academic literature, the former has received far more attention than the latter.

In fact, most existing literature in regard to collective land in the countryside is primarily concerned with the realities of different forms of primitive accumulation, e.g., the process in which land is taken away from agrarian producers for non-agricultural purposes. Hsing You-tien (2010) provides probably the best account of these processes. She has carefully worked out the motivation of a coalition of urban developers and local governments to take the land of villagers close to urban centers. Earlier research on this topic includes the work of (Cai 2003; Guo 2001; Ho and Lin 2003, 2004; Skinner, Kuhn, and Joseph 2001; Wang, Tao, and Tong 2009; Yeh 2005).

Largely ignored by media and scholars until recently, a growing group of landless farmers without urban household registration (and thereby without access to urban social security systems) exists in contemporary China. Tao and Xu cite Chinese sources that estimate that about 34 million farmers lost half of their land or more by 2004 and each year another 2–3 million farmers are added to this group (Tao and Xu 2007, 1306). Sargeson (2012, 764) provides an even more comprehensive overview of several calculations on the size of this group:

> In 2002, MLR [Ministry of Land and Resources] staff estimated that, based on the area of arable land converted for urban and infrastructure construction between 1987 and 2001, up to 35 million villagers had been expropriated and the number was increasing annually by 1.5–2 million. At the end of 2003, however, Song Binwen warned that as many as 60 million might already be landless, and 21 *Shiji chanjing* predicted that by 2030, China could have a population of 110 million land-losing villagers. Yu Jianrong, Director of the Rural Development Institute in the Academy of Social Sciences and one of the most prominent self-appointed champions for villagers' rights argued in 2005 that the population numbered more than 66 million. In 2007, two Communist Party School researchers independently published papers referring to contemporary populations of between 60 and 80 million land-losing villagers.

A popular argument links flaws within the design of the collective land usage rights system to the current primitive accumulation in China. Peter Ho (2001) and his assessment that Chinese property rights are characterized by "institutional ambiguity" is probably best known in this regard. He shows that while farmland in the countryside is legally defined as collective (if it is not owned by the state), the actual ownership rights continue to remain vague. This has led to claims to the land by organizations on various levels of the rural administration from natural and administrative village governments to township and even county-level governments—everyone seems to have an interest in the land backed-up by a legal claim.

The other commodification debate concerns itself with new instruments introduced by the Chinese government to allow the transfer of land usage rights between those individual households holding usage rights to various plots of land and other households or even village-external third parties. Land transfer (*tudi liuzhuan*) has emerged as the potential solution to the question of how to transfer and consolidate farmland into bigger holdings, the basis of any increase in the scale of production. In general, this term describes the transfer of collective land usage rights for a certain amount of time to another party. In exchange, a rental fee must be paid. The legal genesis of this system and its main points will be introduced in chapter 3.

Only a very limited amount of empirical research on this aspect of the Chinese agrarian transition exists in Western literature. Exceptions include the work of economists such as Brandt et al. (2002); Kung (2002);

and Rozelle, Huang, and Otsuka (2005). Brandt et al. (2002, 79) report that in their survey from 1995 only in 71.6 percent of the villages the villagers had complete freedom in renting out their land. They also report very low numbers of rented out land. For example, in 1988 and 1995, only 0.6 and 3 percent, respectively, of the land in their survey villages had been rented out (ibid.). Kung (2002) describes the early developments of this market and its connection to labor migration in China. He points out that the rental rate in 1999 according to a survey of the Ministry of Agriculture already stood at 14.3 percent (for the six provinces surveyed), including a rental rate of 35 percent in Zhejiang. Zhejiang is also the location of an interesting study by Zhang et al. (2004), who show the close connection between off-farm labor and the development of land rental markets there. However, most studies of more recent date available for a Western readership are either only very limited regional case studies or they omit the relationship to the overall changing nature of agriculture (see, for example, Shao et al. 2007).

The focus on limited case studies is also to be found in a substantial portion of the studies by Chinese scholars. An interesting point in case comes from Zhang (2008), who presents single instances of land transfer from all over China. Even more common are policy studies that explain the necessity of land transfers but provide no empirical data (see, for example, Chen 2010). An exception is the monograph by Hu Rongen (2010), who gives a very detailed report on land transfer in Guizhou. He took part in an investigative trip to the rural parts of the Tongren region in April, 2009 and conducted many interviews with cadres, villagers, and entrepreneurs about the emerging market for land usage rights. His book contains numerous contracts and other documents necessary for the management of this transfer. Hu called the transfer of land usage rights a "hidden" or "potential" land market (*qianzai de tudi shichang*). For him, the current practice of land transfer is subject to numerous issues, part of which could be addressed by moving the management of land transfers to the township level. Hu also points to the lack of official documents and procedures that create friction in the process. Prices in the land market he observed were based on the later usage of the land. For instance, in 2009 for farmland rented out for vegetable and fruit production the price paid was about 400 to 500 RMB per mu per year. His sources identify the lack of appropriate contracts as a major issue for further expansion of land transfer. To give one example: one township party secretary told Hu and his group that in his township, having a population of 4,320 households, 558 land transfers took place between 2004 and 2008. Among the participating households only 56 had a proper contract. However, in two-thirds of the transfers the land was exchanged between two families in order to create unified holdings. Only about one-third had been rented out to other parties (Hu 2010, 48).

There are indications in the literature that land rental agreements may become more important in the future. Ray Yep (2013) points to the policy reforms in 2008 as a possible stimulation of the land transfer system. In this context, he mentions three major reasons for villagers to lease their plots. First, given the employment opportunities in the cities, land usage rights may become a burden for households that see their future in an urban context. Second, the huge and still growing rural-urban income gap is a major motivation for many households to leave the countryside. And third, prices for land rentals are rising—making this a stronger initiative for villagers (Yep 2013, 281).

Politics and the Chinese Agrarian Transition

The various perspectives on the nature of the Chinese peasantry and its possible future have influenced arguments on how the Chinese state should or should not interact with villagers and agriculture. Analytically it makes sense to distinguish between state actors at national and provincial levels, who are more involved in policy planning than in its implementation and those on the local level, for whom this order is reversed.

Several authors have highlighted the increased efforts of the Chinese central government to reform agriculture and economic structures in the countryside (Ahlers 2014; Saich 2007; Tian 2007). On the provincial level the experimental zones in Chengdu and Chongqing for rural-urban integration have recently received more attention (Cui 2011; Huang, Yuan, and Peng 2012; Szelenyi 2011). The local state and its role in the most recent transformation of agriculture have less often been the focus of scholarly attention. However, there is a large set of literature that deals with the impact of local state behavior on wider issues of rural welfare (for a summary of the earlier debate see Baum and Shevchenko 1999). Three main lines of argumentation can be identified in the current debate.

Along with the characterization of peasants as victims, the first argument sees the local state as not interested in agriculture or welfare but rather in the maximization of personal economic and political profit. Local cadres defy the well-intended policies of the center and in sum exercise a negative and at times corrupt role for the future development of agriculture. One of the most extreme articles in this regard comes from Katherine Le Mons Walker (2006), who sees the rise of "gangster capitalism"—an unholy alliance between local governments and scrupulous entrepreneurs. More nuanced, yet also with a similarly negative view on the role of local governments for local development, are the contributions by Graeme Smith (2009, 2010, 2011) and Ben Hillman (2010). Much along the line of the "selective policy implementation" argumentation by O'Brien and Li (1999), Smith argues that central initiatives are implemented only if there is enough of a benefit for the local government (or individuals within it) or if the threat attached to non-compliance is too big. Hillman in turn sees "that local politics is driven largely by a competition over spoils and that competition over spoils is organized around a relatively stable system of factionalism" (2010, 1). Another insightful contribution in this regard comes from Zhou Xueguang (2010) who sees structural factors in place that force leading local cadres to collude against higher levels of the administration. Once this collusion is an accepted part of the political game, it is hard to confine it to certain policy fields. All of these accounts are rather skeptical about a progressive and positive influence of the local state upon local development.

Second, an opposing argument highlights the many efforts of local state agents to improve and modernize agriculture in order to improve local livelihoods. Studies in this regard highlight the role of local policy experiments and initiatives. Anna Ahlers and Gunter Schubert provide the first empirical insight into these new initiatives (Ahlers 2014; Ahlers and Schubert 2009; Schubert and Ahlers 2011). In their perspective local cadres are integrated into increasingly effective structures of supervision and strategic project funding, which then leads to improved policy implementation on the ground. Along these lines of argumentation is also the perception that there is a trend of local leaders aiming to transform the local state closer to the ideal of "consultative authoritarianism," by listening with more attention to the voices (and votes) of the general public (He and Thogersen 2010).

Finally, a third line of argument sees the good intentions of the center and the local state to get involved in agriculture in a constructive way but also cautions that one must take into account the limited resources available for most grassroots administrations in rural China. These funding shortcomings would limit the involvement of the local state to a few scattered and dispersed experiments (Wong 2009; Zhao 2007; Zhong 2003).

Structure of the Book

The second chapter will present the theoretic framework and the research design of this book. It will introduce the conceptualization of agrarian transitions of Polanyi and Brenner in more detail and discuss the feasibility of its application for the current transformation of the Chinese agriculture. The second part of the chapter introduces the research design based on *process tracing* and *historical institutionalism*.

Chapter 3 will introduce the institutional framework for agriculture and the management of collective land in China. It starts with an introduction to the initial reforms in agriculture that re-created smallholder farming in China and then continues to trace the struggle of the central political leadership to maintain the system of collective ownership of farmland while at the same time pushing for the modernization and commercialization of agriculture. It thereby shows the influence of new ideas for the gradual transformation of the collective land usage rights system. The chapter also discusses the biggest threat to commercial farming, the transformation of farmland into construction land and legal reform initiatives that address this issue.

Chapter 4 deals with peasant differentiation and the conditions for smallholder agriculture in contemporary China. Using findings from the field sites and secondary literature, the chapter shows the difficulties smallholders face in contemporary agriculture and their reaction to these developments. The chapter argues that these difficulties have triggered a massive out-migration of the most capable members of the workforce and have created huge inefficiencies in agriculture. It also argues that, in the process, the value of farmland for rural families has been affected.

Chapter 5 documents the role of local governments in the agrarian transition. It shows that local governments have become important actors in the transformation of Chinese agriculture because the implementation of policies in this field may help leading cadres to advance in their careers, to improve the financial conditions of their local administrations and also to cater to their frequently expressed wish to improve local livelihood conditions.

Chapter 6 takes a closer look at the commodification of collective farmland. The chapter thereby merges findings of the previous chapters and links them to the commodification process. It shows how the difficulties for smallholders and opportunities for wage labor in combination with limitations of the HRS have created an environment in which farmland is underused—a *tragedy of the anticommons*. In realizing this tragedy, central and local governments have put more emphasis upon a rental market for farmland. The tenants in this market are new commercial agrarian producers who have been able to gain access to farmland under very favorable conditions. Despite their weak bargaining position, peasant households still seem to profit from these arrangements in a financial sense.

The conclusion in chapter 7 is structured in two parts. The first will present a synthesis of the findings. The second part will then discuss the implications of these findings for the debate surrounding the current and future nature of Chinese agriculture and the agrarian transitions in general. An Appendix with more detailed information on data collecting and the field sites concludes the book.

NOTES

1. In this book the term "smallholder" denotes the mode of small and fragmented agrarian production in which the family is usually the main unit of operation. The term "peasant" is used not only to refer to this type of production but also to a certain lifestyle and subaltern social and political position. As Henry Bernstein (2010, 80–81) defines: "Peasant production is small scale, using relatively simple technologies (or, at

least, technologies centred on human energies and those of draft animals), and provides both the 'subsistence' (simple reproduction) of producers and surplus labour appropriated in the forms of rents and taxes by ruling classes."

2. For more information about the field sites please refer to the Appendix.

3. For this book also fieldwork in Shandong Province was conducted.

4. Zhang and Donaldsons's use of the term "vertical integration" is somewhat problematic. The translation correctly points to an important aspect of the current agriculture—the integration of peasants into commercial production and marketing structures, yet at the same time it blurs the changes in the individual parts of this vertical integration. In this book, it is argued that individual smallholders will eventually be replaced in many sectors of agriculture by scaled-up commercial operations.

5. Described in detail in chapter 3.

TWO

Theoretic Framework and Research Design

This chapter serves several objectives. First, it introduces the theoretic framework of this book in more detail. As mentioned, the current changes of the structure of the Chinese agriculture will be explored with a theoretic framework based upon the work of Karl Polanyi and Robert Brenner. Although their work has already played a part in classical debates on agrarian transition, both authors still provide a refreshing and stimulating approach to conceptualizing the emergence of new forms of agrarian production. In a second step, the research design based on process tracing and historical institutionalism will be discussed. In addition, three causal variables identified in the theoretic framework, property institutions, peasant differentiation and rural politics, will be discussed in more detail. Special emphasis is paid to questions of how to identify and analyze the developments within these variables. Finally, the *commodification of collective farmland* as a major part of the agrarian transition and the dependent variable of the research design will be explored in more detail. It is argued here that the commodification process provides a link to tie together the three aforementioned variables and the agrarian transition.

THE EMERGENCE OF AGRARIAN CAPITALISM

Agrarian transition has been defined as a process in which subsistence farming, e.g., farming to satisfy ones livelihood needs, is replaced by farming to produce a monetary profit, e.g., capitalist farming. In the words of Ellen Meiksins Wood (2002, 2): "[c]apitalism is a system in which goods and services, down to the most basic necessities of life, are

21

produced for profitable exchange, where even human labour-power is a commodity for sale in the market, and where all economic actors are dependent on the market."

There is a large body of "transition" literature of both modern and classical origin. In her seminal work on the topic, Wood (2002) examines the most prominent accounts. According to her, much of the debate had long been dominated by the so-called commercialization account. The underlying assumption of this approach is that capitalist and rational thinking have always existed within humankind and only needed to be liberated for capitalism to emerge. In this model, capitalism is always an "opportunity to be taken, wherever and whenever possible" (Wood 2002, 6). She continues to explain this idea in relation to markets. If capitalism is about opportunity, then people have the opportunity to sell their product on the market in order to earn a profit. What is lost in this description, according to Wood, is the notion of compulsion. In capitalism, people become market dependent, they get their means for production and reproduction, e.g., to satisfy their livelihood needs, only via the market. It is also the market to which they then sell their commodities. Finally, "[t]he capitalist market as a specific social form disappears when the transition from pre-capitalist to capitalist societies is presented as a more or less natural, if often thwarted, extension or maturation of already existing social forms, at best a quantitative rather than a qualitative transformation" (Wood 2002, 7).[1]

For Polanyi, there was nothing natural in the transition from feudalism to capitalism. Capitalism could only come into existence because of an earlier rupture in social relationships. Before the advent of capitalism, the central norms of interaction were reciprocity and redistribution (Polanyi 1997, 75). The introduction of legal contracts had a huge impact on these non-monetary relationships. From that point on, the once important social relationships of family, neighborhood, occupation, and religion had to be "liquidated," as they would impede the individual's freedom to conduct business (Polanyi 1997, 225). Consequently, capitalism was characterized by the advent of "fictitious commodities," referring to land, labor, and capital. He called them fictitious because these commodities were not produced for sale (Zmolek 2004, 287). The social consequence of this process was a move from securing one's livelihood to aiming for a profit (Polanyi 1997, 70). In the old mode of production, the market was embedded in society, whereas in capitalism society would become embedded in the market. Polanyi considered the consequences of this process nothing less than disastrous.

For him, capitalism developed in three stages. The first was the *commodification of land*, the second was the explosion of agricultural production to satisfy the needs of an emerging industrial society, and the third was the expansion of this system of production to overseas regions (Polanyi 1997, 245). Polanyi suggested that this new system would exist next to the old methods of production, constantly aiming to get hold of the latter's resources, in particular land.

One of the most interesting of Polanyi's insights is his characterization of the changing nature of the market and the influence of the state upon this development (Polanyi 1997, 93–97). According to him the markets that came into existence before capitalism were not competitive in nature. Quite to the opposite, local markets and foreign trade had mechanisms to reduce the competition as much as possible. Only the later national markets were truly competitive. These, however, were created by the nation-state, which also ensured their continued existence. Consequently, he argues that capitalism and a market economy were not the result of a natural process but the product, among other factors, of continued interference by the state.

Another strong critic of the idea of an inherent capitalist logic in humankind was Robert Brenner. Clearly inspired by Marxist thought, he suggested a very interesting comparison of medieval England to other European nations, arguing that the conditions for the later development of capitalist structures existed only within the English agriculture of that particular time. For Brenner, the starting point of the analysis is "the structure of class relations, of class power, which will determine the manner and degree to which particular demographic and commercial changes will affect long-term trends in the distribution of income and economic growth—and not vice versa" (Brenner 1985a, 11). According to him agrarian class structure emerged in two general types defined along the lines of this split, on the one hand the direct producers, on the other hand a "class of non-producers" (Brenner 1985a, 11) who extract a surplus or constitute the ruling elite. By applying this model of class analysis to medieval England Brenner comes to interesting conclusions.

Capitalism in England came into being, he argues, because of two new developments within the social property system. The first was the extinction of arbitrary rent extraction from the peasants by the nobles. The second was "the undermining of peasant possession or the aborting of any trend towards full peasant ownership of land" (Brenner 1985b, 214). The end of arbitrary rent extractions was crucial in triggering the search for alternative revenue sources among the noble class and finally led to their cooperation with an emerging group of commercial agricultural tenants in the countryside. In other European countries, the nobles continued to have far greater rights to extract from the peasants at will and did not need to care about possible alternatives in order to create a surplus. The second development made possible the reorganization of land into the hands of those who produced the most profitable output. Agrarian producers without their own land had to rent land from the nobles; a leasehold system emerged.

Mike Zmolek, a student of Brenner, explains the role of property in this process in more detail. The turning point was when common law replaced customary law and thereby allowed the creation of leaseholds: "Since peasants holding leases granting temporary possession of strips in the common fields held 'at the lord's will' and could be evicted at the expiration of the lease, such arrangements lost much of the 'extra-economic' character of customary tenancies such as copyhold and took on a more strictly economic character as a contract between buyer and seller" (Zmolek 2004, 283). Peasants holding leases had to produce a monetary surplus to pay for the lease. The leasehold system also introduced competition to agrarian producers, whereby over time only the most productive producers could continue to farm. Wood summarizes this system by stating that the agrarian producers did not have the opportunity to produce for the market, as was suggested by the commercialization approach, but that they must produce for it, "simply in order to guarantee access to the means of subsistence and to the land itself" (Wood 2002, 53). The market now came to dominate every aspect of the production. In this perspective, the commodification of land leads to proletarization of the rural population and thereby becomes a precondition of capitalism itself (Zmolek 2004, 289).

Not unlike Polanyi, Brenner recognizes the importance of the political system for the emergence of capitalism as it shapes the conditions of having access to land. Both authors, however, do not discuss the direct influence of state actors as an important factor in agrarian transitions. This omission is very likely related to the different role administrators played in the English case in comparison to present variants of agrarian transition. Other scholars have given the state a more active role in their conceptualization of the transition process.

Gillian Hart, for example, criticizes studies of agrarian change that do not take into account the role of the state, as "[t]his neglect of power and politics results in an almost exclusive focus on commercialization and technology as the main source of rural change and portrays agrarian change as a unilinear process leading to a determinate outcome" (Hart 1989, 31). As an example of the great influence the state has on agrarian transitions she cites the development in four Southeast-Asian countries in which different kinds of "state patronage" each produced different winners and losers of the transition process. Stephen Wegren argues that state interventions will affect all other rural actors, the rural economic environment and rural social conditions and therefore are of great importance for the performance of the agricultural sector and "political–economic relationships among social actors" (1998, 2). He suggests that new social relationships trigger the emergence of new social groups and classes (Wegren 1998, 8).

Summarizing the framework outlined above, agrarian transitions are conceptualized as a historical shift from small-scale peasant production to large profit-oriented operations of scale. For the latter type of production, all production factors—including labor, land, and capital—need to be commodified. Competitive markets for agricultural products and agricultural land are not only an opportunity for small-scale producers but also make them vulnerable to a new risk. This market risk may turn into market failure and force peasants out of independent agriculture into wage labor. The state can choose to protect smallholders or it could take an opposite stand and promote commercial enterprises. It thereby has a direct influence that may accelerate or slow down the process of agrarian transition beyond its role to create and sustain a market system.

This book is based upon the assumption that the current transformation of Chinese agriculture is a case of agrarian transition as outlined and discussed above. Not withstanding further empirical research, similarities between the Chinese case and earlier transitions seem obvious in four broad categories. First, at the outset of this process we see relatively similar patterns of labor organization. The family is the main unit of agrarian labor organization in pre-capitalism England and present-day rural China. Although Chinese peasant farming reappeared only after the introduction of the HRS, the production structures that followed immediately after these reforms closely resembled those in other pre-capitalist societies. This has been referred to as the reappearance of "peasantness" (Kipnis 1995).

The second similarity is the expansion of market rationality into the rural areas. The market dependency, as outlined above, forces its own logic onto farming households. Most importantly, this implies that the success of agrarian production not only depends upon the amount produced but also upon the farm gate prices realized for these goods in relation to the inputs used. This is the idea of labor and resource efficiency that is taking hold in the countryside and it is markedly different from peasant farming, in which the costs for inputs and especially for labor are ignored. The role of changing farm gate prices and their impact on Chinese farmers have been excessively discussed since the beginning of the reforms, as will be shown in the next chapter.

Arguably, the third similarity is the weak political position of the peasant households and their continued difficulty in resisting economic and political pressures. One example would be their limited influence upon the political conditions of agricultural production, e.g., the amount of subsidies and other financial or political support that affect their livelihoods to a large degree. Another example would be the low likelihood of English peasants to resist the enclosure movement and their Chinese counterparts' equally lacking ability to do so against the land grab of ever-increasing cities and development parks.

Fourth, in several steps the Chinese central state has limited the ability of local administrators to extract direct rent from smallholders. Just as in the English case described by Brenner, the continued existence of smallholder farming has become a perceived economic burden for them. How will the Chinese local administrators react to this change? This has been an important question as it relates to the fate of the potential Chinese agrarian transition.

Still, one might argue that the Chinese case is unique or at least not comparable to the early transitions. Three main categories of criticism seem possible. First, one might argue that the theoretic framework itself is flawed and that China serves as a good example of this. Many argue that the Chinese farmers have started to farm individually on their own.[2] One motivation for this certainly may be the desire to make a profit. In this view, the Chinese case would prove the basic assumption of the commercialization approach—capitalist thinking is part of human nature and people just need to be freed-up to enjoy its benefits. Upon closer examination, however, it seems that this point has little merit. Spontaneous individual farming in China started predominately in very poor areas of China and survival needs rather than profit interests seem to have been the main trigger for this development. Furthermore, peasant farming rather than commercial farming or entrepreneurial farming came in the aftermath of agricultural collectives.

Second, one could argue that the model does not apply to China because critical historic conditions differ. In earlier cases of transition to agrarian capitalism, especially in England, the emergence of agrarian capitalism was part of a general move to capitalism, which was occurring at the same time. In China, we see a process of a delayed integration of agriculture into already developed capitalist structures. The key dynamic for the change of agriculture might, therefore, not lie within the interaction of rural actors and the conditions for primary producers but rather within the effects of an overall commercialization and globalization of the Chinese economy. Peasants as sub-scale smallholders are an anachronism, a historic leftover, which is due to vanish if the economy continues to modernize. In effect, this line of thinking is based on the same assumptions of an evolutionary character of capitalism as the first criticism. Eventually the rural sector in China would catch up to the standards and achievements of the urban areas; it only needs time and more economic freedom (and/or rights) to do so. This argument, however, cannot explain why the transition is happening right now and not earlier. It also fails to see that for many peasants this "evolution" is not so much a process of catching up in improved living conditions but of further falling behind and subsequent forced lifestyle transformations. Crucially, it leaves out the role of the state in shaping the conditions and guiding the direction of an agrarian transition.

A third and more interesting criticism points to the difference in property systems between earlier cases of agrarian transition and China. The present legal configuration of farmland in rural China puts severe limitations on the ability of actors to buy or sell land. Yet, one of the core processes within the transition of agriculture outlined above is the commodification of land, a market-based transfer of access to agricultural land. In England, the main mechanism in this regard was the leasehold system. According to scholars like de Soto the privatization of land is a precondition for market-based transfer to take place and the starting point of economic growth (Assies 2009, 574). How could agriculture in China be on the path to capitalism if there is no legal individual ownership of land? This is exactly the key question this project is interested in.

It is argued here that there are enough similarities between the developments described in the agrarian transition model outlined here and the current situation in China to warrant the application of the model to China. The existing differences between the Chinese case and earlier transitions should become the target of further empirical investigation. These differences may offer insights into the effects of the specific institutions and actor-constellations in China on the transition effect.

RESEARCH DESIGN

This book is a case study as defined by Alexander George and Andrew Bennett (2005). They characterize "a case as an instance of a class of events" (2005, 17). A class of events is then defined as "a phenomenon of scientific interest, such as revolutions, types of governmental regimes, kinds of economic systems, or personality types that the investor chooses to study with the aim of developing theory (or "generic knowledge") regarding the causes of similarities or differences among instances (cases) of that class of events" (George and Bennett 2005, 17–18). In this book, the current transformation of the Chinese agriculture is understood as an instance of the class of agrarian transitions. Among the different approaches to conduct such a case study this book employs *process tracing*, which "attempts to identify the intervening causal process—the causal chain and causal mechanisms—between an independent variable (or variables) and the outcome of the dependent variable" (George and Bennett 2005, 206). More specifically, this book pursues an *analytical explanation*. This approach "converts a historical narrative into an analytical causal explanation couched in explicit theoretical forms" (George and Bennett 2005, 211).

Based on the works of Brenner and Polanyi, with an added focus on the agency of the state, three independent variables have been selected as being of core importance for an agrarian transition: peasant differentiation, rural politics, and property institutions. Although some earlier studies on agrarian transition point to the importance of technological change, this factor is intentionally left out of this study as the Chinese agrarian transition does not seem to be triggered by an emergence of new technologies.

While this book aims to provide a thorough account of the Chinese path of agrarian transition, it makes sense to further specify the dependent variable. As George and Bennett (2005, 248) put it: "the careful characterization of the dependent variable and its variance is often one of the most important and lasting contributions to research." How did other scholars working on agrarian transition choose their dependent variable?

For Brenner the transition process in England was characterized by a change of class relations that made possible the reconfiguration of agrarian production into a dual structure of noble landlords and large capitalist tenants (Brenner 1985a, 214). His dependent variable, in simple terms, was the formation of a new class of producers. For Byres, the dependent variable appears to be the "particular configurations of the relations of production and forms of appropriation" that have emerged where "capitalist agriculture has developed (in say, England or Prussia or France)" or where a "capitalist agrarian transition has taken place (in, say, the USA, or Japan, or Taiwan and South Korea)" (Byres 1996, 8). Akram-Lodhi points out that "[. . .] an agrarian transition requires that production and accumulation be transformed, and that political constraints to the structural transformation of agriculture be eradicated" (Akram-Lodhi 2005, 76). All of these accounts point to the critical changes in production structures and accumulation. Yet, they are only vaguely defined and rather difficult to operationalize.

Hence it seems more suitable to focus only on a particular, easier to operationalize subset of the changes related to the Chinese agrarian transition. For this purpose, the commodification of farmland has been chosen as the dependent variable. The expected variance of this variable includes all legal, market-like transfer activities of farmland that are in line with the legal framework in China. The HRS is still at the core of all management of farmland in rural China and, as long as there is no private ownership of farmland, all transfer activities have to meet its legal requirements. Market-like transfer activities are a commercial requirement of the agrarian transition. Capitalist agrarian producers need to be able to gain access to all means of production through capital investment. If there is no market for farmland, then there is no agrarian transition.

Before the following sections introduce the variables in more detail, some words on the role of institutions in this book are necessary. Although most scholars might agree with the very basic notion that institutions are rules (see the discussion summarized by Steinmo 2010, 123), many have very different ideas of what this entails in practice. The confusion already starts with the question of what qualifies as an institution. Some argue that only formal rules should count, while others emphasize the importance of informal rules. There is also considerable variance in the answers scholars give to the question of how institutions affect behavior and how to explain their change. These different ideas on institutions may have considerable influence on how problems, solutions, and actors are understood.

This book follows ideas outlined by scholars within the *historical insti-tutionalism* (HI) for its understanding of institutions. Hall and Taylor (1996, 937) summarize several main features of this perspective as being an emphasis on the "asymmetries of power associated with the operation and development of institutions" and the role of path dependencies and unintended consequences during the development of institutions. Schol-ars within HI also tend to recognize that institutions do not necessarily translate into particular behavior and that institutional analysis therefore has to recognize the "contribution that other kinds of factors, such as ideas, can make to political outcomes" (ibid.).

HI is part of a new interest in the role of institutions for political outcomes, which has been referred to as "new institutionalism" (Hall and Taylor 1996, 936). In addition to HI there are two other important schools that prominently take institutions into account: rational choice and soci-ological institutionalism (Steinmo 2010, 125). The most important ques-tion for all of these approaches is: "[H]ow do institutions affect the be-havior of individuals?" (Hall and Taylor 1996, 939).

In studies based upon rational choice actors are utility maximizers who always aim for a maximum of personal benefit. In this world institu-tions structure the incentives of actors and determine which kind of be-havior is rewarded and what is penalized. In political science game theo-ry has gained some traction with the rise of rational choice institutional-ism (Scharpf 2000). In sociological institutionalism actors are "neither as self-interested nor as 'rational' as rational choice scholarship would have it (March and Olson 1989), but are 'satisficers' who act habitually" (Stein-mo 2010, 126). Here institutions are conceptualized as roles or norms that provide guidance for actors in their interactions with others. Scholars in HI have an "eclectic" (Hall and Taylor 1996, 940) answer to this question: their actors are understood to potentially behave in both ways. The more important question for a scholar in this tradition is why an actor behaved in a certain way and not in another. Institutions have to be seen in their specific context in order to understand their impact on actors. The context is the historical environment, or as Thelen (1999, 382) puts its, "historical institutionalists see institutions as the legacy of concrete historical pro-cesses." In this historic context an actor's previous social interaction and perhaps even his position within the political system are important fac-tors (Hall and Taylor 1996, 941). In essence HI assumes that not everyone is affected by an institution in the same way and that statements on the effects of a particular institution should be based on empirical studies. Steinmo (2010, 126) explains: "What the HI scholar wants to know is why a certain choice was made and/or why a certain outcome occurred."

In a similar manner these three approaches also have different under-standings of why and how institutions change. In HI the idea of institu-tional path dependencies runs strong. These emphasize the stability of institutions over time. It has been more the idea of persistence than change that has been emphasized in HI. Some even argue that HI offers little to explain institutional change. For a long time, the dominant explanation has been that these institutional paths change only at "critical junctures" and that a political or military crisis may be such a critical juncture (Hall and Taylor 1996, 942). Although it is certainly true that a crisis can initiate institutional change—this understanding takes away the influence of actors upon institutional change and does not explain many other cases of institutional change. Why, for example, did institutions regulating access to farmland in China continue to change at an impressive rate? While the initial change toward the redistribution of land to farming households correlates with a general systemic crisis in China, later reforms refuse to follow a similar logic. Dealing with similar issues Steinmo has suggested investigating the role of new ideas for institutional change: "Bringing ideas into our understanding of institutional change, then, brings agents back into institutional analysis" (2010, 133). For the case at hand, this implies the need to explore how new ideas on the role of the Chinese agriculture have affected institutional change and how this institutional change in turn has affected the behavior of actors related to agriculture. The following overview on the independent and dependent variables aims to take this into account.

Peasant Differentiation

Peasant differentiation denotes diversification of smallholder livelihood strategies and different stages of market integration of agrarian producers. Many scholars, among them Brenner and Polanyi, argue that compulsory market integration of agrarian production is a crucial factor in this diversification. Three different directions of diversification seem feasible.

The first development is a growing dependence on monetary income for smallholder households and unstable or low incomes in agriculture. This may force rural households out of independent agriculture and into wage labor or even into other sectors of the economy. Ellis explains: "Livelihood diversification describes the phenomenon by which peasant households take up non-farm activities, or rely on non-farm income transfers, for the overall standard of living that they are able to achieve" (Ellis 2006, 391). He continues to argue that livelihood diversification has always been a part of peasant farming because the chief reasons to diversify, risk and seasonality, have always existed. However, for Ellis there are now numerous additional reasons for livelihood diversification, such as inflation, decline in farm gate prices or perhaps the end of subsidies. Ultimately, reporting on the case of sub-Saharan Africa, land tenure may "trap people in agriculture." He asserts that if land cannot be sold or rented out for a reasonable price, families tend to split up. One part stays on the land to take care of it, while the other (usually male) part wanders around in search of wage employment (Ellis 2006, 396). Similar behavior is not unknown for China. The question emerges as to how sustainable smallholder farming is when, as Christiansen (2009, 568) reports, many farmers in the countryside use urban employment in order to be able to continue their unprofitable farming activities.

Zhang and Donaldson (2010), in one of the few attempts to conceptualize the recent peasant differentiation in China as part of a rise of agrarian capitalism, report on another development that goes in a similar direction. They argue that contracted farming is becoming increasingly important for Chinese peasants. In some variants of this process peasants become the employees of the contracting enterprise—on their own land. The key in all these accounts of agrarian proletarizaion is the degree to which independent peasant agriculture, e.g., family farming, can provide the means for subsistence and a good life. If peasant farming fails in this regard, invariably the pressure to redistribute land in one way or another increases. The transformation of Chinese agriculture from a socialist mode of production, in which the collective took all risks of failure, to a mode of private production, in which the households now shoulder the risk is especially meaningful in this context (Christiansen 2010, 140). In countries with limited farmland resources such as China only this struggle of some smallholders creates the necessary room for commercial farming. It is their land which is first commodified.

The second dynamic is represented by those households on the other end of the economic spectrum of this diversification process that are willing and able to take a risk and turn themselves into entrepreneurial farmers. Not only do these households occupy a vanguard position in the spread of capitalism to the countryside but they also depend on a commodification of land. Without relatively cheap access to land the opportunities for these households to expand production are limited. A steady increase in the number of these rural entrepreneurs would suggest that a commodification of land is possible and that agrarian capitalism has taken hold in the countryside.

It has to be noted that peasant farming and entrepreneurial farming, as outlined in the previous section, represent two entirely different modes of production and should not be confused with a social stratification of the rural population. In Europe the differentiation between rich and poor peasants is, according to Rodney Hilton, "at least as old as the earliest records we have of them" (Byres 2009, 35).

The third option is actually the absence or only very limited existence of peasant differentiation. In this case peasants are able to continue small- and sub-scale farming either because there is substantial and sustained financial support for smallholders and part-time farming by the state as for example in the Japanese case (Mulgan 2000) or because of other supporting mechanisms (like homestay tourism, see Park 2014).

The consequences of peasant differentiation could be far reaching. Ellis argues that, in regard to the transformation of agriculture, two trajectories dominate the debate. The first is that agriculture becomes less and less important for the rural population. He refers to this process as deagrarianization. The other trajectory would be the "erosion of the family basis of their livelihoods" (Ellis 2006, 388), which he refers to as depeasantization. The answer as to in which direction China is heading needs to be part of an empirical investigation.

Rural Politics

The term rural politics refers to the triad of institutional framework, policies, and the interaction of state and non-state actors in agriculture. Institutions that govern markets, influence taxes and prices, may initiate or delay redistribution of wealth, are likely to become the initial starting point for an agrarian transition. Structural reform programs or development initiatives, as will be seen, can affect the pace or direction of an agrarian transition.

Another key aspect of rural politics is the interaction among various interest groups that pursue their own agenda in the field of agriculture. Four ideal-type actors have been identified to be of importance for the agricultural transformation process. Peasants and entrepreneurial farmers (in whatever form organized) constitute the first two social actors. The differences between the two groups have already been presented. The other two key actors are the national and the local state, especially on the county level and below. Many of the important policies in the field of agrarian transformation originate from the national level in China. It is necessary to separate the local level here because it not only has its own development initiatives but also has great influence on the implementation of the initiatives of higher levels of the administration.

In order to better understand the direction of the transformation of the Chinese agriculture we need to take into account the motivation and distribution of power among its key actors. Seen from this perspective, a commodification of land as part of agrarian change then also becomes linked to politics that promote certain lifestyles. The relationship between state and primary producers is a crucial part of agrarian transition and is seen as a potential major influence in its outcome. If, for example, the political leadership of a nation perceives that a lack of development within agriculture and the rural sector in general can be attributed to deficiencies in structural aspects and people, it is possible that it will aim to correct this. Robert Bates (1984) has shown how modernizing states in Africa have used the "market as an political arena," manipulating prices and taxes to promote urban industrial production and commercial agriculture over smallholder farming. He further argues that development programs in the countryside "create and nurture rural clients, particularly among elite farmers, and thereby encourage patterns of collaboration that bridge the gap between town and county in Africa" (Bates 1984, 44). In fact, survival and prosperity of different forms of agrarian organization often appears to be more related to political decisions than to questions of efficiency in production.

Property Institutions

All forms of farming depend on a set of rules that regulate the allowed use of farmland and protect the rights of the farming entity against other groups in society that may want to interfere with its work or appropriate part of the harvest. These rules are fixed in property institutions and constitute the third variable of the research design.

In his book *Environment and Economy: Property Rights and Public Policy*, Daniel Bromley (1991) develops a very useful analytical framework that may be fruitfully applied for an analysis of the role of property institutions for the Chinese agrarian transition. For Bromley, "[p]roperty [. . .] is a benefit (or income) stream, and a property right is a claim to a benefit stream that the state will agree to protect through the assignment of duty to others who may covet, or somehow interfere with, the benefit stream" (Bromley 1991, 2). In this framework the structure of social relations define a property, not physical possession. Property exist only when society respects the rights of a party to a specific benefit stream and if the state safeguards these rights. Drawing on Hohfeld (1913; 1917) and Commons (1968) Bromley describes rights and duties as a special type of relationship between two parties, which he refers to as Alpha and Beta. Alpha's *right* to a certain benefit stream directly creates a *duty* for Beta to observe this right. Bromley describes this framework as "perfectly symmetrical" insofar as "[t]he legal relation is identical regardless of the position from which the relation is viewed (Alpha or Beta)" (Bromley 1991, 17).

In practice, however, the nature of legal relations is not always transparent and rights may be disputed. Bromley suggests that these disputes fall into either one of the following two categories: two parties claim the same right or two parties claim different rights that are in conflict with each other. In the former case the *validity* of the claim is disputed. An example in this case may be the restitution of collective village land to households in Transylvania described by Verdery (2003), in which many households brought forward claims to the same plots of land. In the latter case either the *validity* of the claim or that the right applies in the given situation is disputed. The frequent clashes between villagers and local governments in rural China on turning farmland into construction land may serve as an example for conflicting claims. Here, villagers have the right to farm their land, but local governments have the right to turn land into construction land (on the condition of doing so for the common good).

A crucial element in Bromley's characterization of property is the underlying triadic relationship between Alpha, Beta, and the state. Ultimately it is the state that grants Alpha certain rights by ensuring that Beta is observing its duties. The state does this, according to Bromley, because it is convinced of the social utility this arrangement creates for all. If the state looses its belief in the benefits of this arrangement, it may discontinue to support some or all of Alpha's claims. Consider, for example, the relationship between the village collectives and the villagers in China in the early 1980s. The reforms that led to the creation of the HRS could also be described as the state transferring some of the collectives' rights directly to the villagers because it assumed this would lead to improvements in general welfare (among other reasons).

For Bromley, relations of rights and duties operate within a *resource management regime*: "The emphasis here is on regimes as human creations whose purpose is to *manage people* in their use of environmental resources" (Bromley 1991, 21 italics in the original). He identifies four distinct regimes: state property, private property, common property, and open access. Within a state property regime the "state may either directly manage and control the use of state-owned resources through government agencies, or lease the natural resources to groups or individuals who are thus given usufruct rights for a specific period of time" (Bromley 1991, 23). In a private property regime individuals control access and use of property. This control, however, is not absolute, as the state may restrict some use cases and may add obligations to others. Common property "represents *private property for the group of co-owners* (since all others are excluded from use and decision making)" (Bromley 1991, 25). Bromley notes that while size, composition, and structure of these groups may vary greatly, they usually share cultural norms, are subject to the same authority system and interact with each other on a regular basis (Bromley 1991, 26). The group may grant one of its members the right to use (parts of) its property under certain conditions or may withdraw such rights. The ability of the group to take decisions on the usage of property is a defining element of common property. Finally, open access regimes differ from all other forms of property management because they do not impose any limitations on the use of property. In fact, in open access regimes property does not exist or ceases to exist (Bromley 1991, 30). In contrast to the presentation of private ownership in classical works on property rights such as Demsetz (1967), in Bromley's framework none of these three forms centered on the notion of controlling access to property (private, state, and common property) is inherently more efficient than its peers in managing resources.

Property, property institutions, and property rights do not exist in a normative vacuum. Especially in countries, such as China, gave witnessed enormous economic reforms but little political change, different sets of norms and values regarding property frequently may be in conflict to each other. Drawing on the work of Verdery (2003) it seems helpful to differentiate at least between three different perspectives on property in China: a Western, a traditional, and a socialist.

Discources within the Western property rights perspective are centered on the idea that setting defining boundaries for access to a commodity allows a more productive usage of this resource. Verdery summarizes this thinking: "[. . .] once we create property rights and deliver them to people, property ideology says that those people will have an incentive to work well and to use access efficiently, disciplined by the market" (Verdery 2003, 15). A focus is put on the definition of property rights, some of which can then be traded in the marketplace. Economists have a clear understanding of how property rights in a market society should be defined: "[. . .] governments intent on fostering a market economy should thus make sure to put an effective legal system in place, one in which property rights are unambiguous, secure and freely alienable" (Rapaczynski as quoted in Smyth 1998, 236). Many scholars see well-defined property rights as a precondition for working capitalist markets. This debate echoes in the political sphere. Here clearly defined property structures and distributed ownership are perceived as one of the pillars of liberal democracy. Based on specific interpretation of the process of industrialization in the West and in England in particular, it is argued that in order to take an independent stand against the government and develop conditions for the emergence of a civil society, private ownership is a condition sine qua non.

In this perspective the value of land is determined by its economic value and may change due to many factors including location of the plots, shifts in farm gate prices of agricultural commodities, access to necessary inputs, the legal protection of land, the provision of agricultural extension services, training and education, political support through subsidies and tariffs, and much more. Of course the economic value of rural land is not limited to agricultural use cases. In fact, non-agricultural interest in farmland renders continued farming unattractive far too often.

If farming households are less integrated in global food chains and capital-intensive farming, the non-economic value attached to land has a better chance to prevail. This non-economic value forms the basis of the traditional property perspective. For example, for many peasants in the Chinese countryside cultivating land is important to sustain a connection to their ancestors, some of whom are even buried beneath the fields. Peasant migration to the home of the ancestors, often many hundreds of years after earlier generations of family have left this place, shows the continued strength of this connection even in contemporary China (see Liu and Murphy 2006).[3] At the core of this perspective is a local group with clearly identifiable membership, built on shared interests and values. The property type most closely associated with this perspective on property is common property (see Bromley 1991, 25).

An argument brought forward by economists against the traditional property perspective and especially against common property is their alleged limited ability to protect scare resources from being depleted (Demsetz 1967). If everybody has the same rights to a piece of land, nobody will have the power to limit the use of said land. This argument misses the point that membership in such groups usually entails both rights and obligations. In fact, the organization of common property regimes may be even more complex than the one in the Western property perspective based on legal clauses. James Scott (Scott 1998, 33–47) gives a great example of the complexity of traditional property system for the management of farmland. Willem Assies (2009) reports that a more traditional perspective of land, which goes beyond mere classification as an economic asset, is experiencing a renaissance in the international development discourse. Here land is related to the basic human rights of security, shelter, and secure livelihoods. For many peasants, land always had these qualities and it is terribly difficult for peasants in China (and in many other parts of the world) to come to terms with the fact that land may have lost considerable importance in this regard.

Compared to these two previously outlined perspectives on property, the idea of property is treated very differently in socialist countries. While the next chapter will introduce the legal specifics of land management in rural China, some more general aspects of socialist property will be discussed here.

Verdery argues that socialist countries "emphasized a different set of property types based on the identity of the owners and the social relation among them" (Verdery 2003, 49). It is not legal rights, although they are defined, that regulate access to property but rather administrative commands within a hierarchical system. Consequently, three main property subjects emerge: "(1) the state (technically all the people in whose name the state acts), (2) socialist cooperatives together with other nonproducing socialist organizations, and (3) individuals and households" (Verdery 2003, 49). All three of these actors become eligible only for specific kinds of property but possess the important right to provide their sub-units with access to parts of their own property as they see fit.

In relation to these three groups of owners four types of property were created: *state property, collective property, private property*, and *personal property*. The first two types included most means of production. State property was controlled by one of the organizations within the state hierarchy. Verdery calls collective property "one of those compromises life so often forces on grand designs" (Verdery 2003, 50) and links its existence to the initial opposition of peasants against the nationalization of all farming plots. Collective ownership emerged by pooling agricultural resources, either by free will or by force, into agricultural collectives. Ownership of these resources remained within the collective—in part to counter fears that the resources pooled would be taken away from the collective. In socialist countries private property covers the limited means of production of small producers, "such as uncollectivized peasants and tradespeople (e.g., tailors, cobblers, and carpenters); such property was likely to be organized in households" (Verdery 2003, 51). This type of property did not exist in all socialist systems. Personal property is only for consumption and in most cases it was forbidden by law to turn it into a means of production.

Socialist property systems, in contrast to the Western property system, did not aim to create a single owner for each object. Rather "the most important relationship after the ownership prerogatives of the state was based on what was officially termed the *right of direct (or operational) administration*, which I call *administrative rights*" (Verdery 2003, 56, emphasis in the original). Organizations and administrations received administrative rights to a given piece of property. Verdery argues that this goes beyond usus fructus rights and comes close to a Western understanding of ownership rights. However, the rights were handed down by a higher-ranking organization or administration and could be withdrawn and given to another organization at any point in time.

At all times the land remained in state ownership. The state could not be expropriated or foreclosed on and regulations for the transfer from one kind of ownership to another usually were biased toward state ownership. During the transition from socialism to a market economy, property institutions have come under scrutiny. While many former socialist countries in Europe, often following the policy advice of international organizations such as the IMF and Worldbank, made considerable efforts to privatize property, China has moved in a different direction by keeping a formally socialist property system in place. The Chinese route implies the continued existence of administrative rights, at least to some degree. An important question for the next chapter, therefore, is to see how the Chinese state incorporated the distribution of private plots to farming households within the framework of a socialist property system.

Commodification of Farmland

Commodification as a process has strong links to the Western Property Rights perspective outlined before. Proponents for a commodification argue that land should be "allocated in order to maximise the benefits that accrue from its ownership and control" (Akram-Lodhi 2007, 1439). Akram Lodhi has called this a "neoliberal enclosure" and points to the failure to recognize a value in land beyond it being an economic resource (ibid.).

Smallholder farming in this perspective has two main shortcomings that necessitate the redistribution of land: small average sizes of land holdings and fragmentation of land. Proponents of consolidating land into bigger holdings, such as Collier (2008), point to the inherent lack of capital of small farms, translating into an inadequate application of necessary production inputs. The lack of modern agricultural production impedes the quantitative and qualitative outcome of this type of agriculture, Collier argues. By allowing the formation of bigger farms production could be more labor-efficient through the usage of machinery, better usage of inputs and better knowledge of modern production techniques. Surplus labor would be free to pursue better-paid, non-agricultural employment. Technical sophistication in agriculture will in turn lead to increased monetary income per unit of agricultural labor.

Countering land fragmentation is another important point for the proponents of a Western property perspective. To create economies of scale in agriculture it is not only important to have a lot of land but also to have it all in one place. For smaller plots, the application of new machinery, tractors, and combine harvesters in particular, as well as the construction of irrigation infrastructure and the usage of modern inputs is either not possible or the costs exceed the potential benefits by far. Kautsky has argued that smaller holdings in Prussia have not led to fewer investments in mechanization (per unit of land) but rather to more, as each farmer needed to have his own equipment. To be more efficient industrial agriculture therefore depends upon the concentration of plots into larger holdings (Kautsky 1899, 130–163).

The efficiency of large landholdings is not undisputed. Those in favor of a return to smallholder farming at times also argue in the terminology of economic efficiency. A popular argument is the assumed *inverse relationship* between the size of the plots used for agriculture and how efficiently land is used (Berry 2011). Smallholders are said to use the little land they have more effectively because labor and supervision costs do not figure prominently. Large farms instead are assumed to be more likely to leave land unused or underused just because they have less urgency to bring it into comparable use. If the land is distributed in an egalitarian fashion this is assumed to carry additional benefits for poverty alleviation. Having access to land the rural poor would be able to secure their means of survival more easily and therefore would be less dependent on transfer payments. In addition, these peasants could rent it out, use it as a security to acquire a loan and, if necessary sell the land.

From a traditional property perspective, therefore, the consolidation of land into unified and bigger holdings (beyond the amount one household can manage) makes little sense. Quite to the contrary, it might have negative effects on smallholders (as argued by Zhang and Donaldson 2010). Smallholders on average have less input and machinery at hand and therefore depend more upon the quality of a given plot of land than commercial farmers do. Small plots of high quality land, under these circumstances, may be better for a smallholder than having a bigger piece of land of mediocre or less than average quality. In this context more land may mean more risks but not necessarily more benefits.

Two possible routes for the commodification of farmland in China seem plausible. In one scenario property rights are taken from communities with some kind of traditional or common property regime by force. This kind of enclosure movement usually entails a coalition of state agents and investors, as in the example outlined by Polanyi. In a second scenario villagers decide to stop working the land themselves and sell or rent their land to someone else. Although this may also be in response to pressure by local governments or capitalist investors, villagers may have at least some say in the process, including that their consent is necessary for any transactions. It is this latter scenario the book is interested in. What makes a rural family give up farming? And ultimately, what makes them give up their land, especially in a country where there is no legal means (yet) to take away the land for economic reasons such as personal debts?

By conducting an investigation into the commodification of farmland in China the book pursues three main goals. Given the little information available on this process to the world outside of China, it first aims to provide a detailed account of current modes of transfer of farmland in China. The second goal is to explore the potential relationship between the pace of the Chinese agrarian transition and the way in which this commodification of farmland is managed. The third goal is a better understanding of the power constellation of different actors in this commodification process and the emerging structure of a post-smallholder agriculture in China.

SUMMARY

This chapter sets the stage for the subsequent empirical investigation and is structured in two sections. It starts with an detailed introduction to the concept of agrarian transition drawn from the works of Polanyi and Brenner and discusses the feasibility of its application in China. Instead of viewing the emergence of capitalism in agriculture as being connected to an inherent capitalist nature or demographic changes, this section identifies peasant differentiation, property institutions, and rural politics as main causal mechanisms within such a conceptualization of agrarian transitions. All three have deep links to the commodification of farmland, which is a critical process of any agrarian transition.

Next the research design of the book as a case study based on process tracing is introduced. The three causal mechanisms of agrarian transitions identified in the theoretic discussion are chosen as independent variables, while the commodification of land is taken as the dependent variable. The section includes a brief discussion of the role of institutions in the book.

The section then proceeds to discuss the four variables and their variance. Peasant differentiation is mainly understood as the increasing compulsory integration of peasants into the market. Market integration brings with it market risks, which may force peasants out of farming. These market risks thereby create opportunities for other actors to fill in—if the institutional framework allows for the transfer and concentration of land. Rural politics is a composite variable covering institutions, policies, and state actor interference in agrarian production that may promote or prevent agrarian transition and also may have great influence on the nature of the transition and who is becoming the driving force of this process. The variable concerning property institutions draws on the work of Daniel Bromley to conceptualize property within an agrarian transition. A second aspect of this variable considers the relationship between property regimes and the value of land. It is argued that the property debate in China shows considerable similarities with the debate in postsocialist societies in Eastern Europe. Here, a traditional property perspective competes with Western and socialist property regimes.

Finally, the dependent variable, the commodification of farmland, is discussed as a process which ties together the three different independent variables and a potential agrarian transition. Market-like transfer activities are a commercial requirement of the agrarian transition. Capitalist agrarian producers need to be able to gain access to all means of production through capital investment. If there is no market for farmland, then there is no agrarian transition. However, if farmland becomes a commodified asset eventually capital will become a major requirement for most types of agricultural production. Hence the commodification of farmland correlates strongly with an agrarian transition. The expected variance of this variable includes all market-like transfer activities of farmland that are in line with the legal framework in China and where land continues to stay within agriculture. The HRS is still at the core of all management of farmland in rural China and, as long as there is no private ownership of farmland, all transfer activities have to meet its legal requirements.

NOTES

1. Another important account of the transition has been the "demographic model," as Brenner (1985a) refers to it. This model relates the emergence of capitalism in Europe to "certain autonomous cycles of population growth and decline" (Wood 2002, 17). In response to these cycles, the emergence of capitalism was a logical consequence of the laws of supply and demand, these scholars argue. For Wood, this is only a variation of the commercialization model, as the underlying rules for capitalism, such as supply, demand, and market dependency, are already assumed to be natural laws.

2. See the next chapter for an introduction to the Chinese transition to family farming in the late 1970s and early 1980s, including a brief account of the debate on who started family farming in the Chinese countryside.

3. In this particular case, the historic background may also be a welcome pretext for economic claims in the present.

THREE
Collective Land and Household Responsibility System

The main narrative of this chapter is the struggle of the central political leadership to maintain collective ownership of land in the countryside while at the same time pushing for the modernization and commercialization of agriculture. Not all relevant political actors in rural China have adopted this agenda. Instead of being able to focus on the modernization of agriculture, the center is forced again and again to curtail the interest of its local agents for alternative and perhaps financially more rewarding uses of the land.

Subsequently, three major themes can be identified in the administration of collective land in China since the early 1980s. The first is the institutionalization of the Household Responsibility System (HRS). It is an attempt to create room for private farming in an economy increasingly dominated by markets while still holding on to a socialist property system. Since its conception several reforms have aimed to further strengthen the HRS and especially the rights granted to farmers within this system. The second theme is the will to ensure the protection of a minimum amount of land for farming by all means available. The continued existence of administrative ownership rights has turned the transformation of collective farmland into construction land into a very profitable endeavor for the local state, individual cadres, and real estate development agencies. The transformation has reached such dimensions that Beijing sees the national food security endangered. The third theme in land administration is the wish to make land within the HRS a more flexible asset in order to suit the needs of a modernizing and commercializing agriculture.

The chapter is organized in four sections. The first section deals with the conception of the HRS and its roots in collective ownership. Its focus is upon the economic effects of the initial redistribution of land to the rural households. The second section addresses major legal reforms in the administration of farmland from 1982 until 2008, the starting point of the empirical work for this book.[1] Many of these regulations aim to limit the loss of farmland to construction projects. The third section will explore this kind of land loss as an important contextual factor for the commercialization of agriculture. The final section of the chapter is an outlook on currently discussed reforms in the administration of collective land.

CREATION OF THE HRS

In the late 1970s production teams in several impoverished parts of Anhui Province started handing out farmland directly to peasant households for independent farming activities. The developments that followed these early experiments not only transformed agriculture but also had disruptive consequences on other parts of the economy, social relationships, and the political organization of the countryside in China.

These reforms in agriculture are among the most well-researched parts of recent Chinese history. As numerous as the studies are, so too are the interpretations of these historic changes. Many controversies circle around the question of who was behind the experiments in breaking up collective structures in agriculture. Less disputed seem to be the economic consequences, or in other words, the enormous economic boom frequently associated with these experiments. However, the connection between the return to family farming and enormous economic growth may be more complex than generally assumed and warrants closer scrutiny if one is interested in understanding the current social and economic trends in the countryside. In the following section, the main narratives concerning the origins and drivers of agricultural reform will be briefly discussed before taking a look at the resulting structures for the management of collective farmland. Finally, the economic effects of the return to smallholder farming will be analyzed.

Jonathan Unger (2002b) offers a comprehensive overview of the available documentation on the movement from the production team system in agriculture toward individualized farming on contracted land in the aftermath of the 3rd Plenary Session of the 11th Central Committee of the CPC in 1978 (see also Watson 1983, 712–718). According to him, party secretaries in rural Anhui Province either began to hand out land to peasant families in order to increase production in these poor townships or colluded with peasants who had already divided the land on their own. Wan Li, provincial party secretary in Anhui at the time, publicly endorsed these developments as early as February of 1979 (Unger 2002b, 100). In the early days of the reform, two alternative experiments in handing out land directly to peasants emerged: *bao gan dao hu* (contracting management to the household), more frequently referred to as *dabaogan* (big management contracting) and *bao chan dao hu* (contracting production to the household) (see Unger 2002b, 96–100). Under the experiment of *bao chan dao hu* the peasant households were contracted to produce goods determined by the production team and received all necessary inputs to do so. After the harvest, the families were remunerated according to quantity and quality of their produced output. In contrast, peasant households within the *dabaogan* system received a share of farming land and perhaps some other resources from the production team but were free to produce as they saw fit and had to sell their harvest on their own (although this happened basically within the state procurement system). In both cases, new freedom came with new responsibilities.

The grain quotas delivered to the state, which in the past had to be fulfilled by the production team, from now on had to be transferred directly to the producers (Kung 1997, 35). The amount of land received by the household was used to calculate the grain quotas and other obligations such as corvée labor. These obligations were fixed in contracts, which formed the basis of the HRS. Nolan and Paine (1987) provide an early contract from Guanghan Township in Sichuan Province. The contract identifies two parties, the village collective and the individual household, and outlines the responsibilities of these two groups. Among the obligations of the village collective, the owner of the land, are land and water conservation, the provision of inputs such as seeds and fertilizer, suggestions and technical guidance, and transparent and democratic management of collective property. The contracting household in turn has the following responsibilities: they must make full use of contracted land, they must follow the lead of the village in their choice for planting, they may not have children in excess of the birth plan, and they must fulfill their rent obligations to the collective on time (Nolan and Paine 1987, 99–101).

The interpretation of the reasons behind the creation of the HRS in the countryside is at the center of much of the controversy about the reform in China. In contrast to the public account of these events published in the newspapers at the time, in which the developments in the countryside are portrayed as a bottom-up movement of emancipating peasants, Unger (2002b) sees the political leadership in Beijing behind these changes. His two main arguments for this are: first, not only did his interview partners report that local cadres decided in most cases on the time frame and the model chosen (*dabaogan*) but second, the rapid implementation of the policy suggests coordinated efforts by the center. Indeed, of the two models the less collective *dabogan* began to dominate quickly. Unger notes "by the end of 1983 97.8 percent of all the production teams in China had parceled out their land to households in the *dabogan* system, according to official Chinese government statistics"

(2002b, 102). One year later, the adoption rate stood at 99.1 percent (ibid.). Cai and Treisman also argue that the source of the dynamism of the reforms should not be seen as "innovative, autonomous local leaders in defiance of an ideologically blinkered center" but rather "as gambits in a game played between competing factions centered in Beijing" (2006, 518). They note that the reforms started early and spread fast in those provinces in which the leading figures such as Wan Li in Anhui and Zhao Ziyang in Sichuan had a close connection to Deng Xiaoping. Finally, they argue that "[g]rassroots initiatives were certainly important, but the main battlefront ran not between the center and regions but rather through the heart of Beijing" (ibid.).

Thomas Heberer (1996) takes a different position and suggests that peasants themselves were the main driving force behind the transformation of agriculture. He argues that most approaches explaining the return of individualized farming in China focus too much on the activities of officials and political institutions. According to him most of these reforms are a reaction to what was already happening on the ground, independent of the debates in Beijing and elsewhere: "[i]n the poverty stricken regions of central and southern China the peasants distributed the land among themselves and returned to family farming" (1996, 3). Many other reforms in the countryside started as illegal actions in a similar vein, Heberer adds, and concludes that "[f]rom this point onwards the peasantry dictated the policies of the Party leadership through continuously renewed spontaneous action" (Heberer 1996, 6). This position is shared by authors such as Kelliher (1992) and Zhou (1996), who also see the reforms as being inspired and pushed through by the peasants themselves. Yuan Cheng (2010) sees a considerable gap between the starting point of the reforms and their official endorsement, which only happened after many localities had already taken steps in this direction. He argues that in effect the statements of Deng Xiaoping and Hu Yaobang around Spring Festival of 1980 and the No. 1 Document of 1982 put an end to 30 years (throughout the collective period) of the illegal existence of *bao chan dao hu* (Yuan 2010, 99).

Yang Dali and Joseph Fewsmith take the middle ground in this debate and highlight the importance of local administrations for this reform. Yang (1996, 178) writes:

> [. . .] the conventional literature errs in its overemphasis on the role of the state, especially that of the central leadership [. . .] I have argued that local initiatives preceded state policies on the adoption of liberal rural policies, leading to the adoption of contracting everything to the household (*dabaogan daohu*). In contrast, even the most "daring" of the reformist leaders, including Zhao Ziyang and Wan Li, toned down rural liberalization in its early days. One contribution of this chapter is to establish that localities responded to factors other than the state and played a key role in forging the path of reform.

And Fewsmith (1994, 19) argues that the reforms "emerged from a highly complex process in which local leaders provided peasants with the opportunity to experiment with reform and then argued, both directly and indirectly, with the central leadership to allow the experiments to continue and eventually to be expanded."

It is important to note that most accounts of the transformation agree that the return to family farming in China had been very popular among the rural population. Whether one agrees with Unger, who notes that "[w]ithin Party cycles, the knowledge that the program was popular among peasants seems to have effectively obscured the issue of whether the change was being implemented voluntarily or not" (2002b, 102) or with Heberer, who sees "a partial victory for the peasants in the form of economic reforms" (Heberer 1996, 3), the fact remains that the reforms had been very popular among villagers. After years of dealing with collective experiments in farming, villagers well appreciated their freedom to do business "on their own," without micromanagement by the local state and without potential "free-riders." Not only did the countryside benefit greatly from the reforms, but the urban population was soon after also able to enjoy an until-then-unknown variety of vegetables and fruits as new farmers went to the cities to sell a part of their products in order to make more money. The new quantity, diversity, and quality in agricultural products available for the urban population may have been one of the reasons that would have made all decisions to end the reforms very difficult.[2]

This is not the place to continue the debate on who started the reforms in the countryside. For the questions discussed in this book, it is more rewarding to examine the post-reform evaluation of the economic effects of this historical change. The reforms and more specifically the return to family farming have been used as a popular explanation for the economic growth in the countryside since the early 1980s. A first look at the empirical data seems to prove this.

In 1978, the average per-capita income of a rural person was 124.05 RMB, of which 15.15 RMB derived from tilling the land and 12.01 RMB came from animal husbandry. In 1985, the basic income had risen to 367.69 RMB, of which 191.46 RMB came from farming and 44.36 from animal husbandry (all figures see National Bureau of Statistics of China 1995, 279). In other words, the monetary per-capita income from farming had increased nearly thirteenfold and revenue from animal husbandry almost quadrupled in only seven years. Rozelle (1996, 64) confirms this growth:

> From 1978 to 1984, per capita rural incomes increased in real terms (that is, after adjusting for inflation) at extremely fast rates. Annual growth in incomes exceeded 10 per cent during this period, while inter-

household income distribution in rural areas remained relatively unchanged.

Some regions, especially in poorer parts of the countryside, may have
had even higher relative growth rates than the national average. Certainly the new freedom of households to manage their own business may
have been a great incentive to increase farming efforts. Nonetheless, new
enthusiasm in farming is only partially responsible for the increased welfare in the countryside. The success of the HRS reform and agricultural
growth was ensured by substantial subsidies to agrarian producers
(mainly via the state procurement system). Moreover, the factor contributing most to improved welfare in the countryside was the emergence of
non-farm employment opportunities, which provided even higher incomes.

The introduction of the HRS reform may never have been primarily
about maximizing the output of agriculture.[3] Zhu and Jiang (1993) note
that, while one of the main goals of the HRS system has been a closer
connection between work and enumeration, other goals such as equality
and fairness in the distribution of land and food security have been
equally important. For the initial distribution varying degrees of the
available farming land in the villages (sometimes all land, most of the
time less) was set aside and rated by villagers and officials. Among the
criteria used for judging the quality of the land was the "soil fertility,
location and availability of irrigation" (Zhu and Jiang 1993, 447). Every
household received plots of varying quality. This led to an average distribution of 0.56 hectare of land, split into 9.7 plots per household (ibid.). In
most cases, households received land based upon the number of household members and not the available workforce within the household,
although the latter variation also existed.

Usually not all of the land was distributed to the households. In the
most popular model, the collective farmland was divided into two parts.
This system was called "two-field system" (*liangtianzhi*). The first part
was the "grain ratio land" (*kouliangtian*), which was supposed to ensure
that households would be able to meet their subsistence needs. The second part of the land, "responsibility land" (*zerentian*) was to be contracted
out to households who agreed to meet part of the procurement quota of
the village set by higher levels of authority. In addition, some villages
continued to have common land or additional reserved land, which
could be contracted out for a fee (called *chengbaotian*) as well as additional
contributions made toward the procurement quotas (Bramall 2004,
129–130). The No. 1 Document of 1984 issued by the Central Committee
of the CPC established a 15-year time frame for the initial land contracts
(Ash 1988, 537).

In November 1982 Du Runsheng, at the time head of the Rural Development Research Center of the State Council and highly involved in the

design of the reforms, gave a speech in which he addressed the scattered nature of the distributed land and its potential impact on agrarian productivity. He argued that this, instead of being an obstacle to the development of modern agriculture, would allow Chinese farmers to better utilize their competitive advantages in labor supply. Instead of relying upon more inputs, as economies of scale in capitalism and socialism do, the Chinese farmer would work the little land he had in the most profitable way. The direct link between output and payoff would eliminate the monitoring issues larger entities had. As an example Du mentions that the grain harvest in some regions after the return to family farming doubled (Du 1989, 39). It is an early and rare argument by a Chinese official in favor of the "inverse relationship" theory (Johnston and Le Roux 2007), which states that the productivity of a plot increases if the farm size decreases.

The available data confirms the difficult state of economies of scale in the early reform years. Although almost right from the start of the reforms it was possible to rent out contracted land in the form of subcontracting, the time frame for these subcontract leases was usually restricted to 1–3 years (Zhu and Jiang 1993, 441). This limitation made it very difficult to create sustainable bigger farms. In fact, even after some restrictions were lifted (see the next section in this chapter) very little farmland was rented out. James Kung (2002, 396) mentions a study from 1995 which states that up until the year 1995 only 3–4 percent of the available land was managed by rental relationships. The scattered nature of the plots, their small size, and the difficulties in the creation of bigger holdings in agriculture led authors like Bramall to go as far as to draw comparisons between the HRS and pre-war farming in China (Bramall 2004, 126).

There are no indications that, after the initial distribution, land was moving toward more efficient users. Quite to the contrary, the initial allocation of land was followed by frequent redistributions in order to preserve the relatively egalitarian patterns of land distribution. Zhu and Jiang (1993, 447) mention an official Chinese survey from 1988 that illustrates the amount of land redistributed in the first few years after the initial distribution:

> The sample survey of the RCRD shows that 65% of the 250 sample villages have redistributed land every 2 years since 1983. The redistribution in 91% of those villages was caused by demographic changes. Only 5% of the villages reallocated land in order to enable farm size to grow and less than 2% did it for plot consolidation (about 3% of those questioned gave no reason).

In another sample there were on average two reallocations between 1982 and 1995, which typically involved two-thirds of the farmland and three-quarters of the households (Brandt, Rozelle, and Turner 2004, 629). A third survey of 271 villages from 1997 found that 80 percent of them had reallocated the land since the beginning of the HRS. Of these villages, 66 percent even reallocated two or more times (Ho 2001, 397).

In 1993 the redistributive nature of the farmland administration was changed. In order to allow more long-term investments by Villagers, the land was contracted to households for an additional 30 years (Ho 2001, 295). The 30-year time frame also entered the revised Land Administration Law (LAL) of 1999 (Brandt, Rozelle, and Turner 2004, 629). This change in the system might have taken place to the dismay of many farmers, who seem to have preferred the frequent egalitarian redistributions (Ho 2001, 397; Unger 2002b, 115).

To what degree have the reforms in the pattern of land management contributed to the enormously positive development of agriculture? Putting aside regional differences for the moment, in the absence of economies of scale in agriculture a lot seems to speak for Du Runsheng and his "inverse relationship" argument. However, if we add other data and policies to the picture, the situation becomes much more complicated and the combined effects of a new freedom in agrarian management decisions and an egalitarian distribution of land lose some of their magic. Important factors for agricultural production, such as investment, weather, and state purchasing may have had a big stake in the economic success story of agriculture in those early days of family farming. Let's look at some of these factors in more detail.

Just before the introduction of the HRS substantial investments in irrigation works and new technologies were conducted in many production teams with most of the corresponding effects taking place only at a later point. According to Bramall (2004, 120) this advent of the "Green Revolution" in China has been largely ignored in the accounts of that historical time. He notes that good weather might have been another important factor in the increased output.

Another important reason for the rising incomes in agriculture in the early 1980s has little or no connection to the introduction of the HRS. Although the agricultural reforms in many regions included regulations that allowed for the reopening of local markets, most core products in agriculture such as rice or corn have had only a very limited direct entry into these markets, as opposed to vegetables and fruits. A procurement system inherited from the collective organization of the economy continued to fix prices for these products. In order to fulfill their grain quota, peasants had to sell part of their harvest at a certain fixed price. After having fulfilled its quota, the household could sell its remaining harvest at the higher "above quota price." Subsistence needs and the grain quota forced many farmers to devote large parts of their land—more than 70 percent, sometimes even more than 80 percent—to grain production. Only the small remainder of the cultivated land could be used for cash crops (Zhu and Jiang 1993, 447). The monetary income of producers was therefore directly dependent upon a set of prices determined by the financial capabilities and the will of the political center, not unlike the economy in the pre-reform times.

In 1979, even before the experiments in land distribution in most parts of China had begun, the state procurement price (*tonggou*) for grain was raised by 20 percent. The above-quota price (*chaogou*) was even increased by 50 percent (Ash 1988, 540). While the procurement prices for agricultural goods increased considerably, the prices for industrial goods remained rather stable. Even more important for farmers was the price drop for important inputs by 10–15 percent during 1979–1980 (Ash 1988, 540). This gap in the development of relative prices turned agriculture for a short time into a comparatively profitable business—even with the little and scattered land available for each household. Ash notes that "[b]etween 1979 and 1981 Chinese peasants received an extra 46,290 million *yuan* as a result of the price adjustments" (ibid.).

Jean Oi (1993, 132) argues that the new procurement prices were the main reason for the rising incomes during the early stages of the agricultural reforms. While Unger (2002b, 111) notes: "[. . .] incomes had begun rising noticeably even before the return to family farming, due to the removal of land use restrictions and this improvement in farmgate prices." Hartford (1985, 56) agrees that the new responsibility system, albeit important, was not the only reason for the increased agricultural output and that, in fact, "[o]ther factors that may have played a role include a jump in producer prices, increased private marketing opportunities, a rise in fertilizer application and a pronounced shift in cropping patterns to capture comparative advantages." For some time, the center was willing to substantiate pro-peasant rhetoric by putting considerable funding into the procurement system.

The phenomenal harvest of 1984 put the state procurement system to a hard test. Sicular (1995, 1023) notes that "[b]y 1984 government spending on price subsidies was 22 billion yuan, equivalent to 14 percent of total government budgetary revenues." In addition, there were numerous reports on the inefficiencies of the state-centered retail system of agricultural goods leading to grain rotting at the storage facilities while at the same time market demand was not being fully met (Ash 1988, 544).

The No. 1 Document of 1985 aimed to address these issues and called for an end of the state procurement system for core agricultural goods. The second major aspect of this document addressed the agricultural taxes. The previous system of in-kind payments was supposed to be replaced by cash payments. Smallholder farming never fully recovered from these changes. In 1985, grain production output shrank by 7 percent and some of the procurement reforms had to be reversed in 1987 (Alpermann 2010, 30–31). Even worse, beginning in 1985 prices turned against smallholders and in 1986 the rapid growth of the Chinese economy led to inflation. The prices for industrial goods, among them important inputs for agrarian production such as fertilizers, pesticides, and machinery (esp. tractors), were rising much quicker than those of agricultural goods. This had considerable impact upon rural incomes, as stated by Rozelle (1996, 64) "[r]eal per capita rural income in China did not increase between 1984 and 1990." And Ash (1988, 548) adds:

> An investigation conducted in Hebei province in April 1986 revealed that in the previous three years, charges for electricity had risen by 100 per cent; for water, by 200 per cent; and for diesel oil, by 300 per cent. The outcome was that in 1985 net income per mu of grain land was 20 yuan less than it had been in 1983.

Wary of the danger of shrinking incomes in agriculture and the potential impact on grain production, Beijing soon reversed some of its 1985 policies, as mentioned above. In January 1988, the Chinese Minister of Agriculture admitted that the 1985 reforms led to numerous problems, and later that year a partial return to the procurement price system and a new round of increased procurement prices were announced (Ash 1988, 550–551).

The political support of agriculture during the first phase of the reform may have been of at least equal importance for rural economic growth and rising incomes as were the new monetary incentives arising from regained entrepreneurial freedom. Many authors note the difficult situation the CPC and the system in general were in after the tumultuous years, which saw Mao's death, the arrest of the Gang of Four, and the struggle of factions at the center to gain control (see for example Heberer 1996, 3). The reforms took away some of that pressure from the leadership and created room for maneuvering. Bramall (2004, 125) therefore argues that "the primary motivation behind the imposition of decollectivization in 1982–3 was undoubtedly political." For him, the reforms were part of the efforts of Deng Xiaoping and his group to build up support in the countryside. He also notes that "[a]fter 1983 there was no going back to collective farming; decollectivization settlement had made certain of that" (ibid.). While the center gained political legitimacy, the reforms came with considerable political costs at the local level. Local cadres, used to adjust labor and production structures as they saw fit, now had lost considerable influence (Zweig 1989, 162).

The introduction of the HRS also brought about a dramatic change in the relationship between agrarian producers and the land. Previously, while being members of the production teams, work ethos and abilities — or the absence thereof — had little impact upon household income. The HRS changed this. Not only did access to personal plots create an opportunity to improve the income via the market, but with the new market dependence also came new risks for agrarian producers. In the booming coastal areas, farmers who failed to cultivate their *zerentian* would be fined (Zhu and Jiang 1993, 441). Although this group was still very likely to make a "good living," for others the introduction of the HRS greatly increased their poverty risk. Families with many dependents but few able-bodied members or households with many elderly members unable to perform farming activities still had the same obligations regarding the procurement quota while also struggling to produce enough food to meet their own needs (Unger 2002b, 109). The introduction of the HRS was therefore not only the beginning of a return to peasant farming but should also be seen as an important milestone for peasant differentiation in the People's Republic.

While the reforms have been a stunning success in raising the legitimacy of the political center and the CPC in the countryside, in the eyes of those interested in economic growth and production output they were far from flawless. Critics pointed to the fragmentation of land, the lack of capital and modern farming knowledge, and the subsequent trend toward demechanization and traditional farming practices—all resulting in a lack of modern economies of scale in agriculture.

Probably the most important consequences of the reforms within agriculture has been their impact on the non-agricultural sectors of the economy (see Heberer 1996, 10–15). The reforms took away the control of the rural labor force from the production team. Villagers were now basically free to do what they wanted in order to make their living. Given the emerging job opportunities in the non-agricultural sector and the comparatively high earnings there, many farming households decided that their main labor force would be better employed outside of agriculture. Especially the younger, more risk-taking villagers decided to leave agriculture all together. Already in very early post-reform studies the wealth of rural households was increasingly linked to non-agricultural employment of household members (Unger 2002b, 111). In 1987, industry already contributed more to rural incomes than agriculture did (Oi 1993, 141–142)!

The new wealth created by non-agricultural labor, however, was very unevenly divided. In 1988, about 62 percent of all wages were earned by the richest 10 percent of the rural population, whereas the poorest 20 percent received only 1 percent of their income through wages (Oi 1993, 143). Brandt et al. (2004, 630) note that for their sample in 1995 "between 35 and 40 percent of the local labor force was employed outside of agriculture either full or part time, a level consistent with that reported at the national level." Off-farm employment of huge parts of the rural society in turn also began to affect the distribution and concentration of farmland. The better the non-agricultural employment opportunities were, the more the mobility and consolidation of land increased (Zhu and Jiang 1993, 441). A survey from 1997 mentions that, of those villages that put an end of land reallocations, 17.1 percent argued to do so because the land had lost importance as the primary source of income (Ho 2001, 398).

At the same time, the collective ownership of the land made it difficult to fully cut the ties to one's village. Villagers were not allowed to sell their contracted plot. Although many scholars argue that this provided the rural population with an additional safety net in case their urban employment opportunities ceased to exist, their continued legal status as rural people (read: peasant, *nongmin*) excluded them from most urban social services and housing.[4] It effectively established a new urban underclass with lower wages and fewer rights. Yet, these new sub-par urban wages handily exceeded most rural wages by far.

TRANSFORMATION OF THE HRS

The introduction of the HRS was a crucial institutional juncture for the administration of land and the legal basis of agriculture. China returned to family farming. A practice with thousands of years of experience replaced 20 years of collective farming in the countryside, as Yuan Cheng enthusiastically notes (2010, 95). Now the institutions from collective farming need to be adjusted to suit this new reality.

This section will review the institutional basis of the HRS and its remarkable metamorphosis from a system of egalitarian distribution of land to the basis of commercial operations in agriculture.[5] In accordance with the overall research interest of this book predominantly institutions of land administration related to farming are explored. Some laws and regulations that primarily target agriculture have been included because of their strong indirect influence on the valuation of land.

This section is organized chronologically. The starting point is the legal basis of the HRS and collective land at the beginning of the reforms in the countryside in the early 1980s. The review of the legal framework ends with the year 2008, the starting point of the research for this book. This section will not focus on the implementation of the legal framework or its effectiveness, as these two points will be addressed later. Still, it is important to keep in mind that in China, like anywhere else, regulations and laws are not necessarily carried out as intended (Bardach 1977). Neither should one ignore the many local variations and vastly different timeline of the implementation. Finally, even though the legal framework for collective land and the HRS may have had substantial influence on agriculture, there are several other factors which have also had great impact on the fate of agricultural production in China. Examples include the general development of the economy, increasing peasant differentiation, off-farm employment and local state interests.

When the central leadership approved the extension and expansion of the experiments in the countryside, it carefully placed them within the existing socialist ownership system in China. Traditionally, this system was based upon only two types of land ownership: state-owned land and collectively owned land. Private land ownership, the basis of capitalist farming in Western countries, was not envisioned or possible from a legal point of view. Furthermore, given that the division between the two types of land ownership was basically a division in space, with state-owned land in urban areas and collective land in the countryside, the new mode of agricultural production would have to be placed within the framework for collective ownership. Article 10 of the 1982 Revision of the Constitution (Quanguo Renmin Daibiaohui 1982)[6] outlines the differences between collective and state-owned land:

> Urban land is state-owned land. Except for those parts that legally belong to the state, rural land and suburban land are owned by the collective (*shuyu jiti suoyou*); housing land (*zhaijidi*) as well as crop- and hilly land for personal needs (*ziliudi, ziliushan*) are also owned by the collective. For public interest (*gonggong liyi*) the state may, in accordance with the law, carry out land requisitioning (*zhengyong*). No organization or individual may seize, buy, sell, rent out or by any other illegal means transfer ownership of land. All land usage by organizations or individuals must be rational (*bixu heli liyong tudi*). (Translation by this author)

The constitution specifies the owner of collective land as all members of the village collective economic group (*nongcun jiti jingji zuzhe*), which is the responsible organizational body for the administration of land. However, in legal terms this village collective economic group is not defined—there is simply no such organization. In other words, the constitution fails to identify a specific actor as being in charge of the administration of collective ownership rights. The seminal work of Peter Ho (2005) explores this legal mystery in more detail. Ho argues that this "institutional ambiguity" is deliberate. In rural practice, institutional ambiguity has led to claims on collective land by many different levels of the administration, among them the natural village, the administrative village, and also even township and county level administrations. Another issue emerged with the usage of "public interest" as a condition for the expropriation of collective land mentioned in Article 10 above. Again, this term was not clarified and thereby gave local governments a lot of leeway in declaring a "public interest" in their development projects. Especially in relation to another policy adopted in 1982 this had profound consequences on farmland in the following years.

This policy from the Standing Committee of People's Congress, called "Regulation for Land Requisitioning for National Construction [Projects]" (*Guojia jianshe zhengyong tudi tiaoli*, 1982 Regulation), not only included stipulations for the procedures to be followed in land requisitioning but also guidelines for the compensation to be paid (Changwu Weiyuanhui 1982). Over time the guiding principles and the calculation of the compensation has seen astonishingly few changes (Yan 2009). Article 9 of the 1982 Regulation states that the compensation for collective land is based on the assumed average annual output value of the farmland in question, multiplied by a factor between three and six. The average annual output value is calculated by using the output of agricultural production for the last three years before the requisitioning, multiplied by a national standard price for rice and then divided by three. This mechanism is used not only for cropland but also for all other kinds of land in agricultural production and even housing land. For land that does not generate any profit, no compensation at all has to be paid.

In addition to the compensation for farmland there is a resettlement fee paid to each member of the household (holding a rural household registration) for each mu of land under agricultural production. According to Article 10 of the 1982 Regulation the fee is based on the same average annual production output already outlined above, multiplied by a factor between two and three. However, the overall fee for each mu of land is not allowed to exceed ten times the average annual production output. For the actual housing, no resettlement fee is given. The provincial level of the government is the responsible body for making the final decision regarding the compensation and the resettlement fee (including the decision concerning the multiplication factor). In case the compensation and resettlement fee given to a household are too small to ensure that the household has a level of livelihood comparable to the situation before the land requisitioning, the authorities can increase the resettlement fee. Still, the fee is not allowed to exceed twenty times the average annual production output value. In the years that followed the adoption of the 1982 Regulation, the connection between agrarian output, compensation, and resettlement fee has led to two problematic developments: the gap between the compensation and the market value of the land after its transformation into construction land has been steadily increasing, and the 1982 Regulation provided local governments with incentives to turn functional farmland into wasteland in order to pay less or no compensation.

The first Land Administration Law (*tudi guanli fa*, LAL) in 1986 was the attempt to provide a more comprehensive framework for the new HRS (Changwu Weiyuanhui 1986; Vendryes 2010, 89). Of special importance for agriculture and the rural population are the parts that entail the idea of land usage rights and the legal limitations for the transfer of ownership and usage rights. Article 6 of the LAL confirms the basic division of land in China into state-owned and collective land, as outlined in the 1982 Constitution. Article 8 specifies that collective land belongs to the villagers' collective (*shuyu cun nongmin jiti suoyou de*). Furthermore, the agricultural producers' collective (*cun nongye shengchan hezuoshe*), the agricultural collective economic group (*nongye jiti jingji zuzhi*), or the villagers' committee (*cunmin weiyuanhui*) are the responsible bodies for the management and supervision of collective land. Article 7 confirms that usage rights for state and collectively owned land can be transferred to other units and even to individuals. The receiving units or individuals have the obligation to protect and administer the land and only use it for reasonable means. Article 9 states that collective land needs to be registered at the county level of the government. The county government is also responsible for handing out certificates and to confirm ownership. All units and individuals with ownership or usage rights need to register with the county government. The regulations regarding the potential use-cases for contracted collective land by units and individuals are entailed in Article 12 and include agriculture, forestry, herding, animal husbandry, and aqua farming. The contracting parties are obliged to adhere to the regulations stated within the contract.

Finally, the LAL included provisions for the transfer of ownership. Article 10 states that such a change must be registered at the county level, and Article 11 notes the general legal protection the owner and holder of land usage rights enjoy. Accordingly, no unit or individual has the right to violate these rights. In addition, Article 15 states that all levels of the government have to work out a master plan for the future land usage, which then needs to be approved by the higher levels. The LAL highlights the obligation of all levels of the government to economize their land usage. In comparison to the later revisions of the LAL (especially that of 1998), the municipalities and districts enjoy much more discretionary power in land acquisition and ownership transfer (Xu, Yeh, and Wu 2009, 902). The LAL (Articles 27, 28, and 29) adopted the regulations regarding the compensation payment and resettlement fees for farmland turned into construction land outlined in the 1982 Regulation, as detailed above.

The 1987 Organic Law of the Village Committees (OLVC, adopted in 1988) was one step further in the process of the institutionalization of the HRS, e.g., turning the HRS into a viable legal framework (Zhuxiling 1987). Article 3 states that the village committee should manage the land collectively owned by all villagers. The village committee should also inform villagers how to make the best use of their land and urge them to protect and improve the quality of their land.

The year 1988 saw the revisions of the Constitution (Quanguo Renmin Daibiaohui 1988) and the LAL (Changwu Weiyuanhui 1988). Although the articles regarding land did not change in the 1988 Constitution, the LAL saw a set of minuscule yet important modifications. The most comprehensive changes took place in Article 2. Although the 1986 version prohibits the occupation (*qinzhan*), selling and buying (*maimai*), or renting out (*chuzu*) of collective land, in the 1988 version renting out was removed from that list (thus making it legal). The other changes of the 1988 Revision mainly addressed the protection of soil from man-made loss. The documentation of the changes regarding the legalization of land rentals has been ignored in most accounts of the land management laws in

China. Yet, they mark an important point of transition in China's land administration policies. Before the 1988 Revision, efforts were made to provide a legal framework for the changes that had taken place in the countryside, whereas this modification is the first indication of a shift in focus toward improving resource efficiency in agriculture.[7] It is the first attempt to allow for the transfer and consolidation of land based upon economic reasoning. The 1988 Revision may also be the first indication of institutional change in land administration triggered by new ideas, as discussed by Steinmo (2010, 133).

The Agriculture Law (AL) of 1993 included many of the regulations previously outlined in the Constitution and in the LAL (Zhuxiling 1993). The crucial concept in the AL is that of the contractor (*chengbaofang*). Article 12 states that all land managed by the village collective economic group can be contracted to individuals or collective units for agricultural use. Once both sides settle on a contract it has the status of a legal document. Article 13 offers more details about the rights and duties of the contractors. While the contractor still has to adhere to duties outlined in the contract, he enjoys decision-making power in production and operation, including the right to market his products for a profit. In addition, the contractor has the right to transfer (*zhuanrang*) the land to other parties—if the party he contracted the land from approves such a move. Article 13 has two more interesting clauses. First, it states that when the original contract expires, the contractor receives preferential treatment in the redistribution of his formerly contracted land. Secondly, if the contractor would die during the contracted time his inheritor (*jichengren*) would receive the contract. These changes show the intention of lawmakers to move away from the system of reallocations of farmland in favor of a greater security for long-term investments for farmers.

The other important change of 1993, outlined in the No. 11 Document, entitled "A Number of Policy Measures by the Central Committee of the Chinese Communist Party of China and the State Council to Economically Develop the Present Agriculture and Villages" (CPC) (*Zhonggong Zhongyang ‧ Guowuyuan guanyu dangqian nongye he nongcun jingji fazhan de ruogan zhengce cuoshi*), follows a similar logic (Zhongfa 1993). The document starts by listing numerous problems and unfavorable developments in the countryside, such as falling rates of productivity in grain and cotton production, growing price differences between industrial and agricultural goods, and decreasing investments in agriculture in some locations (*yixie difang*). These issues would make it difficult for agriculture to catch-up (with industrial production) and needed to be solved to guarantee steady increases in rural incomes. The suggested solution is a move further away from the egalitarian ideal. The HRS system is described as the basis of agriculture in China and needs to be stabilized. In order to do so and to encourage investments as well as to increase the productivity of the farmland, the time frame of the current contracts should be extended by an additional thirty years. The time frame for the contracts for reclaimed collective wasteland or forests could be even longer than that. In addition, the document directly calls for an end to the reallocations of land due to changes in the household composition. In the future, the principle of "more people but no more land, fewer people but no less land" (*zengren bu zengdi, jianren bu jiandi*) should be adhered to. This basically omits all reallocations based on births and deaths within the family. The No. 11 Document also suggests that in regions with a huge percentage of off-farm labor the land could be concentrated into bigger holdings for the sake of more economies of scale in agriculture—if the farmers agree to such a move. Besides regulations regarding collective land the No. 11 Document includes many more regulations to push ahead reform in agriculture, in particular in regard to the procurement system, to promote increases in productivity, and to improve agricultural extension services. The No. 11 Document also points to a second priority of Beijing. In section 11, it calls for the thorough execution of the "Fully Treasure and Reasonably Use Every Inch of Land [and] Feasible Protection of Farmland" (*Shifen zhenxi he heli liyong mei chun tudi, qieshi baohu gengdi*) policy. The LAL should be strictly enforced in order to protect the farmland. More details about the protection would be published in the forthcoming "Basic Regulations for the Protection of Farmland."

The year 1994 saw the publication of these Basic Regulations as State Council Document No. 162 (Guowuyuan 1994) was published. At its core, this document is a set of clarifications regulating which level of government is responsible for the approval of changes to land usage, the monitoring of the current usage plans as well as similar regulations with a focus on the protection of farmland from transformation into construction land. For example, every land usage change involving less than 500 mu of top-quality land needs provincial approval; every change involving more than 500 mu of said land type needs the approval of the State Council. The Basic Regulations also provide hints about the future focus of agriculture. Article 12 outlines four principles for the investment of earmarked funds for the protection of basic farmland. These funds should only be invested in (1) approved new production bases for grain, cotton, and soy bean production as well as bases for agricultural production of famous brands, high-quality products, and specialist production, (2) fields for high-yield and dependable crops and those with a good irrigation infrastructure as well as those mid- to low-level yield fields currently improved by irrigation schemes, (3) vegetable production bases in the vicinity of middle-sized and big cities, and (4) fields for scientific research and experimentation. In addition, earmarked funds should only be invested in level one and level two quality land, e.g., top-quality and good quality land, respectively. The protection of farmland in this case includes a drive for gradual modernization and transformation of the production structures.

In the years thereafter the efforts to strengthen the HRS came to the forefront again. The Standing Committee of the CPC and the State Council jointly published in 1997 a "Notice Regarding Efforts to Stabilize and Perfect the Rural Land Contracting System One Step Further" (*Guanyu jin yibu wending he wanshan nongcun tudi chengbao guanxi de tongzhi*, 1997 Notice) (Zhongbanfa 1997). The 1997 Notice outlines the difficulties the farmers faced during the implementation of the HRS. It argues that in a small subset of places a number of unpleasant developments had taken place: the extension of the original contracts had not been carried out, contracts were subject to frequent arbitrary changes, the land had been re-collectivized and then handed out to farmers on very unfavorable new terms, and finally some regions had conducted efforts to create economies of scale against the will of the peasants. The 1997 Notice outlined renewed efforts to address these unfortunate developments. Introducing a set of rules for handling the "big stability, small adjustments" (*da wending, xiao tiaozheng*) principle in practice, the center wanted to further clarify the limited role it envisions for the reallocations of land in the HRS. Reallocations of land should only be carried out in cases of extreme discrepancies between distributed land and people. The reallocations should by no means turn into an instrument to increase the contract fees for the farmers. In addition, two-thirds of the village inhabitants would have to agree to said reallocation. Finally, it left little doubt as to which behavior the regulations intended to stop: using an official degree to conduct frequent reallocations every few years. All of these changes gave the system of contracted land usage rights a much firmer legal protection.

The 1998 Revision of the LAL (adopted on January 1, 1999) stressed in a similar manner the institutional strengthening of land administration again (Guowuyuan 1999). The law stated more directly what should be considered state-owned and collectively owned. Land ownership, usage rights, and any change regarding the two from now on would need to be documented. No unit or individual is allowed to infringe on these land rights. The law confirms the role of the county level as the responsible level for land administration. Important decisions, especially regarding the land requisitioning, need to be approved by higher levels.

The 1998 Revision also dealt with the process of land requisitioning (*zhengyong*), e.g., changing the status of collective land to state-owned land, in order to use it for other purposes. The county level would now be required to outline a master plan for land usage (*tudi liyong zongti guihua*) for the next 15 years. The county level master plan must differentiate between farmland, construction land, and land without determined usage. From the master plan, an annual land usage plan (*tudi liyong niandu jihua*) is derived. All ownership and usage conversions must strictly follow these two plans. Land conservation, the process of turning wasteland into farmland, is one of the few mechanisms that provide local governments with some flexibility. Up to sixty percent of the area of the regained farmland can be used elsewhere for additional land conversion projects.

While not reversing the decentralized nature of the land administration of collective land, the 1998 Revision clearly limits the legal rights of local governments in managing collective land. Several scholars see in this policy a sign of renewed centralization of the land management (Ho 2001, 404). The most prominent display of these changes might have taken place in the legal process of collective land requisition. In order to take collective land from a farmer, two processes need to take place: first the ownership status needs to change from collective to state ownership and second, a formal change of usage needs to take place. Xu, Yeh, and Wu (2009, 902) argue that the revision of the LAL put these two processes firmly under the control of the center again. Municipal governments from now on could convert land only in accordance with the above-mentioned restricted top-down quota and the annual plan. These plans need to be approved by authorities at either the national or provincial level.

The year 1998 also saw the revision of the OLVC (Zhuxiling 1998). Although this law did not directly change the regulations of land administration, it did strengthen the rights and opportunities of villagers to participate in important decisions affecting the village. Article 19, for instance, states that if matters arise that affect the interests of villagers, the elected village committee must refer these matters to the village assembly for discussion and decision making (*bixu qing cunminhuiyi taolun jueding*). The article includes a list of such matters. On that list: cases in which land contracts (*nongmin chengbao jingying fang'an*) or housing land (*zhaijidi shiyong fang'an*) have been affected.

There are indications that the 1998 Revision of the LAL and many other reforms up to this point were triggered by two problematic developments in the eyes of central administrators: the massive loss of farmland and inadequate economic structures in agriculture for further growth. The new master plans and other elements of the 1998 Revision provided agriculture and agricultural land with an additional layer of legal protection. Other legal regulations, such as the OLVC, were supportive in this regard. A constant stream of modifications and efforts to stabilize the HRS might point to the dissatisfaction the central leadership has had with the economic development in agricultural areas. In fact, structural reform in agriculture (*tiaozheng nongye jiegou*) became a dominant idea in the years following.

The "Opinion Regarding the Work to Complete in Agriculture and the Countryside in the Year 2001" (*Guanyu zuohao 2001 nian nongye he nongcun gongzuo de yijian*), jointly published in 2001 by the Central Committee of the CPC and the State Council, provides a first in-depth statement on the structural problems that the center perceives within the countryside and agriculture and a policy outline to address these issues (Zhonggong

Zhongyang and Guowuyuan 2001). The outline starts by indirectly admitting that past reforms have left agriculture in a weak spot. The incomes of farmers were unsatisfactorily low and, instead of catching up with urban areas, the gap between urban and rural incomes was even increasing in past years. The only way out of this mess and thereby maintain stability in rural areas would be to conduct a thorough structural reform of agriculture that put emphasis on both quality (*suzhi*) and efficiency (*xiaoyi*) of agriculture. Quality refers here first to the quality of products produced but also to the methods employed during the production process. More market-oriented and technology-based production was deemed as higher quality production. Efficiency refers in this context to the still low labor efficiency in agriculture. In order to raise rural incomes, a huge part of the rural population would have to move out of farming and shift to wage earning in local enterprises and in urban settings. The 2001 Opinion states quite frankly that "if 900 million peasants do not change their ways of earning a living, peasant prosperity will never take off, and the modernization of the countryside will be difficult to realize." Over are the days in which the central leadership emphasized "inverse relationship" inspired ideas on the superiority of smallholder farming.

While quality and efficiency in production are the important goals of a structural reform, the 2001 Opinion at the same time clearly expresses the intention that all transformations of agriculture must respect the HRS and the 30 years of unchangeable land usage rights for farming households. The tension between these two goals became a dominating element in the administration of agriculture in the years following—up to the present day. All legal reforms to ease the transfer and consolidation of farmland that followed were bound by this formula. The 2001 Opinion offers some ideas concerning the actors that should drive the structural transformation of agriculture. Newly formed Dragonhead enterprises should take the lead in all aspects of food processing, including added labor, taking care of the distribution and marketing as well as other necessaries of a commercial agriculture. The document includes a vision for agriculture that is based on the cooperation between these Dragonheads and the households as primary agrarian producers. In addition, governments on all levels should support peasants in providing market information, know-how, agricultural extension services, and similar beneficial activities.

The next major step in land administration was the formulation of the 2002 Law on the Contracting of Rural Land (*Nongcun Tudi Chengbaofa*, LCRL, adopted on March 1, 2003) (Zhuxiling 2003). Although the LCRL integrates many parts of the existing legislation for land usage contracts, in several important aspects it goes beyond these earlier frameworks. The most significant additions fall within three categories: further legal protection for those holding land usage contracts, basic guidelines for the transfer of land usage rights between the contractor and a third party, and a detailed framework on how to deal with conflicts of interest in the field of land administration.

In regard to improving the legal protection for land usage rights, for the first time emphasis has been placed upon the protection of women's rights in land contracting, prominently stated in Articles 6 and 30. Women marrying into a new village keep their original contracted land if the new village is unable to provide them with adequate land. Similar regulations should protect them in case they seek a divorce or are widowed. Other articles stress the importance of the public and democratic nature of the process of handing out land contracts. Western property rights scholars stress the importance of Article 21, which states that the contracting of land must be documented in written form (Vendryes 2010, 90). Article 23 notes that certificates for contracted land must be handed out and that this service must be free of charge for the contractors. The LCRL also outlines the conditions under which contracted land returns to the village collective economic group—which are limited to very few cases. For example, Article 26 states that if a household changes its residence permit (*hukou*) from rural to urban, the land returns to the collective. If the household only moves to the nearby town (which does not involve a change of residence permit) and settles there, it keeps its contracted land (even if it is rented out). Finally, Article 16 confirms the legal right of the contractor to receive part of the compensation if his land is requested by the state.

Another important part of the LCRL is the outline of a framework for the transfer of land. It mentions several different ways to do so: subcontracting (*zhuanbao*), lease (*chuzu*), exchange (*huhuan*), or transfer (*zhuanrang*) and leaves the door open for other ways (in regions with the appropriate conditions). The law provides a general set of principles that must be adhered to in all cases of transferring land usage rights to a third party. Important regulations are outlined in Article 33: (1) fair bargaining in all aspects of the sub-renting is required, (2) the character of the land and its agricultural nature may not be changed, (3) contracted land can only be rented out for the duration of the contract and not longer, (4) the party that receives the land has the right to manage it, and (5) under comparable conditions villagers from the same village receive preferential treatment in the search for a subcontractor. Article 36 states that the amount of rent paid for the sub-contracted land should be the result of mutual consultations. These subcontracts also need to be documented in written form; exceptions are only allowed for cases in which the land is rented out for one year or less. The new subcontractors themselves have the right to rent out the land should they decide to stop farming for any reason. The LCRL requires that, if land is rented out to a third party from outside the village collective, two-thirds of the village assembly and the township government must approve this move. The final section of the

LCRL details legal regulations in case there are conflicts in the management of land contracts. The major addition to former laws is the inclusion
of judiciary means in the arsenal of conflict resolution. Explicitly, the
illegal infringement on collective land is classified as a punishable act
that either may lead to sanctions of higher organs or even entail legal
investigations.

The 2004 Revision of the LAL continues the line of argument formulated in the documents preceding and adds little new content (Changwu
Weiyuanhui 2004). The only significant difference concerns the fourth
paragraph in the second article. Instead of stating that the state can request land only for public interest (*zhengyong*), the new version now
states that land expropriation (*zhengshou*) in the public interest is possible
but compensation must be paid.

The more interesting policy change in the year 2004 is the "Decision of
the State Council to Deepen the Reform of a Strict Land Administration"
(*Guowuyuan guanyu shenhua gaige yange tudi guanli de jueding*) (Guofa
2004). In very strict language, the 2004 Decision aims to address several
worrisome developments in farmland usage, in itself more or less being
an admission that previous policies failed to provide the necessary protection for arable land in China. Despite efforts to constrain and limit the
conversion of farmland to construction land, including a moratorium on
all land conversions in 2003, problems such as blind investment, construction of low quality buildings, illegal expropriation, and a chaotic
and abusive usage of farmland continued to persist in the countryside.
The 2004 Decision calls for the strictest administration and control of the
usage of farmland possible (*zui yange de tudi guanli zhidu*). For this purpose, a set of twenty articles cover a broad range of measures, from
general aspects such as raising the awareness of the legal framework for
the administration of land to very detailed regulations for the process of
land conversion. The latter include passages on the compensation that
should be given to the households for their land. In principle, these have
to be in kind, e.g., converted farmland must be replaced by land of the
same quality. The decision also stipulates that any unit or individual
starting construction work without proper approval crosses a "red line."

While the protection of agricultural land continued to be a priority,
the increasing commercialization of agriculture moved more to the center
of attention for policy makers. The center aimed to walk the narrow line,
on the one hand reinforcing the rights granted within the HRS to create a
stable framework for investment, and at the same time pushing ahead a
modernization of agriculture toward more labor-efficient economies of
scale. For the latter goal, more flexibility in the access to land was needed
to allow the emergence of entrepreneurial agriculture and the withdraw-
ing of households from agriculture to use their labor resources elsewhere
with better remuneration.

In 2005 the Ministry of Agriculture published the "Procedures for the Management of the Transfer of Contracted Usage Rights for Rural Land" (*Nongcun tudi chengbao jingyingquan liuzhuan guanli banfa*, 2005 Procedures) (Nongyebu 2005). The 2005 Procedures state as their goal the aim to provide better guidelines for the process of transferring farmland in order to protect the legal interests and rights of the two sides involved and also to promote further development of agriculture and the rural economy. The point of reference for the Procedures is the HRS, which should be further strengthened in the process. Therefore, all legal transfers of land usage rights need to be based on fair bargaining and the legal framework, be voluntary in nature and include a compensation for the land given away.

The 2005 Procedures identify five distinct ways of transferring land usage rights but leave room for other methods that are in accordance with the general legal requirements. The five methods are a permanent transfer of contractual rights (*zhuanrang*), the transfer of usage rights for a limited time (*zhuanbao*), the swapping of land usage rights between two members of the same agricultural collective economic group (*huhuan*), pooling of land usage rights in a shareholding system (*rugu*), and renting out land usage rights for a fixed time in exchange for a compensation fee (*chuzu*). Of these five methods only the permanent transfer of contractual rights and the swapping of land usage rights affect the HRS contract. In both cases, the household that gives the land away loses all rights and obligations from the former contract. The permanent transfer of land usage rights requires the approval of the administrative body that handed out the contractual rights in the first place and is only possible if the household in question is either engaged in a stable non-agricultural profession or has another stable source of income. The transfer of usage rights for a limited time can only take place between two members of the same village collective economic group. The underlying rights and responsibilities of the original contract are not affected. If the intended time for *zhuanbao* is less than one year no written contract is needed. If farmers decide voluntarily that they want to pool their land usage rights into a shareholding system they are free to do so. The shares should be organized in a shareholding company or cooperative. If the shareholding arrangement is dissolved the land usage rights must be returned to the contractors. Finally, *chuzu* allows for the transfer of land usage rights between the contractor and a third party for a fixed time and compensation fee. Again the underlying rights and obligations of the original contract are not subject to change. The household that receives the land usage rights within the *zhuanbao* or *chuzu* method has the right to use these methods as well, if the original contractor agrees to such a move. Should the subcontractor invest in the land and thereby raise its overall quality, he is eligible for some compensation when the land is transferred back to the original contractor. Another modification concerns the role of intermediary parties in land rental transactions. The legality of such operations is now recognized but they are required to register at the relevant governmental bodies at the county level. Unless otherwise noted, all transfers of land usage rights require documentation in writing. This requirement includes the use of standardized forms. Finally, one of the most important conditions of all the transfer mechanisms outlined in the procedures is the continued usage of the land in question for agriculture.

The 2007 Property Law is seen by many as a hallmark legislation for China (Vendryes 2010, 90; Zhuxiling 2007b). Although most of the changes seem to affect only urban areas and state-owned land, the law also includes interesting additions to the heretofore mentioned legislation for collective land in rural areas. Article 42 lists new compensation details for expropriated collective land. In addition to a general compensation fee for the land, a resettlement compensation, and a compensation for the constructions and seedlings currently on the land, a social insurance provision and stable livelihoods for the expropriated farmers must be ensured. Article 126 points out that, after the original contract for collective land ends, the contractor, in accordance with national guidelines, continues to contract [this piece of land]. This removes the time frame limitation from all contracts. Very interesting in light of the (current) debates on further reforms in land administration are Articles 180 and 184, which both explicitly exclude collective farmland from being able to be used for mortgage purposes.

The continued institutionalization of the HRS and an improved legal protection of land usage rights of the rural population surprisingly come at a time the center has begun to aggressively move away from the subsistence and sub-scale farming household as being the centerpiece of agricultural production. The 2008 "Decisions of Central Committee of the Communist Party of China Regarding Several Big Issues in Pushing Forward the Reform and Development of the Countryside" (*Zhonggong zhongyang guanyu tuijin nongcun gaige fazhan ruogan zhongda wenti de jueding*) outline this vision of an alternative future for agriculture in China and the role the HRS plays in it in more detail (Zhongfa 2008a).

A structuring element is the vision of modern agriculture. This variant of agriculture is defined by high yields, high quality, high levels of efficiency in the production process, the protection of environmental resources, more security for the producers, the use of scientific methods and modern equipment, and the integration of food production and processing—in short a thorough modification of the whole system of agricultural production. A fully commercialized agricultural production is seen as key to raising rural incomes and narrowing the rural–urban gap. For this purpose, more and bigger Dragonhead enterprises should be created and promoted to allow for more standardized production but also in order to establish well-known brands for agricultural products. Given the difficult natural endowments for agriculture in China, in the future the potential for more use of science and technology should be used to its full extent.

The HRS is fully integrated in this vision. Building on this legally well-developed instrument the center hopes that the modernization of agriculture will not infringe on two other important political goals, the legal protection of the farmers interests, important for social stability and the containment of the transformation of agricultural land into non-agricultural use. Regarding the latter target, the decisions now mention the new goal of keeping a minimum of 1.8 billion mu land for farming, the so-called Red Line, which entered the debate via the adoption of the 11th Five-Year-Plan in the previous year. It also calls for a stricter inspection as to whether or not the necessary requirements for the approval of a conversion of land to construction land are truly met—especially the condition of being in the public interest.

While the HRS is seen as a necessary tool to protect the farmers' interests and to stop land loss, the current distribution of land following the HRS is deemed unsuitable for modern agriculture. The 2008 Decisions therefore envision the "creation of a 'perfect market' for the transfer of land usage rights" (*jianli jianquan tudi chengbao jingyingquan liuzhuan shichang*). The use of all methods of land transfer (as outlined above) should be encouraged. Wherever the proper conditions exist new operations of scale should be installed, such as specialized households (*zhuanye dahu*) or specialized peasant cooperatives (*nongmin zhuanye hezuoshe*). Rural finances are mentioned as being at the core of a modern rural economy. The 2008 Decisions demand for an all-around structural change of the rural financing system. Besides raising the level of investments the creation of modern financial instruments such as village credit cooperatives, markets for futures/options for agricultural products, and insurances for the risks of production are called for.

The framework outlined in the 2008 Decisions does not stop here. For example, it calls for a comprehensive system of subsidies and guaranteed prices in agriculture to protect the production of important agrarian products such as grain and rice, as food security remains an important political goal in China. The 2008 Decisions note that the Chinese decision to promote more grain production and international cooperation in this field "is a contribution to improve the global food supply" (*wei gaishan quanqiu liangshi gonggei zuochu gongxian*). The subsidies system should also encourage further activities in environmental protection. The Decisions encourage return migration of successful migrants, which should use their know-how to start a business in their rural hometowns. Finally, much of the document goes beyond agriculture and addresses changes for the whole countryside, e.g., integration of rural and urban administration, extension of urban services to rural areas, and in general a reduction of all differences between the two.

Similar-sounding goals are found in all so-called No. 1 documents since 2006, when the term *Building a New Socialist Countryside* (*shehui zhuyi xin nongcun jianshe*, hence XNCJS) entered the debate for the first time.[8] These No. 1 documents emphasize or re-emphasize important goals in rural development. They are called No. 1 documents because they are the first formal joint publications of the State Council and the Standing Committee of the CPC in each year, although most of them were approved in December of the previous year. The name may also indicate a higher importance of these documents.

The 2006 No. 1 Document (Zhongfa 2005) includes, among many other visions to modernize the countryside and improve the living conditions of the rural population, an outline for a comprehensive makeover of agriculture in China. The *New Socialist Countryside* provides a comprehensive and integrated framework for many ideas and concepts brought forward already in the previous years. Strong calls for the application of more technological and scientific innovations in agriculture intertwine here with a push for the creation of integrated commercial production structures in agriculture. Dragonhead enterprises, cooperatives, and households should be linked to each other and join forces to create the economies of scale needed so much. Local and national agencies should support the development of commercial agricultural development and research centers with subsidies and tax breaks wherever feasible. Mechanization in agriculture should be vigorously pushed forward. Schemes to spread new technologies among farmers need to be encouraged and further subsidized. In regard to the management of collective land, the 2006 No. 1 Document encourages more transfer of land usage rights—if conducted according to the law, based upon the free will of the peasants and adhering to the compensation principle.

In the course of this discussion of the reforms of the HRS since its introduction in the early 1980s, we can identify three important themes. First, there are continued efforts to stabilize and improve the legal framework of the HRS system, culminating in increasingly urgent and unequivocal calls to improve the legal protection of contractors. Second, there is a strong emphasis upon the goal of protecting the remaining farmland and recovering lost land for agriculture as part of a national food security policy. The central piece of this aspect of the land administration is the *Red Line* of 1.8 billion mu for farming. The third and final aspect is closer to the main topic discussed in this book. It is the idea that a commercializing agriculture needs more flexible access to farmland. The way in which commercialization should be achieved, however, is a strange concept strictly confined by legal path dependencies in land administration. Repeatedly it is stated that the individual contracting household must be the basis and starting point for all efforts to transfer and concentrate collective land for farming purposes. The central leadership in Beijing seems therefore not to concur with the analysis of Peter Ho, who in the conclusion of his book (2005, 190) noted:

> It seems unlikely, however, that in the course of economic develop-
> ment land lease can continue unless the ownership question is re-
> solved. As the basis of the Household Contract Responsibility System
> is unclear, there is no chance of further commercialization of land lease.
> And this will seriously impede rural economic development. There are
> clear indications that a critical moment has been reached and further
> delay in institutional reform in the land administration system will
> have grave consequences.

LAND LOSS AND AGRARIAN TRANSITION

In December of 2011, a village near Shanwei City in Guangdong Province made national and international headlines for being the site of a standoff between its inhabitants and a troop of riot police several thousand men strong. Wukan Village is a rather typical case for one segment of the Chinese countryside in which villagers and state officials are in confrontation about the expropriation of collective land. Only the dimensions of the protest and the media attention it received distinguished this case from many others in the countryside. Protests in Wukan started as peaceful petitioning but quickly turned into violent riots, forcing an expulsion of all cadres and a several-week-long siege of the village (Lasseter 2011; Moore 2011a). In contrast to many other places in China, the villagers in Wukan skillfully included national and international media outlets in their quest to regain possession of the land. Ultimately, a formal investigation in the land deals of local cadres was launched and the protest of the villagers was given the label "rightful" (Blanchard 2012). Many have wondered whether Wukan was the sign of the beginning of a new form of interaction between villagers and local governments (He and Xue 2014). One year later, and six months after the village elected a new party secretary, the results still were not decisive. Only 600 ha of the 3,200 ha farmland converted to construction land by the former village government (despite the illegality of doing so) were returned to the villagers (Fung 2012). Amnesty International is even more skeptical about the progress in Wukan, claiming that so far there has been no investigation into the death of the villager who died in police custody and also that no land has been returned at all (Amnesty International 2012).

Less well known is the case of the villagers from Haiyang in Liaoning Province. On April 13, 2010, more than 1000 former inhabitants of Haiyang Village (now a subdistrict) went to Zhuanghe City to plead their case against illegal expropriations. In their desperation, they resorted to a dramatic yet peaceful form of protest and knelt down in front of the main government building for about 30 minutes. All of them had lost their land and had received little or no compensation in return (Cai and Fu 2010).

It is difficult to judge the frequency of cases like Wukan and Haiyang Village in the Chinese countryside of today. Statistical data is at best contradictory but in most cases simply missing. The loss of agricultural land due to construction projects may be the biggest threat for the commercialization of agriculture in the Chinese countryside. Given this background the following section aims to provide an overview of the most important developments in this regard. The focus is put on the conditions at the time research for this book was conducted. For several national and international scholars and officials within the political system, illegal expropriations of farmers appear as the dominant and sometimes only relevant issue when it comes to land policies in China. A number of important studies on the topic have been published recently, although most of the empirical data precedes the time frame of this book (Cai 2003; Hsing 2010). In order to include up-to-date information, this overview mainly uses newspaper reports and to a lesser degree academic references. This was also done to portray the mainstream debate in China.

According to official statistics the arable area decreased by 218,000 ha annually between 1978 and 1996, adding up to about 4 percent of the total arable land (Ho 2001, 395). Another source states that between 1987 and 2001 in total 2.26 million ha of cultivated land was lost and that 70 percent or 1.58 million ha of this was collective arable land lost due to land requisitioning (Ping 2011, 626). As documented in the previous section, laws and regulations have become tighter since then. Unfortunately, this has had little impact on the conversion process. An article in the *China Daily* states that between 1997 and 2009 China lost an additional 123 million mu (8.2 million ha). In 2010, the remaining arable area stood at 1.826 billion mu and thereby came very close to the Red Line of 1.8 billion mu. Officially three main reasons for this enormous loss of land have been identified: construction purposes, forestry or grassland replanting programs, and natural calamities.

Land conversion for construction purposes can largely be divided into two categories, demand for the projects of local governments and new housing projects by the villagers themselves. Limited data exist to judge the amount of the latter development. Newspaper reports suggest that especially in better-off localities villagers proceed and construct new houses as part of life cycle planning (e.g., housing for the next generation of the family) at the expense of arable land. Supposedly, this has its roots in the custom that men, if they want to marry, need to have their own house in order to be considered being a good catch. Demographic developments and most profoundly the introduction of birth control policies and practices have decreased the number of women entering the marriage market and thereby increased male competition, raising the importance of good housing even more. Several government regulations aim to address this new construction boom in the villages (see, for example, Liu 2011).

However, the real danger for agriculture and collective land seems to be rooted in land expropriations by local governments. According to official data the Ministry of Land and Resources uncovered 37,000 cases of illegal land use in the first three quarters of 2011, in total involving 246,000 mu land. There are clear regional trends in this appetite for collective land. About 80 percent of the illegal land grab in 2011 took place in Western and Central regions of China (Wang 2011). Another news report argues that, while in 2011 (compared to 2010) in Central and Eastern China the size of the illegally used land was declining at the rate of 1.2 percent and 12.5 percent, respectively, it increased in Western China by 50.6 percent (see Wang and Guo 2011)!

The regions mostly affected by land grab are now the main bases of agricultural production. The developments in 2011 represent a 10.8 percent increase as compared to the previous year (Xinhua 2011a). However, in the first nine months of 2010 about 85,000 mu of illegal land conversion was uncovered, which was back then called a 10.4-percent decrease compared to the previous year (Xinhua 2010). Not only do these numbers show substantial year-to-year changes, their general usefulness might be doubtful, too. For example, it remains difficult to judge how many agrarian producers are negatively impacted by land conversions and land grab. One of the very few reports available in 2012 suggests that 43 percent of all farmers are affected by land grab (AFP 2012). Although not directly related to agricultural land use, it is important to mention that the land grab does not stop at the farmers' fields. In fact, demolitions of village housing appear to be the most problematic factor in the expropriation of collective land and currently are seen as the greatest threat to social stability in the countryside (Yan 2011).

What drives this gigantic illegal land grab? According to most Chinese sources it is the mismatch between supply and demand of construction land in China. At a Forum to celebrate the 21st National Land Day (*Di ershiyi ge quanguo tudiri*) in Nanjing the then–Minister of Land and Natural Resources, Xu Shaoshi, outlined this thinking:

> Given the increasing progress of industrialization, urbanization and the modernization of agriculture, the demand for construction land is rising. With the tightening of land control becoming more visible, the basic condition of this country given its developmental stage determines that in the future the Chinese land usage conditions will be even more severe. The contradiction between demand and supply of land will become even more prominent, making it difficult to continue development based on enormous consumption and low efficiency of land. (Ruan 2011)

Minister Xu hinted in this comment that the enormous momentum in land conversion may not always have been based upon a genuine demand. In a recent article, Ping (2011) took a closer look at the demand side of land conversion in Guangzhou and arrived at surprising conclusions. For his field site, he concludes that "the supply of development zones had not been met by a corresponding demand, resulting in a considerable amount of idle land" (Ping 2011, 645). The most striking and tangible example for this waste of agricultural land might be the capital of Inner Mongolia, Ordos, with its many empty streets, unused housing, and gargantuan office buildings.[9]

If land grab is not driven by demand then why do local officials engage in this high risk and illegal activity? Ping argues that numerous incentives and rewards exist that contradict the strict regulations in land policy. A comment in *Renmin Ribao* by the Tsinghua University professor and Director of its Politics and Economics Research Institute, Cai Jiming, discusses these institutional issues and identifies several root causes for illegal land expropriation: the conflicting legal regulations, the layered nature of local governments leading to limited checks and balances, the monopoly access to construction land of local governments, their revenue scarcity, and the huge difference between the value of the land and its net costs (Cai 2011).

Certainly the legal context of land expropriations is confusing and makes illegal conduct easy. In the focus of the discussion is the condition of public interest (*gonggong liyi*). As outlined in the previous section, all land conversion projects must meet this condition. However, there are still very few guidelines on how to judge whether or not a project is in the public's interest (see for example Jinan Ribao 2011). Cai Jiming argues that the legal confusion regarding the legality of land conversion is deliberate and a necessary step to keep the government's monopoly on construction land sales intact. Not only do local governments have a monopoly on the sale of construction land, the layered structure of their organization makes it much more difficult to install a system of checks and balances or to monitor land sales, Cai adds. The local office of the Ministry of Land and Resources receives its orders from the local government, in many cases directly from the vice mayor responsible for big construction projects. This vice mayor himself receives his orders from the mayor or the party secretary, who has the final say in all land approval. The power to conduct land deals therefore remains in the hands of a very small group of persons, increasing temptations for them massively (Cai 2011).

The economic value a piece of land has immediately after being turned into construction land is staggering. A report mentioned previously points to the differences between the compensation for a piece of land given to the peasants and the monetary value of the same land sold to real estate development agencies. For each mu of land converted and sold, the local governments received on average 778,000 RMB, whereas the compensation of villagers per mu, again on average, was 18,739 RMB or about 41 times less (AFP 2012). Gao Liangzhi (2008) compared average land prices in Nanjing to the compensation given to villagers. In his examples, the price for one mu of construction land in Nanjing in 2007 was between 330,000 and 2 million RMB, whereas the maximum compensation for one mu was 48,750 RMB. This gap between compensation costs, part of the net costs for land expropriation and the revenue certainly is a major driver for land expropriations. Yan Jinming (2009) from the Public Administration Institute of Beijing University reminds us that the compensation paid today is still defined by rules originally set in 1982. Many protests in rural China, such as the one in Haiyang mentioned before, erupt because even this little amount of compensation is not handed out to the villagers on time.

The economic difficulties of many local governments, especially since the 1994 tax sharing policy, have created a dependency upon land sales. Local governments receive only 45 percent of all tax revenues but have to cover 75 percent of all local expenses (Cai 2011). According to Cai, tax sharing is not only responsible for triggering land sales, it may also be the reason for continued real estate development by local governments. In the tax-sharing provisions, local governments receive revenues from the land use tax (*tudi shiyong shui*), the housing tax (*fangchan shui*), the stamp tax (*yinhua shui*) and the land-value increment tax (*tudi zengzhi shui*)—and higher prices for housing thereby translate into higher local government tax revenues (ibid.). All of these tax revenues are related to construction projects.

These extra-budgetary income sources are necessary to perform basic government functions and to sustain operations. The center knows this and has already devised ways to use this circumstance for its own policy goals. According to new regulations from 2011 about 45 percent of the revenue from land sales are already fixed: 15 percent go into funding for agriculture, 10 percent into rural housing, 10 percent into education and another 10 percent into irrigation infrastructure (Yang 2011a). Only the remaining funds are to be split within the different levels of (local) government. Lin (2007, 1832) argues that about 30–70 percent of the income of urban governments derives from land sales. Given these figures it comes as no surprise that the Vice-Minister of Land and Resources, Lu Xinshe, admits that officials would (only) be prosecuted if the illegal amount of the land converted to construction land would exceed 15 percent of the total converted land, thereby officially granting even local administrations some leeway (Xinhua 2009).

The mix of legal blurriness and dependence on extra-budgetary revenue opened Pandora's box. This dependence of the whole local political system on land sales and their integration in normal day-to-day business makes it difficult to pinpoint corruption cases exactly. In many harmful

land operations, the personal benefits of leading cadres might not sur-
pass certain limits. It is that the whole political system and local development depends upon unnecessary development and a culture of wasting
land resources (Ping 2011). However, there are certainly also numerous
cases of personal corruption (Cai 2003; Hsing 2010; Le Mons Walker
2006).

REFORMS

In this last section reform initiatives and visions for the future of collective land administration in China will be discussed. Again, as in the
previous section, this discussion mainly draws on newspaper reports and
policy papers published. It is intended as a summary of intentions to be
taken up in later empirical sections in this work. The main argument of
this section is that the center continues the three big strands of the Chinese land administration policy but that there is more emphasis on aspects of social stability than previously.

A recent report and comment from *Jinan Ribao* (2011) republished on
the website of *Renmin Ribao* provides an interesting inside view on how
the issue of land expropriation is discussed within central political organs. Four big issues in regard to land requisitioning are identified. First,
the scope of the land expropriated often would exceed legally allowed
limits. Relevant legal limitations installed in the previous years, for example that two-thirds of the villagers need to approve the land requisitioning, are ignored and have largely proven ineffective. The report notes
that in many cases coercion is used to remove farmers from their land.
The second issue mentioned in the report is that of the compensation
handed out to villagers. The already mentioned Cai Jiming from the Economics Department of Tsinghua University is quoted to argue that the
compensation payments are too low to allow families a successful start in
a new location. Peasants without land, without employment opportunities, and without social protection via the insurance system might turn
into a "hidden danger" (*yinhuan*) for social stability, he adds. Third, the
confusing legal framework would ease land expropriation. In many
cases, the farmers would have been tricked into handing over their land.
Fourth, national guidelines regarding the compensation of housing constructions on the collective land would still be lacking. Sun Jiye, Vice-
Head of the Provincial Supervision Bureau in Shandong, provides a quite
cynical and illuminating quote in the report: "[. . .] in some regions the
compensation for 1 sqm is as low as 400 RMB, which means that rural
housing comparatively is worth less than an urban restroom." The article
frequently mentions that the State Council is working on a solution regarding these issues. How to address these problems?

Former President Hu Jintao himself provided a first glimpse at the future of reforms in regard to collective land at a meeting on the topic of land administration on August 23, 2011 (for all of the following statements see Xinhua 2011e). Under the reanimated slogan from 1993 to "fully treasure and properly use every inch of land" (*shifen zhenxi he heli liyong mei yi cun tudi*) he identified four main priorities for the rural land administration, which are mostly based upon previous policy initiatives:

The first priority is an even stricter and complete system for the protection of land. Hu argues that the protection of arable land is the basis for Chinese food security. To ensure this goal, land rehabilitation (*fuken*) and the protection against natural catastrophes also need to be strengthened. Second, institutions that promote the most efficient land use must be created and implemented. Compared to past policies the strong focus on this topic is a new aspect in rural Chinese land administration. Third, Hu puts emphasis on strengthening the rights of villagers during the land requisitioning process. Land usage under the label "public interest" must be strictly limited, and expropriations and demolitions, if truly necessary, should comply with national standards. In addition, he calls for an improved supervision of land usage and better rights protection. Finally, he stresses the need for a reform of the land administration system, e.g. the completion of a comprehensive and strict system for land administration including a quick reform of the land requisitioning system and a deeper integration of the principle of giving compensation for the land taken from villagers. Hu Jintao's remarks provide a good overview of the main directions the reform of the rural Chinese land administration will take in the coming years. Let's have a closer look at the details of each of the reform policies he has outlined and some aspects not mentioned in these remarks.

It could be argued that the center has developed a sense of urgency in regard to the expropriation of collective land. The calls for an even stricter system have remained nearly unchanged in the past years—and already have reached the stage of the "strictest feasible system of land administration." A crucial legal loophole that experts and officials alike have identified is that of lacking transparency in attaching the status of public interest to construction projects. Currently, due to a lack of regulations that clarify the meaning of this condition, its effectiveness tends to be limited (Jinan Ribao 2011).

In addition to issuing tighter rules for land usage the national level continues to issue "strike hard" campaigns against illegal land seizures every once in a while (Xinhua 2011d). Scholars such as Li Chang'an call for the inclusion of higher levels of the administration (up to the provincial level) in investigations of all problematic land deals, as in the past strangely only low-ranking cadres were found guilty for infringing upon land usage rights (Jin 2011b). Another strategy that started in 2010 is the documentation and registration of all collective land usage in the countryside. The Ministry of Land and Resources argues that this would improve the protection of farmers rights to their land (Xinhua 2011a). The Ministry also issued plans to investigate how efficient the various regions in China have been in their efforts to protect the land (see Jin 2011b).

Recovering lost land for farming certainly has become a high priority in land administration. The Ministry of Land and Resources issued a statement in 2011 that, given (incomplete) official data, China has lost more than 130 million mu land due to construction, industrialization, and national calamities (Liu 2011). More than 100 million mu of farmland went into construction and about 20 million were lost due to natural catastrophes. The Ministry was confident that about 90 million mu of this lost farmland could be reclaimed for agricultural production, whereby 60 million mu would be suitable for grain production and 30 million could still be used for other agricultural purposes such as fruit trees. The Ministry mentions that up until 2009 already 30 million mu of farmland had already been recovered, leaving an additional 100 million mu to go. Using this land would help to maintain the *Red Line* of 1.8 billion mu of farmland. Yet, the report also warns that China continues to lose several million mu of land each year due to construction. An earlier report from 2009 states that in China each year about 4 million mu of land are reclaimed for agricultural production (Xinhua 2009). In July 2011, during heated public debates about the loss of arable land in China, the Ministry of Land and Resources mentioned that China still has about 7.3 million ha or 109.5 million mu of "reserve land," which could be developed into arable land (Xinhua 2011b).

However, efforts to reclaim the land lost to farming previously seem somewhat pointless while at the same time a good proportion of the available land is not used adequately. Idle land has become a big issue in contemporary rural China. It is estimated that between 10 and 15 percent of the arable land in China lies idle (Ruan 2011). An article in *China Daily* provides more information on this aspect. Accordingly, 46.6 percent of the arable land in 16 provinces in southern China lies idle during the winter, whereas in the past it was planted with rice during the winter season. In some regions, such as Hunan, up to 15 percent of the land was not planted for winter crops. The same report mentions a huge increase in imports for corn and wheat for 2010, 1,892 percent (almost 19 times more) and 36 percent, respectively (Jin 2011a). In addition, parts of the available farmland show enormous levels of pollution. Official sources admit that "in total about 10 percent of farmland has striking problems of heavy metal levels exceeding (government) limits" (Buckley 2011).

The reforms in land administration not only address the physical resources affected by the land expropriation but also aim to reduce their potential to destabilize rural society. Compensation payments have been identified as one crucial aspect in this task. Given the emphasis of the "with compensation" (*youchang*) principle mentioned in every recent policy paper on this topic, it is safe to assume that in the present situation land requisitions without proper compensation are a common issue. A reform of the compensation scheme is frequently discussed in the media.

The ideas here start with modest proposals to increase the amount paid by 20 percent up to 100 percent more. However, within the Ministry of Land and Resources more thorough reforms are at least being discussed. Substantial changes to the current system, for example, are suggested by Chen Xiwen, Vice-Head of the Leading Group for Rural Development and the already mentioned Sun Jiye, Vice-Head of the Provincial Supervision Bureau in Shandong. Chen Xiwen argues that compensation paid for collective land should be based on the same regulations as those of the compensation for state-owned land issued earlier in 2011. This is another way of saying that the market value of objects should be used to calculate the compensation. Because collective land does not have a direct market value, villagers and the local state should get together to find an approximate and realistic price point, his suggestion continues (Yang 2011a). Sun Jiye goes even further in his suggestion and argues that villagers who lose their land should receive a social insurance and that the compensation should be based upon their inherited net costs and not on a calculation based on the approximate outcome of future agricultural production, as stated in the 1982 Guidelines. In this way, villagers would directly benefit from the modernization and urbanization of the countryside. In the past, an important conflict in regard to compensation was the question of how to recognize the (housing) constructions and plants on the expropriated land. Many villagers claimed that the monetary value of these things had been insufficiently covered by the compensation they received. Sun Jiye suggests that the compensation for housing should be based on the market value of similar structures (Jinan Ribao 2011).

The National Deputy Inspector for Land Supervision, Gan Zangchun, also outlined new ideas for the compensation scheme. He explained that a reformed compensation should consist of three parts: a compensation for the lost land usage rights, a compensation for housing and a compensation for other structures. Furthermore, the resettlement of the expropriated farmers must follow the principle of social fairness and an urbanization of land should be followed by an urbanization of the people. Accordingly, the expropriation process would not only involve changing the household registration of these villagers but also granting them the same benefits the urban population enjoys, including education, health care, as well as provisions for unemployment-, old age-, and social insurance (Jinghua Shibao 2011).

These new regulations should in part also provide an antidote against the threat of social instability that forced demolitions represent. As mentioned earlier, demolitions have become a major source of conflict in the countryside. In early July 2011, the central government issued a statement that all resettlement schemes in the future should follow the principle of "relocation first, demolition later" (Xinhua 2011c). A few weeks later the Supreme People's Court published an urgent notice that demolitions must be stopped if residents threaten to commit suicide (Zheng 2011). Public acknowledgement of the necessity of such drastic measures may have been triggered by the case of Tang Fuzhen, who in 2009, in her despair over the forced demolition of her home, set herself on fire. Since then Amnesty International has counted 41 self-immolations triggered by forced evictions in China (mostly in the countryside) (see Moore 2012).

If we recall the root causes of the boom of land expropriation identified by Cai Jiming in the previous section, it is striking how few of the reforms in this section seem adequate. Professor Cai himself suggests several measures, all structural and institutional, to cut the Gordian knot. According to him, the monopoly of governments on construction land needs to be broken. An important step toward this would be to provide much clearer legal definitions and limits for legal conditions of "public interest" that allows the expropriation of farmers. The compensation for these kinds of land expropriations needs to be fairer. He further suggests that, when village land is turned into construction land but (the legal requirement of) specific public interest is not a given, the ownership of said land should not change and the villagers should therefore reap the benefits of the land sale. These structural reforms would only work, however, if the funding of local governments improves and they would not have to depend upon land sales to fund their operations. In other words, the responsibilities and the funding of local governments need to match better. Cai also mentions the need to improve the supervision and monitoring of high-level cadres, as all unchecked power may promote corrupt behavior (Cai 2011).

Finally, at some point the debate to reform land usage rights usually turns to the issue of privatization. While in the early 1990s (especially before tenure of the land usage rights contracts were increased to 30 years), much of the privatization talk was inspired by the idea of improving tenure security (Cheng and Tsang 1995), today privatization is primarily mentioned as a means against the problem of land expropriation. When the issue of privatization came up in the interviews conducted for this book, the most frequently mentioned reason given in favor of privatization was to improve the rights of farmers and to provide them with a better legal basis in the conflicts of land requisitioning. During an interview session with scholars from the Department of Economics of Guizhou University (Guiyang, September 10, 2010), one of them argued:

> What the state wants to do, he will do. If he wants to have some houses demolished and the inhabitants resettled, then he will just do so. Privatization will not protect the houses of the villagers, but private ownership will give peasants a basis to make their stand against this development (*you kangzheng de liyou*). We define the land in the village by usage rights, but this definition is incomplete. Peasants have usage

rights, but they are incomplete (*bu jianquan de*). Peasants cannot use the land usage rights as a security for credits, because they are not allowed to sell their land. In reality [the current model] is a hidden and incomplete type of private ownership. It is exactly the incomplete nature [of ownership], which allows certain interest groups to infringe on the interests of peasants.

Almost all of his colleagues disagreed with this position. Three main overlapping counterarguments were formulated. First, a privatization of land may turn the peasants into an even more vulnerable group for expropriation and land loss, as the legal system is biased against them. Second, if many more peasants decide to leave agriculture permanently and move to the city, then this might put even greater pressure on urban centers, especially in regard to social security and social stability. Third, pressure on social security may also emerge even if privatization leads to higher compensation payments, as many peasants may not spend their new wealth wisely and end up becoming dependent on social security.[10]

While the reforms in land administration dealing with the loss of agricultural land have moved to the center of media and scholarly attention in China, the reforms to allow more transfer and consolidation of agricultural land for the purpose of agrarian commercialization have not stopped or slowed down. Of particular importance in this field is the continued stream of ideas in the already mentioned No. 1 Documents.

The *New Socialist Countryside* outlined in these documents aims to restructure almost all social, political, and economic relations in the countryside and also includes a set of particular ideas about agriculture and the role collective land should play in it. It is the idea that local governments should encourage the creation of markets for land usage rights. The No. 1 Document from 2009 (Zhongfa 2008b) even suggests the creation of service companies for that purpose in regions that meet the conditions. The documents also call for more integration of Dragonheads, cooperatives, and households within agricultural production.

Experimentation in land administration and ownership continue in the countryside. High-ranking officials have recognized that the transition to commercial agriculture demands more funding, the concentration of land and ultimately a transition of the majority of remaining peasants into some form of urban employment. Zheng Hui, Head of the Chinese Development Bank, has identified the collective land usage rights as an untapped source of funding to grease the wheels of modernization. His idea envisions using land usage rights as a form of security for loans (*chengbao jingyingquan diya daikuan*). Not only could these loans contribute to speeding up the industrialization of agriculture and the creation of economies of scale, they would also be an important instrument in raising rural incomes and a channel for creative financial services for the countryside (*nongcun jinrong jigou yewu chuangxin de yitiao yujing*). He highlights the importance of such loans, especially for independent commercial farming households (Wang 2011).

Experiments in this direction have been reported from all over China. In Shaanxi Province, for example, 32 households received a set of three property rights certificates (*chanquanzheng*) for their collective land usage rights and housing land. This allowed them to use their new ownership rights as a security for loans, albeit exact conditions of this experiment remain vague. It is, for example, doubtful that the underlying legal procedures have been changed and therefore questionable whether the land certificates could really be used as a security (Chen 2011).

Another perspective on using agricultural land as security, albeit without changes to the agricultural nature of the collective land, is put forward with the so-called land-credit cooperatives (*tudi xinyong hezuoshe*). This is another variation of pooling land usage rights of the villagers from the same village. The pooled land could then be used as a security for loans. The interests of villagers should be preserved and their provisions with social insurance ensured. Finally, villagers should start to pick up non-farming work and the land-credit cooperatives should transform themselves into a shareholding framework (Chang 2011b).

Experimentation in land administration in order to ease commercial transformation and modernization of agriculture is an important feature of the current Chinese political system. For the near future, this does not imply that popular local solutions for land transfer and the consolidation of holdings will go beyond the legal framework outlined earlier in this chapter. The HRS framework remains the starting point for all reform efforts.

SUMMARY

This chapter introduced the institutional framework of collective land and the HRS and their transformation over the years into the basis of a modernized and commercialized agriculture. Despite changes in the mode of operation, the underlying property institutions of a socialist economy continue to persist. In a strictly legal sense, China continues to only have state-owned and collective land. Yet, the system of contracting collective land to farmers and thereby granting individualized land usage rights has greatly evolved in recent years. Market structures that one would only expect in economies with private landownership have evolved in China. However, there are important caveats.

Throughout this analysis of the current state of land policy in China it becomes clear that all efforts to modernize agriculture in China and to create a market for land usage rights compete with other legal and illegal use cases for the farmland. With a constantly changing legal framework for land administration the interpretation of this framework by local actors becomes crucial. How do farmers and local officials perceive the conditions for the pursuit of commercial agriculture? How do markets for land usage rights develop, given that local officials would benefit to a much higher degree if the same land would be converted to construction land? These are the questions that will be pursued in the next chapters.

The chapter was organized in four sections. The main argument of the first part was that initial HRS reform was not primarily about maximizing output of agriculture but rather about political stability. Frequent redistributions of land ensured the continuation of an egalitarian distribution of land. The new freedom to till "one's own" land and generous sponsoring by the center led to annual growth in rural incomes between 1978 and 1984. Yet, the initial implementation of the HRS has created a set of limitations for the long-term commercial development of agriculture. Especially the small scale and fragmented nature of the plots has made it difficult to create economies of scale in agriculture. These limitations may have been causal for the fact that the biggest institutional factor in increasing rural incomes has been the new freedom of peasants to engage in non-farm employment, e.g., the freedom to stop being peasants.

Based on the analysis of 20+ laws and regulations the second part of the chapter argued that the continuing stream of reforms in the administration of land since the conception of the HRS in the early 1980s is based upon three pillars. First, there are continued efforts to institutionalize, stabilize, and improve the legal framework and protection of the HRS. Increasingly urgent and unequivocal calls to improve the protection of contractors dominate this aspect of land administration policies. The second pillar consists of efforts to avoid further loss of farmland and to recover land lost for agriculture as part of the national food security goals. Finally, there is a third pillar in the reforms of rural land administration. Based upon a framework of agricultural modernization and commercialization, numerous efforts have been put into place to ease the transfer of farmland from traditional farming entities to modern economies of scale. The unique Chinese path of farmland transfer allows for the commodification of land for agricultural use within the limitations of the HRS and collective ownership. Collective ownership of land is unlikely to be only a short-term transitional stage in rural land administration.

The third part of the chapter showed the connection between collective ownership of land and the difficulties to protect farmland and farmers. Construction projects may be the single most important threat to the commercialization of agriculture in China. The regions affected today are core agricultural production bases in western China. The coexistence of an upward trend in the expropriation of land and the tightening of laws may come as a surprise to external observers. Nonetheless, the new laws do little to change the structural funding difficulties of local governments or the profitability of the expropriation process. Most local governments depend upon land sales to finance their day-to-day business. Policies to further improve the supervision of land are unlikely to succeed if not matched by efforts to tackle underlying structural funding imbalances.

The last part of the chapter took a look at the current discussion regarding further reform of land administration, as observed in newspaper articles and interviews between 2008 and 2012. In the Chinese mainstream debate, there are no plans for major changes to the current property institutions. The lack of legal protection for the collective land usage rights and rising anger about low compensation payments are attributed to bad management practice and not yet seen as being connected to the general institutional framework of collective ownership. Therefore, the majority of present reform initiatives aims to further strengthen the HRS and the legal protection of farmland within this framework, mostly by improving supervision of the local land administration. In addition, alternatives to the existing system of compensations for requested collective land are being publicly discussed. Outside of the mainstream debate several scholars are suggesting that a privatization of collective land may substantially improve the bargaining position of the current land usage rights holders.

NOTES

1. Later reforms and their impact are discussed in the empirical chapters as encountered in the field sites.

2. On the pre-reform conditions see Smil (1981) and Skinner (1978). Personal communication with Prof. Heberer, November 8, 2012.

3. In contrast to the first HRS experiments in poverty regions, which may have had that priority.

4. See the literature review in the introduction for more on this position.

5. If not noted otherwise, all legal documents were accessed through the Wangfang Database (via crossasia.org).

6. To cite legal documents the official abbreviations, e.g., Zhongfa, have been used where available. In all other cases, a short handle for the issuing institution is used. For the full title of the institution and a translation, please see the references.

7. In other words, decreasing the amount manual labor used to work a given plot of land while at the same time increasing its output.

8. The term disappeared from the No. 1 Documents again in 2011 and 2012.

9. Another good example is mentioned by Wang Qian and Guo Anfei: "With only 10 legal golf courses, nearly 600 golf courses had been illegally built and operated across China as of the end of 2010, *People's Daily* reported in June" (2011).

10. Note the similarity of these arguments to the various perspectives on the rural population outlined in the introduction.

FOUR

Peasant Differentiation and Smallholder Frustration

Previously this book identified peasant differentiation as an important part of agrarian transitions. In fact, the integration of smallholders into markets and their growing dependence upon monetary income is the initial stage of an agrarian transition. The more independent the small-holders from the market are, the less likely it is for a transition to commercial agriculture to take place. Only if peasants turn to new employment opportunities, irrespective if they do so voluntary or not, land can be rearranged in a non-violent manner. Given the current Chinese legal framework and its renewed emphasis upon strengthening the access rights of villagers to their land, peasant differentiation appears to be the only road to a commercial agriculture that does not bring further tension to the relationship between villagers and local administrations. This chapter primarily deals with the relationship between peasant differentiation as found in the field sites and the other two variables of agrarian transition, rural politics and property institutions. Furthermore, the chapter aims to trace the links between peasant differentiation and a potential commodification of land. There are two main arguments presented here.

First, while the Hu/Wen administration had a strong pro-smallholder rhetoric, the economic context for unspecialized small- or sub-scale farming has not been very favorable. The arrival of new subsidies and earmarked transfer payments has not significantly improved the conditions for smallholders and the gap between rural and urban income is still continuously widening. The negative environment for smallholding drives many former smallholders into wage employment—either in the cities or locally. Second, the financial devaluation of smallholder farming is reflected in an economic devaluation of land for smallholders. Verdery (2003) has argued that such an economic devaluation of land is the precondition for changes in the moral value of land—and may perhaps ease the moral side of the transfer of land for these smallholders. Idle land and the absence of resource (including labor) efficient farming are the indicators of this economic devaluation.

The chapter is structured in the following way: The first section will discuss how most villagers came to become increasingly dependent upon monetary income. The following section will describe the forms of peasant differentiation encountered in the four field sites. The third section introduces a set of factors in smallholder agriculture that is seen as having considerably influenced this shift. The final section provides the main argument of this chapter in the form of two hypotheses concerning the effects of current differentiation of the peasantry for the commodification of land in China.

For some questions in regard to peasant differentiation the villagers themselves would be the best source of information. Yet most interview partners in the main four field sites were officials, who did not talk in depth about the new financial needs of the rural population. This section is therefore also based upon the experience of earlier fieldwork as well as upon secondary literature.[1]

A NEW DEMAND FOR MONETARY INCOME

During an interview with a female household head and her two daughters in a small and poor village in Qinghai Province I asked all family members what their dreams for the future would be. Almost immediately after I had raised that question the oldest daughter started to cry and began to argue with her mother. As it turned out, her biggest wish was to continue her education—in school she had done exceptionally well so far. The mother argued, however, that the family was too poor and could not afford the tuition fee and the additional costs. Although Beijing has taken away the burden of the primary education tuition fee, higher education in China—especially for many rural households—continues to be very expensive. And not only the tuition fee but also the related costs for books, public transportation, school dorms, etc., need to be taken into account.

Further peasant differentiation in China (and elsewhere) is connected to the monetary income needs of rural households. The expansion of services and opportunities for consumption for the rural population since the start of the reform policies in the late 1970s has nurtured a new demand for monetary income. Opportunities for villagers in education (especially in regard to high school and college level education) and health care, for example, have greatly expanded—but so have the prices for these services. These two examples, education and health care, will be briefly discussed in the following section.

Numbers on the proportion of rural income spent on education vary considerably among various sources. Official data, according to Wang and Moll (2010), state that the average spending for education in the countryside was 306 RMB per capita or 9.5 percent of the total income in 2007 and for Guizhou, their field site, 147 RMB or 7.7 percent of the total income. However, not every household has school-aged children, thus has to pay for education, and in addition there are huge differences in income among households in the countryside. Wang and Moll (2010, 357) calculated that the 793 households in their sample paid for primary education between 254 and 335 RMB, for secondary education between 1,580 and 2,248 RMB and for a type they called secondary and higher education between 3,750 and 6,500 RMB per year. Using income data, they divided the 793 households into five similarly sized groups. The average per capita income in the poorest group was 1,012 RMB and 2,690 RMB in the richest group. The poorer households in the sample had a much higher likelihood of having education expenses (70 percent) than the richest group (41 percent) (Wang and Moll 2010, 357). They show that education spending is a great liability for rural households with children. Hannum and Kong (2007) confirm this with their data on education expenditures in Gansu. While in 2000 the average total enumerated semester costs for a sample child household was 356.77 RMB, by 2004 this figure had risen to 910 RMB. They conclude that these costs, given an official average rural per capita net income for Gansu in 2004 of 1,852 RMB, are a huge burden for rural households.

Paying for health care has become another major expenditure for the rural population. The Ministry of Health (Weishengbu 2009) conducted a survey of 56,456 households with 177,501 persons in 94 counties in 2008. The average rural net per capita income for these households was 4932 RMB, of which 3728 were spent. Among the expenditures of these households health care amounted to 11.6 percent and education to 15.5 percent (Weishengbu 2009). Having a low income or living in poverty greatly increases the chances for further impoverishment through health care spending, as this usually involves out-of-pocket spending (Blumenthal and Hsiao 2005; Liu, Rao, and Hsiao 2003). However, the introduction of the *New Cooperative Medical Scheme* (*xinxing hezuo yiliao*) might have reduced the magnitude of the health care question. Li et al (2012, 641) show that, since a peak in the year 2000 in which 60 percent of health care expenditures were out-of-pocket payments, this rate dropped to 35 percent by 2009. Still, the survey from 2008 indicates that 24.9 percent of all villagers and 28.1 percent of the villagers in the poorest villages ended medical treatment early because they could not afford it or thought it was too expensive (Weishengbu 2009, 41).[2] In a great contribution, Lora-Wainright (2011) shows how a perceived low effectiveness of medical treatment in combination high costs deters many rural indiduals to consult medical services. In addition, even an article by Li et al., which mainly highlights recent improvements in rural health care provision, exemplarily shows that in one county-level hospital investigated revenues from hospital stays and prescription fees exploded from 4.6 million RMB in 2008 to 25 million RMB in 2010. This came along with an increase in the average hospitalization bills from 741 RMB to 3,068 RMB (Li, Chen, and Powers 2012, 638).

These two brief examples of education and health care should show that the need for more monetary income in the countryside is tremendous. The following section will discuss how peasants have addressed this need in the four field sites.

PEASANT DIFFERENTIATION IN THE FOUR FIELD SITES

The new demand for monetary income had a huge effect upon the economic strategies of agricultural producers. Two important variants of peasant differentiation are of particular interest. In the first variant, farmers are integrated into the market via an increasing specialization of their production. These farmers primarily produce for the market and the object of their operations is similar to other commercial enterprises: they engage in agriculture primarily in order to make a profit. In the second variant, smallholders discontinue independent farming and become hired workers. Whether or not they keep their agricultural land in their home village does not influence their occupation and main source of income to a large degree. In their seminal work, Zhang and Donaldson (2008; 2010) discuss the various stages in the spectrum between the traditional smallholder and wage labor without any land usage rights.

The differentiation of the peasantry in more entrepreneurial forms of agrarian production was already an important factor in the local economic mix in all field sites. In Suining, less than one-third of the rural income was generated from traditional peasant products such as grain (rice) and small poultry. Already a third was derived from economies of scale in pork production. Another third was created in services. The head of the Agricultural Commission in Suining especially highlighted the importance of the pork industry there. For those families who did take part in this commercial endeavor, the average income rose by 680 RMB in 2009 (from 2008, see cf019). Income increases for the rural population in Laixi exceeded even the aforementioned numbers. Commercial farming and wages were the drivers of this increase in income, too (cf022). A township official in Anju District outlined the many sources of income of their local peasants nowadays: renting out land, working in local companies, carrying out small sideline agricultural production, or cultivating fruit trees in the mountainous parts of the villages. In the last two years alone, the income in his township has increased by 15 percent and now (2009) the average is 5,340 RMB. Around 20 percent of all villagers here have an annual income exceeding 10,000 RMB (cf012).

Yet, most local wage income opportunities diminish in contrast with the incomes that can be earned beyond the village borders. Labor migration has become one of the biggest threats to smallholding in China. During the interviews in Sichuan, Shandong, and Guizhou, it became clear that one day of hired work (*da gong*) pays between 30–140 RMB, with skill and gender having a great impact upon the actual amount paid (cf021, cf020). This amount is magnitudes higher than what could ever be earned in traditional family farming. Using data from a survey conducted in 1999 by the Ministry of Agriculture, Kung (2002, 401) argues that the wage differences and an emerging non-farming labor market are the main drivers for labor migration and land rental. In his survey, unskilled work pays roughly double of what can be earned as a peasant. The empirical data for this book suggests a much higher degree of imbalance.

In an interview with the head of the Agricultural Commission in Suining he stated that the average grain harvest for one mu of land was around 600 kg. Given the 2009 increase for the procurement price from 0.7 RMB to 0.9 RMB kg, these 600 kg would translate into 540 RMB revenue, from which production costs still need to be deducted (cf019). In the same interview, he argued that, despite guaranteed minimum procurement prices for grain, a farmer could earn no more than 400 RMB per mu, whereas with cash crops it could exceed 2,000 RMB per mu (cf019). One has to keep in mind that in the Suining area farmers have on average little more than half a mu (0.58) per capita (cf006). A party secretary from a village near Suining City even argued that with the local rice variety (*huanggu*) the harvest could possibly sell for only 300 RMB per mu. After paying for production costs, no income at all would remain (cf021).

Using the above data a conservative estimate on the income imbalance between smallholding and wage labor would be a ratio of 1 to 5, but 1 to 10 and higher seems very possible, too. For example, if a migrant worker has employment for 250 days at an average of 80 RMB/day, he ends up with 20,000 RMB, minus the costs for living and travel expenses. A net profit of 15,000 RMB seems to be a reasonable figure. Now compare this with 400 RMB per mu in grain and per capita average land usage rights of roughly 0.6 mu in the regions of Sichuan, where our field sites were located. A family of four, having 2.4 mu (4x0.6), would make less than 1,000 RMB (960) per year. To this amount, the revenue from small livestock farming needs to be added—however, the total revenue for such a family is very likely to be below 3,000 RMB. A negative view on small-scale grain production was shared by a group of villagers during one of the interview sessions. In reflection on past times (before they had their land transferred to an agricultural enterprise), this group provided the following nice, paradox statement: "In the past, when we cultivated grain, we didn't have enough to eat" (cf014).

We need to compare these returns to those possible with cash crops, of which fruit trees have been a very tangible trend in the field sites. One official in Suining explained that the local variety of oranges was good for more than 10,000 RMB per mu and, after deducting costs, a net income of 6,000 RMB per mu would remain. With grapefruits even up to 8000 RMB per mu would be possible (cf019). Specialized livestock farming is even more profitable. Taking an example from the pork industry, the same official explained the enormous developments taking place:

> By 2015 we aim to create a Dragonhead enterprise that can process as many as 10 million pigs [a year], the production output having a value of several hundred million RMB [. . .] 54.9 percent of all pigs are raised as part of economies of scale; that's more than 20 percent above the national average. In Suining the pork industry adds about 76 percent value to the livestock industry. The livestock industry itself adds about 63 percent value to the overall agricultural output for Suining. Along this line of thinking one could say that the pork industry produces half of the production value output of agriculture in Suining (cf019).

However, there are several hurdles for smallholders who want to engage in these more profitable sectors of the agriculture. In fact, many villagers have opted for a perhaps easier way to improve their income by going to the cities as wage laborers. As one village cadre in Anju explained: "This year [2009] even more have left the village; for them there is nothing left to do in agriculture, so they look for work elsewhere" (cf021). In this particular village at the time of our interview, 618 people (of a total work-force [18–60 years] of 823 villagers), or 75.1 percent, had left the village to search for work elsewhere (cf021). A township official nearby summarized the local conditions in the following way: "We still have 11,000 people working the land. Most of them are old, women or children" (cf011). In other villages visited, the development may not have been as dramatic. However, in all villages around 30 percent of the labor force at minimum did not engage in farming anymore and had already left their village (cf018). It could reasonably be argued that the transfer payments of the urban labor sustain the village life in the field sites visited.

But it is not only different income levels between urban and rural areas that trigger this migration. For some peasants, rural life itself, with its exhausting work in a closed social setting, is rapidly losing its attractiveness. A new generation of migrants, as Austin Ramzy (2010) argues, is turning to the cities to take part in a more urban and modern life, which they are unable to find at home; they are going "for fun." This is in line with a cadre's statement from the Agricultural Office in Anju, who mentioned that during the financial crisis in 2008/2009 the number of return migrants was higher and the local labor situation was briefly bad.

However, "even if it was [bad] like that, they would not return to work their fields again" (cf009).

The financial crisis in 2008/2009 provided a brief window into an alternative universe without enough urban jobs for the would-be labor migrants. Governments in Anju and Xifeng, for example, responded and tried to bridge the timespan until the economy recovered by providing training and giving financial and political support to start-ups in specialized agricultural production. In the end, however, officials seemed very relieved when the economy kicked back in and the *nongmingong* (migrant workers) left the villages again (see cf030 or cf009).

Having guaranteed access to collective farmland seems not to have affected the decision of villagers to go to the cities and towns in search for employment to a large degree. The diversification of income sources, with non-agricultural income taking up a bigger portion, arises out of economic necessity. The following section will examine this economic phenomena. In particular, it will deal in more detail with the hurdles for smallholders wanting to become commercial farmers.

THE CONDITIONS FOR SMALLHOLDING IN THE FIELD SITES

Land Distribution

The size, quality, and distribution of plots directly affect the profitability of farming activities. Whereas the third chapter has provided detailed information on the institutional context, the focus here is upon the existing conditions found at the grassroots level. There is considerable variance in the per capita land available in the field sites. In some regions in Sichuan, it was down to as little as 0.3 mu (cf010). In 2009, one leading cadre in Suining put the average there at 0.56 mu. He also mentioned an international minimum amount of land necessary for food security of 0.8 mu (cf019). A year earlier another cadre put the figure for Suining at 0.58 mu and made reference to a security line of 0.8 mu from the United Nations (cf006). Sustainable traditional agriculture seems very difficult under these conditions of land scarcity. In the Shandong field sites, peasant families had much more land on average, in one case up to 2.2 mu per capita (cf026).[3]

The size of the plots is not only very small already, but is also continuously shrinking. For example, from 1978 to 2007, acreage in Suining shrunk by 19.8 percent (from 193,172 mu to 154,994 mu) (Suiningshi Tongjiju 2008, 286). While Laixi, according to the statistics, actually saw little change in the acreage between 1991 and 2010 (from 71,713 hectare to 71,154 hectare), the whole administrative region of Qingdao lost 20.87 percent of its cultivated area in the time between 1978 and 2010 (from 531,300 hectare to 420,400 hectare) (Qingdaoshi Tongjiju 1992, 90; Qingdaoshi Tongjiju 2011, 212). Public outrage and a number of recent state policies calling for better protection of land use rights and peasant agriculture seem to be based on a tangible of all too common cases of land expropriations throughout rural China.

The nature of land as a fixed asset makes agrarian production vulnerable to numerous external influences. For traditional small-scale producers, two of these influences are of extraordinary importance: weather conditions and environmental pollution. Obviously weather greatly affects the harvest in quality and quantity. Although weather conditions seem at first glance to be beyond the influence of farmers and local governments, many of its hazardous influences originate from manmade changes to the natural environment or a lack of proper precautions. The case of water is probably the most important and very illuminating. Water is a constant source of sorrow in China, always seemingly lacking just the right amount or quality of it. Whereas urban areas struggle with the quality (Wang and Li 2011), rural areas seem to have either too much or too little to sustain production (Larson 2011; Wong 2011). Despite enormous investments in water irrigation in many parts of rural China, weather and water scarcity in particular remain an important and incalculable part of agricultural production. Although major draughts or floods have not hit the field sites recently, the lack of water is perceived among cadres to be problematic and a potential obstacle for future agricultural modernization (cf021 and cf012).

Recovering wasteland, cleaning polluted fields, and making land reusable for agriculture has become an activity many local governments engage in. Officials stated that land rehabilitation is an important means to address shortages of decent quality agricultural land. The task at hand is twofold: to improve the land quality and to reclaim land for agriculture (cf004). Programs for integrated agricultural development often include attempts to improve conditions for agricultural production and initiatives to upgrade the quality of land feature prominently (cf025). For smallholders, there is an important caveat to these land improvement investments: most of them are targeted to reach already existing larger holdings of farmland or to create them. If smallholders want to improve their land quality they have to make considerable investments by themselves.

Land rehabilitation has also become an important part of agricultural modernization. Not only does newfound environmental consciousness motivate local governments but also the less obvious opportunity to turn additional farmland (elsewhere) into construction land. If there is enough newly recovered land to keep the amount of agricultural land at roughly the same level, lucrative land usage transformation is possible (cf023 and cf004). The target for the Anju District, for example, was to recover 10,000 mu by the end of 2008 (cf004).

Due to local conditions and the differing nature of targeted land, the costs for these land rehabilitation activities may vary greatly. One official in Anju put the costs for one mu of reclaimed land at 12,000–15,000 RMB (cf008). A township cadre argued that the costs are much higher and put the figure at 1–2 million RMB per mu. In fact, given the unfavorable land conditions here this money, the cadre continued to argue, would be better used for road construction or in regions with better conditions. In his township, all such investments were just a big waste of money (cf011). The costs of land rehabilitation were split between the center and local subsidies. In one of the locations, the costs were divided according to a formula wherein the national level covers 30 percent and the local state 70 percent. In addition, in this particular location 15 percent of the revenue for any sold construction land is also used for land rehabilitation purposes (cf004).

SUBSIDIES

The negative prospects for smallholders seem somewhat surprising in light of the official rhetoric of support for the countryside. In recent years, the Chinese central state and, to a much lesser degree, local administrations have engaged in a confusing and sometimes contradictory pattern of agrarian subsidies. They are considered to be part of the *sannong* policies and its successor, the *Building of a New Socialist Countryside* (Yu and Jensen 2010). Do these new subsidies improve the competitiveness of small-scale family farmers?

In the field sites this hardly seems to be the case. At most, these subsidies slow down the pace of agrarian change among traditional peasant farmers. The positive impact on entrepreneurial farmers tends to be much stronger. In the following section, the subsidies given directly to the producers will be dealt with, but first a clarification regarding the term is necessary. Agrarian subsidies relevant to small-scale family farming production can be broadly divided into five categories: a) subsidies for certain crop varieties and livestock, b) subsidies for seeds, c) subsidies for inputs such as fertilizer and herbi-/pesticides, d) a guaranteed minimum price for certain crops, and e) subvention for agricultural machinery. Yu and Jensen (2010, 349) provide data on annual subventions for agriculture. Accordingly, "Together, [. . .] subsidies totaled CNY 26.2 billion in 2006 and were expected to reach CNY 42.7 billion for 2007, which implies a per mu subsidy of CNY 27 nationwide (CNY 30 for main grain production provinces and CNY 20 for other provinces)." Lin and Wong (2012) have used a different way to calculate the subsidies and report a much steeper increase. According to their data, in 2003 the total of all central level production subsidies stood at 10.6 billion RMB. By

2009 these subsidies in five sub-categories[4] for agrarian production increased to 139.02 billion RMB (Lin and Wong 2012, 29).

The numbers for the field sites show considerable variance, even within the same location and time. In 2008 in Laixi, a leading official presented these figures: Rice subsidies had been 16 RMB per mu in the past and in that year rose to 70 RMB per mu. For wheat and corn, there were subsidies of 10 RMB per mu. In addition, there were also subsidies for apple tree planters, including a subvention for "bagging" of fruits. He called these agricultural subsidies a rather forceful instrument for the future development of agriculture and, in part, a solution for rising commodity prices, the "peasant burden" and insufficient investments (cf022). In 2008, another official in Laixi estimated the amount of subsidies per mu in grain production to be in the range of 100 RMB. He contrasted this to a tax of around 7–80 RMB / mu which the farmers had had to pay earlier (cf024). Officials from Anju put the figure at around 80 RMB subsidies per mu grain production (cf020).

Several local officials criticized the usefulness of these agricultural subventions. As one township party secretary explains:

> Within one year our township hands out subsidies totaling 3 million RMB. If we would not directly give this money to peasants and use all of it for paving roads with cement, we would be able to finish this project in two years. For roads connecting all villages! If you give the money to the people—one villager receives around 200 RMB, a family around 1,000 RMB—the money is quickly spent [to no use] (cf011).

The same sentiment was echoed in Xifeng. A county cadre there said: "grain subsidies have a bigger political than practical significance" (*liangshi zhibu de zhengzhi yiyi da yu shiji yiyi*) and also wished to be allowed to put these funds to more efficient use (cf030).

Although these subsidies amount to considerable sums in the eyes of cash-starved local administrators, they pale in comparison to investments in modern, integrated agriculture. In Laixi, for example, investments were made in two different kinds of greenhouses, one at a cost of 6000 RMB per mu and subsidized with 1,000 RMB and one with costs between 30,000–50,000 RMB and subsidized with 5000 RMB. After the deduction of the production costs, annual revenues of 10,000–20,000 RMB and 20000+ RMB are likely. Those who have the skills and funds will also receive generous subsidies to start their own businesses (cf022). The same pattern is visible in the livestock industries. In Laixi, the city of Qingdao handed out 400 RMB per cow purchased in 2007 and increased that sum in 2008. There are also substantial subsidies for pigs purchased (cf024).

In contrast, those engaging in low profit agriculture have little support to gain from the state subsidies in order to continue doing what they do. These findings mirror those of a recent study by Lin and Wong (2012, 39), who found that central level subsidies and the matching local funds on average would increase the income of a village household by 304.8 RMB in 2005 (85.8 RMB per capita). However, there are huge differences in income among the recipients, as already noted in the above interviews. Lin and Wong (2012, 43) state that "[a]n increase of 10 per cent in per capita income will provide a 1.9 per cent increment in per capita subsidy." To summarize the findings above, subsidies for agrarian production in China are already in large scale directed toward commercial agriculture. Smallholders do benefit to some degree but the subsidies do not turn smallholding into a substantially more profitable business.

INPUTS

The limited effectiveness of subsidies for smallholders is also related to another important change in Chinese agriculture. Not only subsidies have reached new heights. Production costs in agriculture, especially for certain inputs like fertilizers and pesticides have grown even quicker. These chemicals have become the nuts and bolts of Chinese agriculture. Given the shrinking size of the plots and the enormous population density, the application of agricultural chemicals tends to be seen as the only means to raise production output, ensure food security, and increase peasant incomes.

Unger (2002a) once argued that in many locations in rural China the difference between poverty and medium income is already decided by whether one has the resources to purchase enough chemical fertilizer or not. *China Daily* reported in October of 2011 that the average use of pesticides in China is three to five times higher than the international average. The same article quoted the then–Vice-Minister for Agriculture Wei Chao'an as saying that China's consumption of chemical fertilizer now "constitutes 35 percent of global market share, equal to the US and India combined" (Yang 2011b). The enormous amount of chemicals used in Chinese agriculture have raised serious food safety concerns in China and abroad (Klein 2013; Yan 2012).

Nevertheless, the application of fertilizers, pesticides, and herbicides has become an important part of the calculations of farming households in China. In 2008, one official in Laixi argued that, while in the past the costs for fertilizer may have been around 10 RMB for a typical farmer, they would now exceed 200 RMB. He continued:

> We now do have a lot of favorable policies for peasants from the center, which are really good. But seen from another perspective, the costs in agricultural production in general and for the necessary inputs have increased too fast, so that, in reality, the rural population does not experience any tangible effect from these favorable policies (cf024).

These costs in production have turned agriculture into a capital-intensive business. Unfortunately, ever since the reforms started, capital has been a very restricted resource for individual farmers in China.

Lack of Capital

How to solve the farming households' need for fresh capital remains one of the biggest open questions in rural China today. Official loans usually require some kind of security, which these households do not possess. Some regions in China started to experiment with using collective land usage rights or housing as security. One scholar in Guiyang mentioned a recent reform that would allow farmers close to urban areas to use their land as collateral, albeit the law actually prohibits this (cf017).

Zhang Hui, head of the Chinese Development Bank, also argued in a recent talk for the use of collective land usage rights as a security for peasants to tackle the question of loans lacking in the countryside. However, he did not really touch upon possible constitutional implications attached to this move and only briefly mentioned the risk of even more "three-nothings farmers" (no land, no job, no insurance) (Wang 2011). As of the time of the writing of this book, all initiatives in this regard seem to be isolated experiments, with the possible exception of Zhejiang, according to Prof. Yu Jianxing.[5]

What other sources of capital are there for villagers? Lynette Ong uses survey data and interviews to discuss a number of rural credit institutions and their ability to provide loans for the rural population. She concludes with a devastating verdict: "[. . .] a whole range of rural credit institutions that are intended to serve farmers' credit demands have failed miserably in their missions," and "[a]dditionally, it is noteworthy that cropping was the single most important use of informal loans among those in the poor locales, underlining the fact that the formal credit institutions are unable to meet the basic credit demands of households in the economically deprived areas" (Ong 2011, 62). In his book on political reforms in the cotton sector and their implementation, Björn Alpermann discusses in detail different sources for capital open to local cotton entrepreneurs. The situation in this sector is somewhat comparable to the one in agriculture in general. His findings suggest that the center plays a negligible role in this regard. Only in relation to the Dragonhead enterprises serious funding was provided. Other more important sources for funding were usually savings, informal financing, and official loans (by local governments) in a supplementary role (Alpermann 2010, 145–146).

During the fieldwork in Jianzha County in Qinghai Province it became obvious that almost all households interviewed (n = 23, in three villages) had some kind of informal loan, usually with horrendous interest rates attached to them. Here the main drivers for the debts were costs for education and health care[6]—nobody mentioned investments in agriculture.

Modern Farming Skills and Cooperation

In addition to the factors listed above, villagers sometimes simply lack the necessary skills to transform their business. With the exception of a very small but well-educated and connected group of specialized farmers, many households do not have the proper knowledge and training to engage in more profitable sections of agricultural production. Several cadres argued that traditional farmers also lack a proper mindset, one that is oriented toward the future and modernization:

> [. . .] the more you guide them to cultivate a certain seed, the more they will refuse to do so. This has something to do with traditions being passed down of being used to grow [only] one seed (cf022).

Modern agriculture is based in part upon the scientific application of inputs in the production process. This is especially the case with fertilizers and herbicides. Although yearning for higher profits might be the main reason for their overuse, the lack of knowledge on proper application is certainly also a big factor (Yang 2011b). From the viewpoint of local governments, it is difficult to teach these households new approaches because the young, risk-taking, and receptive members of these families all too often already left the villages long ago. A generation of 50+ year olds that takes care of their grandchildren is not necessarily the group most likely to engage in high-tech capital-intensive agriculture. Improved education also seems to be a precondition for all plans to move forward with urbanization. The "2011 Blue Book on the Overall Integration of Rural and Urban Areas" promotes the education of the labor force as an important aspect of economic transformation (implying an integration of the rural economy into the overall economy) (Chang 2011a).[7]

Cadres frequently pointed out the need to educate villagers on how to cooperate more. Earlier studies have mentioned the importance of social capital for development (a good literature review can be found in Das [2005]; on the importance of social capital for cadre-villager interaction see Tsai [2002]). Cadres in our field sites echo these sentiments.

> In the village, for example while paving a small road, it is not enough to just pave the area around your own doorstep. Several families and households cooperate with each other and make it into one [unified] case. In reality, this is an educational process, teaching villagers how to collaborate in a unified way and how to become a "civilized countryside" (*xiangfeng wenming*) (cf028).

Not only peasants may lack knowledge or motivation. Local governments often fail to provide required services, as they are lacking either the resources, the manpower or the will to do so. Smith, for example, notes that "[. . .] *during months spent in township* [agricultural] *extension stations, I did not encounter a single ordinary farmer"* (Smith 2011, emphasis in the original).

TWO EFFECTS OF SMALLHOLDER FRUSTRATION

In the previous section the difficulties of sustaining smallholder farming in rural China such as the limited amount and poor quality of land, the ineffectiveness of subsidies, the rising costs for production inputs, the lack of capital, and the gaps in knowledge and motivation needed to create a modern agriculture have been discussed. These many difficulties and frustrations of traditional independent small-scale production seem to be a persistent feature of modern-day rural China. Already in a 1991 survey among 7,448 rural households in 274 villages throughout China the respondents mentioned the following five main problems facing farming households:

(1) shortage of funds to purchase inputs; (2) lack of know-how; (3) insufficient supply of improved seed varieties; (4) inability to purchase sufficient chemical fertilizers and pesticides; and (5) shortage of resources for farmland capital construction. (Selden 1998, 32)

Two major reactions to the frustration of smallholders in farming have become visible in the field sites: first, the continuation of peasant differentiation, including further labor migration of the young and skilled and second, an economic devaluation of land for traditional small-scale producers.

Leaving Smallholding Behind

During an investigative field trip to Qionglai, Sichuan, in 2008, to examine a local "social-insurance for land" policy experiment, I asked a roadside villager about the amount of land he owns. He waved me off and said that he neither cared about this nor really knew the amount of land he still has usage rights for. "Farming is a thing of the past," he added, showing me his little shop selling home appliances. "That's what I'm doing now." He may not be alone.

The close relationship between low incomes in smallholding and high migration rates in the countryside has already been outlined in this chapter. Urban life tends to be seen as the only valid future in the eyes of leading cadres, scholars, and also a rising numbers of villagers, the latter of whom have already voted with their feet. In fact, Henry Bernstein, refers to this diversification process as "footloose labour" (Bernstein 2006, 403). Statistical figures leave no doubt about the massive nature of this process. After the initial round of land reforms was completed in 1983, the share of the urban population was at 21.62 percent. In 2010, about 52 percent (680 million) out of 1.3 billion Chinese lived in cities (National Bureau of Statistics of China 2010). Between 1990 and 2000 alone, the urban population rose by roughly 10 percent, to 36.2 percent (Chan and Hu 2003). Li Changping, recalling his time as a township party secretary in Hubei, argued that in his township the difficulties for farmers became so severe in 1999 that by 2000, 25,000 out of 39,000 inhabitants had left. The labor force had been reduced from 18,000 to 3,000 (Li 2003, 200).

Obviously this modern-day mass migration has also had a tremendous impact on the rural social structure. To give one example, a leading cadre put the number of "left behind kids" for his township at 80 percent (cf013). The 23 million children of Chinese migrant workers who, according to a report by *The Telegraph*, grow up without both of their parents may even be a rather optimistic estimate (Moore 2011b; see also Branigan 2011). In fact, in our field sites local governments started to provide services for those family members who stay at home (or are "left behind," if you will), thus encouraging the main workforce to work elsewhere (cf011).

Moreover, many lifelong peasants do not want their children to live the same life they had (see, for example, the position Xin's father takes in Ngai and Lu 2010, 505–506). Every household head I interviewed in Qinghai did not want his or her children to continue working in the fields, and education was seen as the (only) way out. The saddest group of villagers was the one who could not afford to pay for the education of their children.

Devaluation of Land

In a country such as China with its scarcity of agricultural land, high rates of labor migration and the difficulties to transfer farming land caused by the property institutions lead to the very strange and problematic situation that a considerable amount of fine agricultural land is not properly worked (Ruan 2011; Zhang, Ma, and Xu 2004). While in many other countries smallholders who quit farming have sold their land, this is not really an option in the Chinese system (for the Vietnamese case as an example of this process, see Akram-Lodhi [2004]).[8]

It seems that the higher the amount of labor migration, the higher also the proportion of inefficient land usage. This is a view frequently put forward by local officials. As one township official said, "We have a lot of people who work outside, the land of these people lies idle. It is especially bad, when the whole family moves" (cf014). Other cadres confirmed the seriousness of the issue (cf006, cf018). On June 25, 2011, during the festivities of the 21st "National Day of the Land," Xu Shaoshi, the Minister for Land and Natural Resources, estimated that in China 10 to 15 percent of agricultural land lies idle (Ruan 2011).

It appears that land rights have become an obligation for many. What were the former smallholders supposed to do with them? Sometimes the land was used for sideline production by the remaining household members, sometimes it was given to family and friends. In all cases, however, land had lost its importance as the main means to create a living for the household. This trend affected the way these former smallholders thought about their land usage rights. The economic devaluation of the peasant lifestyle led to an economic devaluation of the land usage rights. Smallholders became more willing to temporarily or permanently give up their land usage rights in exchange for monetary compensation—which is a precondition for a commodification of farmland not based on primitive accumulation.

The devaluation of land in rural China is remarkably similar to developments in other post-socialist countries. In some of these locations, farmers have also begun to question the value of a continued life in agriculture.

> Life is better without land because you have fewer worries! Will it rain, will there be a flood, and so on. You're working so hard you haven't time to sit and chat, knit, relax. That's not for me. And besides, we calculate that with cereal prices so low, it's cheaper to buy wheat than to grow it. (Verdery 2003, 181)

However, according to Verdery this was a rare view in her field site and it might not be that common among those who continue to stay in the Chinese countryside either. We should not forget that, as outlined in the theory section, the value of land does not correlate only to its economic value. Even if the context of the collective land usage rights is taken into account, value assessment is still very personal. Especially older peasants are emotionally attached to the land of their ancestors. They are also (rightfully) afraid that they do not have the skills and resources necessary to thrive in the new capitalist economy. This feeling among the peasantry, however, might be subject to change in the future, as noted by a scholar we met in Guiyang:

> First, we should directly stress the function of land as insurance or maybe as a type of psychological dependence. In reality this insurance function has been fully weakened; the second and third generation of peasant labor migrants already have no affection for their land left. Now, at this time, the state needs to carry out a few things, on the basic level the system needs to change. If not, the land will become dormant and cannot be effective (cf017).

SUMMARY

In the first section it has been suggested that the occupational structure of rural population in the field sites is already highly diversified. The main argument of this section is that new income opportunities and a rising demand for monetary income have proven to be powerful triggers for smallholders to move away from small- and sub-scale farming. Two options for these smallholders emerge: specialization of agrarian production including an expansion of the scale or wage labor (and perhaps leaving the village for urban employment). Specialization of agriculture has enormously progressed in the field sites in recent years. While production of fruits, vegetables, cash crops, and meat has exploded, the production of grain, a major product of the traditional smallholder agriculture has stagnated and has become a less important source of monetary income over the last few years—indicating structural changes in agriculture. Labor migration, however, has proven to be an even more popular variant of peasant differentiation in all visited locations. In some villages, most if not all primary members of the workforce have left to look for wage labor elsewhere. The difference in income between smallholding and even unskilled wage labor is striking.

The second section has shown that this differentiation of the rural workforce is not only based upon free will but is also the result of a particularly bad environment for the continuation of smallholding—at least in the field sites but very likely also in most of China. The amount of farmland available for each household had been continuously shrinking since the beginning of the reforms in the early 1980s. Government supported investments to improve the quality of the land, for example via irrigation, tend to be directed toward the most productive agrarian producers while smallholders lack the capital for these improvements. The new wave of subsidies for agrarian producers mainly helps richer and more specialized agrarian producers. The subsidies certainly do not turn the tide in favor of the smallholders. Given that the prices of many inputs have increased much quicker than the subsidies, the effects of this new attention by the center to the needs of primary producers were limited. Capital, a major factor for all commercial enterprises, is still critically lacking in the countryside. Some households appear to have substantial informal loans, which are used to pay for critical needs. Access to formal alternatives and especially loans to buy inputs for commercial agriculture is strictly limited for most households. The lack of specialized expertise among the remaining smallholders has become another major issue for those with ambitions to modernize agriculture. All of these factors come together and turn smallholding into a very frustrating experience in China.

The frustration of smallholders can only be understood if one includes the context of the primary farming institutions in the analysis, as would be required following an HI approach. Although all villagers in China[9] have received collective land usage rights, these land usage rights are placed within an economic and political environment that makes it increasingly difficult to fully take advantage of them. Only during a brief period in the early 1980s did the state ensure low prices for inputs and high procurement prices, and as a consequence, there was a real income increase for those working in agriculture. This has been documented in chapter 3. Later on, procurement prices, especially for grain, did not increase by the same degree as the prices for inputs and non-agricultural goods and services (especially education and health care). Many villagers either lacked skills or capital or both to transform their farming into economies of scale. They had to turn to alternative sources of income and thus left their fields behind.

The third section of the chapter identifies two main reactions to the shortcomings of smallholding in the field sites. First, the differentiation of the peasantry and especially the labor migration of the young, skilled, and well educated will continue. This has already become obvious through the rapid increase in the proportion of the urban population in the last years. This mass migration also has a tremendous social impact because some parts of the family (children, grandparents) usually continue to "left behind" in the village. Second, this migration of a huge portion of the primary labor force and the present structure of handing over long-term stable land usage rights leads to the fact that huge amounts of the land are not adequately worked on (in terms of resource efficiency). The lack of an immediate need for this land has created a devaluation of land, which has turned land usage rights transfer into a feasible option for many villagers.

NOTES

1. During that fieldwork, I went to three different villages in Jianzha County in Qinghai Province and talked to a random set of 23 households. All of my interview partners were ethnic Tibetans. The interviews were conducted in Tibetan—my assistant translated questions and answers from Chinese to Tibetan and vice-versa. The main themes of the interviews were livelihood risks and risk management.

2. This matches my experience in Qinghai, where I encountered a man who had broken his leg two years earlier while working as a construction worker but could not afford the hospital care at the time. Because the leg was never correctly treated the bones fused at an incorrect angle, effectively crippling the man. He then began saving for an operation, which he expected would cost him more than 10,000 RMB.

3. For more detailed information, please see the section on the field sites in the appendix.

4. Well-bred seeds subsidy, direct subsidy for grain production, subsidy for purchase of agricultural machinery, subsidy for agricultural inputs, and subsidy to promote use of an agricultural insurance.

5. Personal communication on June 21, 2011, in Duisburg.

6. A surprisingly high number of villagers mentioned that they or their relatives had hepatitis (*ganyan*).

7. However, the biggest issue for rural–urban integration, the Bluebook argues, is to create a stable social insurance for unemployed farmers without land (*shiye shidi nongmin*).

8. Although there is one variant of land transfer, *zhuanrang*, in which land usage rights are permanently transferred for a one-time payment, this seems to be very unpopular in rural practice.

9. With the exception of government officials and public servants, such as teachers, and cadres from outside of the village.

Greenhouse farming on rented land in Laixi. *Photo provided by author.*

Commercial production of mushrooms on rented land in Anju. *Photo provided by author.*

姓　名	土　地　名	面　积	出租金额	签　字
█████	加担田	0.58	232	███
	下大烂	0.79	316	███
	下大烂 加担田	1.16	464	███
	下大烂	0.32	128	███
	啄啄田	0.58	232	███
	大方田	1.27	508	███
	啄啄田 千担田 下牛角 大塝秋	1.49	596	███
	啄啄田 一从角秋	1.57	628	███
	大塝秋 四亩八大田	2.42	968	███
	妖堰田	1.21	484	███
	加担田	0.86	344	███
	四亩八大田	0.76	304	███
	妖堰田	1.10	440	███
合　计		14.11	5644	███

注：1、此名册为租地合同附件与合同一道具有法律效力。

　　2、名册签字人可以是户主也可以是其家庭成员。

　　3、此表面积单位：亩，出租金额：人民币元。

The first page of a rental contract from Anju. Villagers signed the contract with their signature and thumbprint. *Photo provided by author.*

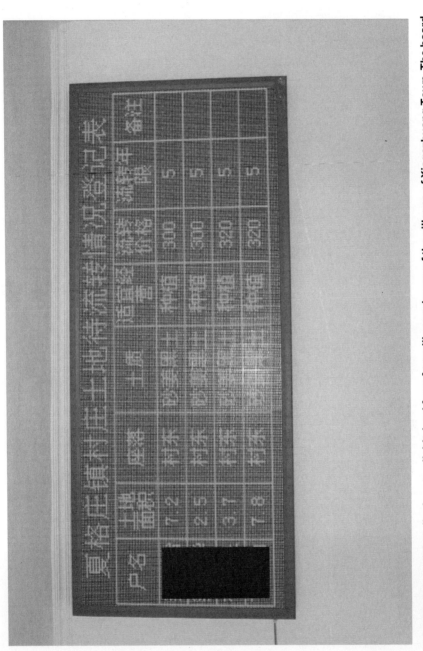

An electronic board that displays available land from four villagers in one of the villages of Xiagezhuang Town. The board advertises the size of the plot (between 2.5 and 7.8 mu), location, quality, rental fee (300–320 RMB), and the intended duration of the rental arrangement (here 5 years). *Photo provided by author.*

This painting from a township office in Anju shows the expected benefits of the "Building the New Socialist Countryside" program, here depicted as a pig, for the countryside. Among other aspects this policy is expected to help improve market information, financing, know-how, technology, culture, and education. *Photo provided by author.*

A picture of a photo op the local government prepared in order to celebrate the completion of new rural housing in Anju. Sadly, very few of the new houses were inhabited yet and these old ladies were the only ones around willing to be in the photo. *Photo provided by author.*

FIVE

Local State and Agrarian Transition

In this chapter the role of the local state and its agents in relation to agrarian transition is discussed. While the implementation of policies is addressed to some degree, the main focus is to gain a better understanding of the reasoning behind the activities of local cadres, who in many locations of rural China seem to be pushing for more and quicker agricultural change.

In recent years, the Chinese local state has come under enormous political, financial, and moral pressure. A system of political supervision has been established that constantly monitors the behavior and actions of government organizations and leading cadres. Although now every project may enhance one's chances to rise within the hierarchical nomenclature system or to be rewarded with new funds and bonus payments, small mistakes may also in theory immediately put an end to promising administrative careers. Financial conditions for many grassroots level governments are disastrous. Numerous reforms of the tax system have been emphasizing a move away from direct taxation of the rural population. These reforms have thoroughly affected the nature of local public finance and political dependencies. And while new transfer payments have become a welcome source of funding, they are usually tied to specific political and financial demands. Finally, the corrupt behavior of some cadres, a tight budget for local public services as well as reliance upon extra-budgetary income (mainly from land sales) has increased the tension between local officials and the rural population. It is argued here that promoting agrarian transition has turned into a favorite solution for local governments to address all of these issues at once.

The chapter is structured as follows: First, the above-mentioned political, financial, and moral pressures on the local state and its officials are discussed in more detail. The next section shows the opportunities that

101

arise for local governments to address these issues if they choose to adopt an agenda of agrarian change. In the final section, the chapter hypothesizes that agrarian change has in fact become a favorite policy for many local administrations and discusses briefly several instances of this strategic change in local practice.

LOCAL STATE UNDER PRESSURE

This section is divided into three parts addressing respectively financial, political, and moral pressure on the local state in rural China. Unsurprisingly, the financial conditions turned out to be a core element in all discussions with members of the grassroots level of the government. It therefore seems to be a good fit to start here.

Financial Pressure

The financial difficulties of lower levels of the Chinese rural administration have been widely discussed in scholarly literature (Wong 2009; Zhao 2007; Zhou 2010; Zhou 2012). The proliferation of new government initiatives such as the *New Socialist Countryside* (Ahlers 2014; Schubert and Ahlers 2012) and a substantial rise of transfer funding (documented by Lin and Wong 2012) have triggered a debate as to whether there have been meaningful changes to the fundamental structural problems discussed in these earlier works. Do township- and county-level administrations still shoulder most costs for public services, social protection, health care, and infrastructure investments at the grassroots level—given all the negative financial consequences for them, as described by Christine Wong (2009)? Linda Chelan Li and Wen Wang (2014) have pointed out that the Chinese state has begun to use massive amounts of earmarked funds to close, for example, the gap in education. Indeed, project-based and earmarked funding as two important trends in the countryside may have considerable effects on the structure of local funding in the long-run. Yet the lack of adequate budgets and revenue sources remained an important issue at our field sites and was especially tangible at the township level.

A leading township cadre in Sichuan, for example, noted that his township government was ordered by higher-level administrations to improve (among many other things) the transportation infrastructure—irrespective of the financial difficulties of this location to fund the construction of roads on their own. Another higher-level infrastructure initiative was to improve the land quality. Given the funding limitations the township government had to prioritize some policies (roads) over others (almost everything else) (cf011). Fieldwork in poorer locations such as in the field sites in Guizhou and Sichuan Province has shown that central policy initiatives, such as the above-mentioned New Socialist Countryside, are carried out only if additional funding is provided and in many poorer locations tends to be limited to show cases (cf019; Ahlers 2014; Ahlers and Schubert [2013]).

The provision of public services is another major drain on local funds and even the wealthier localities are struggling with these obligations. In Laixi, the richest of our field sites, a cadre complained:

> For the two administrational levels of county and township govern-
> ment the wages for teachers are a great financial burden. We have here
> some townships that had to use all of their financial income this year to
> just pay the teachers' wages (cf024).

In the same interview the cadre noted that of the 861 villages in the administrative region of Laixi only about one-third are self-reliant, meaning that these villages were able to cover their expenses with their own means (cf024). A township cadre from Anju mentioned that, compared to all other costs, the wages of the cadres and work expenses still account for the largest part of expenses. This is the case despite strict supervision of all expenditures and very low wages (cf027).

The many financial obligations compare very unfavorably with the available income of local administrations. One example from the field sites may clarify the great difficulties local governments find themselves in. In one of the townships visited, the monthly available operational funds stood at 59,000 RMB, of which 54,000 RMB went directly into minimum social insurance allowances (*wubaohu, dibao*) (cf011). The remaining operational costs hovered at 45,000 RMB per month, and therefore this township alone had an average operational loss of 40,000 RMB per month (cf011). In many locations, township governments do not even have their own banking account. All of their financial affairs are managed at the county-level (cf013). In one Anju township, cadres complained that they do not have any independent income at all and completely depend upon transfer payments from higher levels of the administration (cf021).

Smallholders, in the past at least to some degree responsible for funding local government, are now largely exempt from all tax obligations (cf024). Recent tax reforms have taken away this major funding source for local governments and in addition, especially mentioned by county-level administrators, have introduced considerable obligations to transfer taxes to higher levels of the administration (cf013). A cadre from Laixi pointed out that they had collected two billion RMB in taxes in 2008. In his understanding, this sum would be enough to solve, for example, all problems of funding in the field of education. However, most of these collected taxes, which represent a 30 percent increase from the previous year, had to be transferred to the center (cf024).

Leading local cadres argue that, as a consequence of the mismatch between numerous policy obligations and insufficient funding, they have

incurred enormous debts. A cadre from Anju District estimated the collective debt of all townships to be around 200 million RMB (cf029). The
growing debt of many township governments and their lending activities
have recently been discussed by Liu Yia-Ling (2012). Liu provides an
interesting quote from a township cadre that shows how normal deficit
spending has become for this level of the administration:

> We township cadres take turns as either guarantors or borrowers to
> receive loans from the credit cooperative. In this way we have accumu-
> lated more than 2.9 million yuan of debt so far. You know, C township
> is not the only one to bear debt in Ruian City, Wenzhou. As far as I
> know, every township here, regardless of whether it's rich or poor, is in
> debt (Liu 2012, 334).

Zhou Xueguang notes the great influence several national infrastructural
policies have had on the development of the "collective debt" in the
countryside (Zhou 2012).

At the field sites, another important recent trend in the finances of
rural administrations, in part related to the New Socialist Countryside,
was also clearly visible: the rise of project-based funding. Zhe Xiaoye and
Chen Yingying provide one of the best introductions to this development
(Zhe and Chen 2011). They describe project-based policy implementation
as a process in three stages. First, higher levels of the administration
prepare a set of projects local administrations can apply and compete for
(*fabao*). Second, county- and township-level governments combine these
different projects into integrated packages (*dabao*). These packages basically represent a coordination of several independent projects and funding sources to achieve a shared objective. Third, villages can compete for
these packages, whose contents might change again by the time the projects reach the village (*zhuabao*).

In the eyes of local administrators, a particularly frustrating aspect of
the current system of transfer payments in rural China is that of matching
funds. As a rule, most earmarked or transfer funds have to be matched
locally. In other words, higher levels will only match the amount the local
administration can invest by itself. These "forced" matching funds (*qiang-
xing peitao*) leave cadres little choice but to withdraw from less important
projects in order to get priority projects started (cf027).

The structural imbalance has also led many local governments to the
development of creative funding mechanisms. Almost all field sites reported how they have to combine different projects to achieve their targets. For example, poverty alleviation funds, infrastructural funds, and
minority funds are in the end all used for the construction of the same
road (cf013). To cover the costs for bigger infrastructure projects, for instance, townships have tried every possible means to acquire funding,
including asking villagers for contributions (cf016). One of the townships
in the field study developed another creative (or desperate) way to re-

ceive funding. It asked migrant workers, who had left for urban employment long ago, to fund a portion of its local projects (cf018). The tight
financial situation of many local governments also puts them in direct
competition to each other. In Laixi, for example, officials noted that they
compete with other county-level administrations over transfer payments
from Qingdao. Without participating and succeeding in this competition
they would have considerably fewer funds (cf022).

The enormous financial pressure has also contributed to the proliferation of questionable practices in policy implementation, spending, and
resource acquisition (Wong 2009, 949). Graeme Smith has argued that
local governments basically only start the implementation of new projects if it helps them to gain new funds for the local government or for
their personal benefit or if non-implementation is sanctioned with severe
punishments via the annual assessment system (Smith 2009, 30). Questionable practices of local funding are well documented for the whole
country. As noted in the previous chapter, in many locations sales of
former farmland turned into construction land account for between 30
and 70 percent of all government revenues (Lin 2007, 1832). The profitability of land sales and the limited dependence of the local state on the
opinion of the rural population certainly have contributed to the wide-
spread nature of these practices (Ping 2011).

Several recent studies argue that high demand for additional funding
sources by local governments are not rooted in a genuine demand to
improve service provisions and infrastructure investments but are more
or less the result of a corrupted incentive structure for local cadres, their
distance from the needs of the general public and a failing system of
supervision (Hillman 2010; Smith 2010; Zhou 2010). Although this might
certainly be true for a subset of the locations in China, it does not diminish the fact that there are considerable structural imbalances between
financial obligations and resources for local administrations.

Given these tight financial conditions for many local administrations
in China, the numerous development initiatives in the field of agrarian
commercialization and the continued modernization of the countryside
come as a surprise. All of the townships visited during fieldwork engaged in at least one if not more large development projects with regard
to commercial agriculture. How can one make sense of this mismatch
between a lack of funding for basic services and continued investment in
prestige projects? Why do local administrations invest scarce resources in
fancy and perhaps risky projects?

Political Pressure

A preliminary and simple answer to the above complex questions
may be that local administrations have little leeway in their decision to
participate in regional and national development programs. The local

state is integrated within a very complex system of near constant supervision and monitoring of all its activities. Several previous studies have already pointed to the importance of this system for the strategic planning of local cadres (Edin 2003; Gao 2010; O'Brien and Li 1999; Whiting 2001, 2004; Zhong 2003). The author of this book was part of a team that investigated this system and its implications on the local level, using data from the same field sites in China (see Heberer and Trappel 2013). In this article, we concluded that the evaluation system should be seen as fulfilling more functions than just keeping up pressure on leading local officials—albeit this continues to be one important function of the system. The discussion of the evaluation system here will only focus on this particular aspect and the connection between the monitoring system and career advancement.

The Chinese administrative monitoring and evaluation system seems to be inspired to some degree by the global trend of *New Public Management* (Kipnis 2008). These systems have been established to act as an institutional solution to one of the main issues in a principal-agent constellation: lacking trust of the principal in the conduct of the agent. However, as Power (2003, 189–190) has noted, many of these evaluation systems have taken on a life of their own. Instead of measuring the quantity and quality of the implementation, they lead to a shift in behavior of those evaluated to focus only on the relevant targets within this system (and not the real issues) (compare this to Scott 1998; Hood 2006).

Local governments are subject to three different evaluation procedures: an evaluation of the execution of political programs (*mubiao kaohe*), a performance audit of leading cadres (*lingdao ganbu kaohe*), and the so-called *One Item Veto-Rule* (*yipiao foujue*). Each year all levels of the administration at the local state will outline (in communication with their higher-ups) targets in several important policy fields. At the end of the year the performance in these respective targets is evaluated and graded into excellent (*youxiu*), qualified (*hege*), and not qualified (*bu hege*) (cf001). The county level evaluates the performance of all leading township cadres whereas the prefecture or the province evaluates cadres at the county level. Although most of this evaluation process is based upon an exchange of numerical data among various levels of the administration, additional on-spot investigations are conducted in order to discourage the transmission of incorrect data. The grading is important, as those units with better evaluation results will receive additional funds in the next year.

In a similar spirit the individual performance of leading cadres at the township and county level is evaluated. Performance is measured within several broad categories: compliance with the policies of superior echelons, capabilities, work attitude, performance, and integrity. Only cadres that are given a rating of "excellent" (*youxiu*) two or more times in a row can be promoted. Township cadres with the best evaluation results are more likely to return to a position at the county level, while the county leadership might even move further up.

Finally, all targets that have the status of a One Item Veto-Rule must be achieved, otherwise the local leadership and all organizations may in theory become subject to severe punishments and sanctions. In addition to national targets in this field, such as the one-child policy and provincial add-ons, for example targets related to energy consumption (Kostka and Hobbs 2012), many counties have a set of hard targets mirroring local priorities (see Heberer and Trappel 2013). In Guizhou, a county cadre listed the following six hard targets: one-child policy, *Clean and Honest Government* (*dangfeng lianzheng*), [combating] drugs and substance abuse, public order and responsive government, and secure work environment and social stability (cf001). Among these hard targets the one-child policy was mentioned most frequently during fieldwork and seems to carry the most severe consequences for local officials (see also cf011).

Cadres in our field sites repeatedly argued that priorities stated in the evaluation system would also be among their top priorities. In one township, public security was the top priority and social stability was ranked second. Improving the financial conditions ranked only third (cf027). The aforementioned Liu Yia-Ling notes in her case study that having a balanced household was worth only fifty points—out of more than one thousand points in the performance evaluation of the local government (Liu 2012, 333–34). Our interviews also have shown the large number of items measured in the evaluation system. In Laixi, more than one thousand different items were evaluated (cf025).

While one should not immediately draw direct conclusions from the targets included in this system in regard to the priorities of local cadres, they create considerable pressure and may indicate new trends. For example, some administrations have recently experimented with modifications of the evaluation system that aim to increase the role of the local population's satisfaction with government action. In Laixi, a rather progressive example, 10 percent of all evaluation points are already formally linked to the opinion of the local population (Xifa 2009). Several township cadres noted that they are in constant fear of locals petitioning at higher levels as this may have a direct impact on their work—even if the complaint does not relate to their own work but rather involves other government agencies (cf011). However, villagers petitioning to higher levels seems to carry a direct danger for local officials only if they complain to the center in Beijing or to the provincial level, as one leading cadre from a county level petitioning office explained (cf015).

At the same time the evaluations provide these cadres with a framework to get ahead in their careers. Heberer and Trappel (2013) argue that, when facing evaluations, cadres have three options: They can decide to stick to policy solutions they already know to work to some degree; they can opt for new and innovative solutions, which may carry more potential risks but also could be more rewarding; or, they can collude in an attempt to deceive the evaluators.

Moral Pressure

This book argues that, in addition to financial and political pressure, local administrations and their leadership face considerable moral pressure. There are perhaps three main sources of this pressure. First, there is a carefully designed narrative by the center that links most political corruption to the local state. Second, the many reports of clashes between local administrations and the rural population, especially in the field of land sales, increasingly undermine the legitimacy and authority of the local state in many locations. Third and somewhat neglected in the discussion so far, the leadership of local governments has a very different and positive perspective on its role in rural society. Many cadres argue that they have taken on a position within the government to improve local conditions. In the following section these three aspects of moral pressure will be discussed in more detail.

Especially within the Chinese academic literature we find many accounts that link the local level to corrupt behavior. Zhao Pan (2010) describes the great harm corruption inflicts at the grassroots level from the perspective of the state. Ultimately, he argues, corrupt behavior will erode all possible moral authority held by the local political leadership. Moral authority, however, would be crucial in efforts to transform traditional practices in agriculture (referring to traditional small-scale farming) and therefore necessary for all economic improvements. A very bleak picture of corruption and the conditions in the Chinese countryside comes from Le Mons Walker (2006), who links this level of the administration to a rise of "gangster capitalism." Li Lianjiang (2004) shows that the rural population has very little trust in the local state and its motivation (as opposed to generally high approval rates for the central state). Christian Göbel (2012) notes the existence of a careful narrative of the center that paints the peasants as victims of corrupt behavior by local administrators who do not implement beneficial policies for the rural population as they should.

The second aspect, the frequent clashes between local governments and the villagers, is another source of great moral pressure for local governments (in addition to the political pressure arising as a result of their inability to manage social stability, which usually is a hard target). Ray Yep (2013, 278–280) has compiled an impressive list of recent clashes over land deals in rural China. He argues that there might not even be an upward trend in land grabs and that these protests might instead be the sign of a new rights consciousness of the villagers (along the lines of O'Brien and Li 2006). Nevertheless, news about these clashes harms the reputation of all local cadres. Incidents like those in Wukan and Haiyang

Village detailed in chapter 3 may permanently disrupt the relationship between villagers and the local state.

The third aspect has to do with the self-perception of cadres. One township cadre responded to the question of his motivation to become a cadre: "To develop ones' native place; one [main motivation] is to see that the native place is good, that family and friends are happy and harmonious; that is giving [me] a good feeling" (cf025). Although certainly a cadre can argue in this way and still be corrupt, we should acknowledge that many of them see themselves in the role of a harbinger of modernity. They see the justification behind their work in improving rural living conditions; in their view it's them who bring civilization and higher incomes to the villagers. In public statements, many cadres feel the need to express their great struggle to bring their community ahead and to improve its living conditions.

THE OPPORTUNITIES OF AN AGRARIAN TRANSITION

What are the options for the local state and its leadership to react to these multifold pressures? This chapter argues that fading out smallholder peasantry and supporting the creation of a commercial agriculture may allow the local state to address all of the above-mentioned financial, political, and moral pressures at the same time.

Financial Opportunities

Given the tax exemption for smallholders in agriculture the promotion of commercial agriculture seems to be an obvious solution to raise the tax income of local governments. However, the tax benefit from promoting agricultural enterprises is not as clear-cut as one might expect.

Although commercial farming, which falls within the scope of enterprise taxation, seems to be booming in the locations visited, the actual tax revenues in many locations shrank in 2011. The situation in Laixi provides a good example for this development. All sectors of agriculture there reported a growth in GDP for 2011. Cash crops and livestock industries, for example, grew by 4.1 percent and 6.2 percent, respectively. Still, this does not seem to translate into higher taxation revenues. While the overall financial revenues of Laixi have increased by an astonishing 30.1 percent and reached 2.96 billion RMB in 2011, local taxation revenues have been decreasing by a similar impressive 23.2 percent (down to 1.00 billion RMB) (Qingdaoshi Laixishi Tongjiju 2012).

There are several possible explanations for this. The first and most obvious is a general tax cut approved in 2011. Furthermore, the calculation of taxes has changed and more items have been added to the non-taxation revenues (Jingji Cankao Bao 2012). This may imply that questionable income sources such as land sales have become even more important. Another possible explanation for this might be tax competition among various localities, e.g., the practice of temporarily granting tax exemption or a reduction of taxes for investors in return for their willingness to invest locally (Ahmad 2008). Irrespective of the actual reason for this mismatch, the data from Laixi shows several things. First, it illustrates the shrinking economic importance of even a successfully modernized agriculture. Despite a growth in output value in 2011, agriculture is no match for other sectors of the economy growing at a much higher rate (Qingdaoshi Laixishi Tongjiju 2012). And second, the anticipation of a higher tax income through a restructuring of the local economy and in particular through the shift toward operations of scale in the Chinese agriculture may perhaps be a valid long-term strategy, yet in the short-run taxation income of local governments does not increase substantially. Given the continued existence of the unfavorable tax-sharing pattern, it is even more questionable that local governments would benefit much financially from a structural change in agriculture.

However, there are two other important sources of income attached to agrarian transition: more transfer payments from higher levels of the administration and direct financial support of the newly found enterprises for the benefit of local governments and individual cadres.

The local state, and especially the township level, is given considerable funding to push forward policies to transform agriculture. Even if most of these funds are earmarked, they are a welcome means of improving the local GDP and the rate of investment (see cf009, cf022, and cf024). Still, assessing the financial support from higher echelons of the administration remains difficult. A substantial part of the funding in agriculture in recent years has been hidden within the program called *Building a New Socialist Countryside* (XNCJS), making it extremely difficult to identify the amount of investments in specific sub-divisions of this policy. It was also the case that the local Bureaus of Finance in all field sites were among the most difficult interview partners. One high-ranking official within the administration of Suining City explained the sources of funding for XNCJS in the following way: 10 percent comes from the center, the province contributes about 40 percent, the city/prefecture gives another 10 percent, and the county level contributes the final 40 percent (cf006). An article by Lin and Wong (2012) shows the rising level of central subsidies for rural development but remains also relatively vague about the contributions of the sub-national level.

To understand the true financial importance of the changing structures in agriculture for local governments we have to look beyond the immediate and institutionalized financial benefits. Having more successful local enterprises (to which the new enterprises in agriculture belong) brings many financial benefits in addition to or beyond taxes and transfer payments. In a world where local governments and villagers often lack funds to pay for infrastructure and other public services, it is entrepreneurs who step in with their donations.

In several locations these companies or individual entrepreneurs have invested considerable amounts in new infrastructural projects (cf021). Sometimes these contributions to the efforts of the local state are organized in quite rigid ways and entrepreneurs are systematically asked to donate rather large sums. These contributions seem to fall within the category of "obligatory donations" which are paid "so as not to lose *Guanxi* and to circumvent administrative capriciousness" (Heberer 2003, 223). In Laixi, these "contributions" provided a substantial part of the funding for a local development initiative called *Five Changes (wuhua)*. In a campaign-style approach, all local entrepreneurs were asked to select one village which they "volunteer" to support financially in its efforts to improve infrastructure and to raise living conditions. In 2008, the total investment in this program was 120 million RMB, of which enterprises put in 30 million and the peasants themselves added another 22 million (cf025).

In conclusion, the shift of the agriculture toward more commercial structures may provide local governments with new means to support their local economy and in the long run the tax income from these operations may be important. In the short-run, however, the financial contributions of successful local entrepreneurs might be a more interesting financial aspect.

Political Opportunities

Promoting agrarian transition fits nicely within the policy agenda of the center. For leading cadres at the township and county level, aligning themselves to the national policy is a precondition for all career advancement. During the interviews, two frameworks are frequently mentioned and seem to stand out in their relative importance.

First, there are the so-called No. 1 documents of the center, introduced in more detail in the third chapter, which explicitly target the countryside and agriculture. Although at times during the interviews literally every local state activity seemed to belong to the New Socialist Countryside introduced in these documents, this framework is usually seen as an attempt to establish more advanced and specialized economic structures, to improve infrastructure and, moreover, to ensure an increase in rural welfare (Ahlers 2014; Saich 2007; Schubert and Ahlers 2011, 2012; Tao and Xu 2007). In addition to the No. 1 documents, the spirit of the Third Plenary Session of the 17th CPC Central Committee is frequently mentioned in relevant local documents existing after 2009 (Xinhua 2008a). The essence of this Third Plenary Session is captured in the "Decisions of the Central Committee of the Chinese Communist Party on a Number of Important Questions Regarding Pushing Forward the Reform and Development of the Countryside." Key targets in this document are a modern agricultural production and rising monetary incomes for the rural population. The document also provides a glimpse at the future of rural reforms. By the year 2020, in addition to these targets, China wants to: create a basic system of rural–urban integration of economy and society; sustain grain security and the balance of supply and demand of important agricultural products; greatly increase levels of rural consumption; strengthen grassroots organization in the countryside and improve villagers self-administration; establish a fairer distribution of public services between rural and urban areas; improve rural cultural life and ensure that basic cultural rights and interests of peasants are taken care of; ensure that everyone in the countryside receives a good education; improve social protection and health care; create a resource-aware and environmentally friendly agrarian production and thereby create the conditions for sustainable development (see Xinhua 2008b).

Central policy frameworks provide the local state with tools, terms, and sometimes even funds to play with. The guiding principle in many of these initiatives is the concept of a highly efficient (*gaoxiao*) agriculture. During the interviews with members of the local state, this highly efficient agriculture is dominated by commercial enterprises, scientific/modern production, and a separation of land, labor, and capital. Every location we visited had a detailed plan on how to further develop commercial agriculture. All of these plans included binding targets to increase the capacity for specific cash crops, fruits, vegetables, livestock industries, food processing, and other aspects of agriculture. Showing that one is pursuing this model of rapid development of a commercial and highly efficient agriculture could be very rewarding for one's career.

In Anju, the following quantitative targets had a high priority in the annual evaluations: GDP growth, investments and attraction of investors, average peasant income, government revenue, and fixed investments/assets (cf027). In particular, investments in modern agriculture and livestock industries are among the top priorities of the annual evaluation process, as one township cadre explained (ibid.). For many cadres in our field sites, finding investors, achieving GDP growth and raising peasant income translates into pushing for more commercial farming. Particularly interesting has been the inclusion of land transfer cooperatives in the evaluation system in Anju (cf009). Xifeng also had a very elaborate system of monitoring all variants of land transfer (and not only land transfer cooperatives) (Xifengxian Tudi Liuzhuan Zhongxin 2009b).

In Laixi every step in building agricultural economies of scale is rewarded in the evaluation. In the evaluation scheme for township and street office cadres, these cadres can gain more points for modernizing agriculture (55) than for the implementation of the *Five Changes* program mentioned earlier, which was among the most important local policy initiatives (Laixishi Renmin Zhengfu 2009a). Specific measures mentioned by the evaluation system in Laixi included Biogas facilities, greenhouse construction, installing cooperatives, planting orchards, and many more similar items (cf022).

Moral Opportunities

In addition to the obvious political and the less obvious financial opportunities in an agrarian transition this structural change entails numerous moral opportunities for the local state. At the core of all these opportunities is the shared wish of the center and the rural population to raise the incomes in the countryside. Rightfully or not, the local state sees itself as the only actor who is able to bring about this change. According to the cadres interviewed, in order to achieve this goal all local actors in agriculture need to accept the fact that the organizational basis of agriculture must be transformed. Furthermore, they need to accept the guidance of the local state in this endeavor.

Tania Li has found a similar mindset among grassroots officials in Indonesia and coined the phrase "will to improve" for it. Her research is concerned with the rationale of development schemes to improve the livelihood of the rural population favored by administrators. In particular, she is interested in the "inevitable gap between what is attempt and what is accomplished" (Li 2007, 1). Although she develops her model within a different context, it is a useful analytical tool for assessing how local cadres deal with some of their moral pressure. Li argues that those with the wish to improve local conditions take on the mindset of *trustees*, which according to her can be identified ". . . by the claim to know how others should live, to know what is best for them, to know what they need" (Li 2007, 4). Due to routine activities and membership in the same organizations trustees have developed a certain set of practices in their work. Two of these practices, Li argues, are of particular importance: "problematization" and "rendering technical." Whereas the first practice identifies certain shortcomings in people and their lives, the second practice develops technical steps to deal with these problems and "confirms expertise and constitutes the boundary between those who are positioned as trustees, with the capacity to diagnose deficiencies in others, and those who are subject to expert direction" (Li 2007, 7). In China, the local state frequently turns into a *trustee* (in the sense outlined above) for all actors in agriculture.

Many leading cadres stated in the interviews that peasant production based upon household labor and tiny plots of land is ill-suited to incorporate modern production processes and does not provide the means to increase rural incomes. The persistence of smallholder farming is often connected to "traditional" lifestyles of the rural population. Consequently, cadres dealing with the modernization of agriculture inevitably find themselves on a mission to likewise modernize the lifestyles of the rural population. Teleological arguments regarding the need to modernize agricultural production and the rural population dominate the official Chinese discourse not only on the national but also on the local levels.

Virtually all officials interviewed began with a summary of their activities to create a modern countryside and their efforts to overcome the remnants of traditional agriculture (*chuantong nongye*). A township mayor in Anju, while proudly presenting a newly built pig husbandry, explained: "In the past our mode of production was a few dispersed households raising livestock, no economies of scale and not much of a profit." He continued:

> Now, after founding this company, our peripheral masses (*zhoubian de qunzhong*) get to know technology. From this they can learn that livestock industries are not about, again and again, raising just one pig and that's it. They can learn how to raise pigs and how to make a profit from their production [. . .] (cf012).

This is the essence of the new agriculture: not feeding people but making profits and raising monetary incomes. This thinking explains in part the omnipresent usage of the term "high efficiency" (*gaoxiao*). Efficiency here implies the effective use of resources, including labor, in order to produce a maximum of output (cf006, cf012, cf018).

New business practices unknown or unpopular among peasants are frequently presented to them as a necessary part of this shift. Examples in this regard include the transfer of the land usage rights of households to other entities, which are then able to create economies of scale and in turn may then offer wage employment with a secure and stable income for those former smallholders interested in it. According to many local cadres these changes require substantial ideological work (*sixiang gongzuo*) to convince the villagers and to ensure a smooth implementation (cf016). A city level cadre from Laixi explains:

> Personally, I think that the current modus operandi somehow restricts the development of modern agriculture. The thinking of peasants is just not conform [to a modern, specialized production]. For example, in grain cultivation, if there would be only one product in the village, the modus of production would be the same for everyone; farming would be easier, too. The various seeds/plants would not be mixed, there would be a unified planting of seeds. In this way the production would be efficient and labor could be saved, and certain quality standards in production could be guaranteed. In reality the current situation is not like that; between the two of us you would use this seed and I, very likely, would not agree [. . .] the more you guide them to cultivate a certain kind of seed, the more they will refuse to do so. This has something to do with the passing down of the tradition of growing just one seed (cf022).

Traditional farming and traditions have become terms used to devalue the work and lifestyle of peasants. Local officials have a vision of how proper life in the countryside should look. In our interviews, only one situation emerged in which local cadres found welcoming words for smallholder farming with relation to the economic future of villages and this was in the context of rural home-stay tourism (*nongjiale*) (cf012, cf018).

Leading local cadres can easily connect these discourses of a necessary change in rural lifestyles to concepts promoted by the national level. Especially the debates surrounding the term "population quality" (*suzhi*) have proven useful for local cadres (Kipnis 2006). All local governments, without exception, have campaigns and conduct trainings to raise the *suzhi* of the rural population. A village official gives us a glimpse at the content and conduct of these *suzhi* trainings:

> [. . .] generally speaking, all training of villagers takes place in the big meeting hall. In terms of content it is party policies, government policies, the official line [of argument] and knowledge regarding *Building a New Socialist Countryside*, agricultural technologies and the one-child policy (cf016).

Tania Li uses the term "closure" to denote processes that try to eliminate "political-economy questions—questions about the means of production and the structure of law and force that support systemic inequalities" (Li 2007, 11). In China, the *suzhi* discourse might qualify for this. It blends out the weak legal and political position of the rural population by setting the agenda on which of "their shortcomings" should be addressed.

The obligation to raise rural incomes also comes in handy for doing away with ideological paradigms of past epochs, for example the long-standing ideal of *food security* in China. In the new agriculture, as the Head of the Bureau of Agricultural Affairs in Laixi explained, raising the income of the rural population is the only thing that counts. Instead of *food security* now *food safety*, or, in other words the quality of the produced food, has become the central priority. Raising the quality, in his opinion, demanded a standardization of the food production according to scientific regulations (cf022). As another official pointed out: "Those who only till the land will not become rich" (*guangkao zhongdi bu keneng zhifu*) (cf024), and "One could say that in growing grain nobody becomes rich" (*keyi shuo zhong liangshi shi fu buqilai de*) (cf019). Subsequently, among many of the new local leadership generation agriculture has almost completely lost its former food security rationale, which occupied rural cadres' thinking on agriculture for decades and still has an important role in official documents. Nowadays agriculture is often seen simply as a normal industry, lacking any revolutionary importance. Links to the pre-reform past are used in a superficial way and rarely carry any practical meaning (cf022).

PUSHING STRUCTURAL CHANGE IN AGRICULTURE

This chapter argues that opportunities for local administrators associated with an agrarian transition have in all field sites examined proven to be a powerful incentive in pushing forward structural change in agriculture. In other words, the local state has become one of the major supporting forces for agrarian change in China. Success in this field is seen as most important for reaching the goal of *Building a New Socialist Countryside*, as one leading cadre from Laixi argued. He added:

> Our biggest success is raising the level of agricultural industrialization (*nongye chanyehua de shuiping*), raising the income of the villages, developing Dragonhead enterprises. Our biggest problem is that the funds for *Building a Socialist Countryside* are not enough. Because of these investment needs, the financial power on every level of the administration is not sufficient (cf033).

Some strategies have proven to be particularly popular among these local administrators. In the following section, three of these strategies will be briefly presented. These are the continued emphasis upon Dragonhead enterprises, the substantial promotion of all activities in the field of land transfer and strong informal financial and administrative support for new enterprises.

Dragonhead enterprises have been frequently mentioned in the interviews as being among the most important tools of the (local) state to promote commercial agriculture (cf024). As discussed in the literature review, these enterprises have been instrumental in the creation of an integrated agriculture in China. For instance, in the pork industry in Suining Dragonhead enterprises established long-term supply contracts with farmers, provided food processing services and took care of selling the final product (cf019). A similar practice is visible in Laixi. Here Dragonheads help to organize the production of beef, milk, pork, poultry, vegetables, fruits, and peanuts (cf025). Our interview partners suggested that Dragonheads and the type of development they represent are all part of a bigger urbanization scheme called "creation of [urban-like neighborhood] communities in rural areas" (*nongcun shequ jianshe*) (cf031). In the field sites, they have been a favorite means of the lower level of the administration to push for change in the structure of agrarian production.

Local cadres have adopted the idea that, in order to push for structural change in agriculture, not only integrating peasants in production chains is necessary but also that replacing the small-scale nature of the present production is a precondition. In order to achieve this target, agricultural land needs to be concentrated into bigger holdings. This insight and the lack of alternative actors in this field due to the current legal framework have turned the local state in many locations into a major player in arranging and preparing land transfer solutions. In effect, in many locations, the local state has become an intermediary actor between the villagers and new parties having an interest in agricultural land for farming.

In addition to these methods of direct support for commercial farming, local governments provide substantial informal support. For instance, they provide information about loans and subsidies to key commercial activities in their localities. Even if they themselves have no funds to invest, they might use their social and political capital to assist. A township party secretary in Anju recounted in great detail all the wining and dining with officials and experts that went into the creation of a specialized agrarian production in his township.

Although agrarian change might have become a favorite policy for local administrators, not all stakeholders are similarly enthusiastic. In response to the endangerment of their lifestyle and values, peasants resort to all kinds of protest. While protests triggered by new rounds of land expropriation frequently make the news, there also exists a current of substantial but subtler rejection of agrarian change in the countryside. This may include playing with language; for example, the term *suzhi* is used by the villagers themselves to avoid being drawn into the agenda of officials: "Our *suzhi* is too low, we therefore cannot do. . . ." Protest may take the form of not using the benefits of development projects in the ways devised. For example, many new houses we visited remained empty shells with only one room used, not to mention the numerous newly built houses nobody wanted to move into.

SUMMARY

This chapter argues that promoting agrarian transition policies may perhaps be an answer to financial, political and moral pressures many local administrations currently face. The first section of the chapter introduced these pressures in more detail. Local administrations seem to be structurally lacking funds to start independent initiatives and continue to run the administration. In addition, local administrators find themselves in a strict hierarchical system for career advancement. In order to get ahead, they need to perform well within a very detailed and complex monitoring and evaluation system. Finally, local administrations and their leadership have come under great moral pressure in recent years. Reports on corrupt behavior and the frequent clashes in the countryside have given this level of the administration a bad reputation. This reputation, however, differs from how these administrators see themselves and how they want to be recognized by the public.

The next section of the chapter showed how pushing for agrarian transition may help local administrations address all of these various pressures in a single strike. Financially they profit from informal and "voluntary" contributions from the new entrepreneurs to local development projects. From a political and career perspective, leading cadres increase their chances for promotion if they closely follow the national agenda of modernizing the agriculture and the rural economic structure. Pushing for an agrarian transition also helps local administrators define themselves as positive agents of change. Only because of their involvement could the incomes in the countryside be raised. At the same time the national emphasis on raising rural incomes allows these cadres to coerce rural actors into accepting change. Especially the *suzhi* discourse, which seems to be handy for these administrators.

Finally, it is argued that the many benefits entailed in pushing for a change from smallholder to commercial farming have led to strong adoption by local administrations. Three aspects of this adoption which seemed most significant during the fieldwork are mentioned: the further creation and support for Dragonhead enterprises, a new pro-active role in land transfer markets, and strong informal support for new agricultural enterprises in the countryside.

SIX

The Commodification of Farmland

The previous chapters covered the frustration of smallholding house-holds, the interest of the central government in Beijing and of local governments in developing a modern agriculture and the legal institutions that provide a basic framework for the transfer of land usage rights. In this chapter, these developments meet and form the contours of an emerging market for farmland. The chapter will cover the empirical reality of a commodification of farmland as encountered in the field sites in Shandong, Sichuan, and Guizhou.

In a strictly legal sense the commodification discussed here is based upon variations of a rental system for collective land usage rights, a framework whose genesis was documented in the third chapter. The term tenants will be used to refer to those individuals or organizations which rent the agricultural land from the households for some kind of compensation. Lessors are those households that rent out their collective land usage rights. Intermediary actors are those actors who arrange or facilitate the transfer. The usage of the term "large-scale transfer" in this chapter is based upon the Chinese term *guimo liuzhuan* and refers to all variants of land transfer beyond the immediate family and friends, the details of which ideally have been fixed in a contract. The term market is used in a very narrow and descriptive sense to capture institutionalized and repetitive exchanges of land usage rights on the basis of consultative price finding.

Three main arguments in relation to the empirical findings are developed in this chapter. The first argument concerns the existence of strong asymmetric power relationships in the emerging market for farmland. Peasant households are very likely to not only receive a rental fee that does not reflect the economic usage value of the land but also to accept one-sided contracts with unfavorable terms. Nevertheless, given the present institutional configuration, in the end the former holders of land usage rights still may benefit from these arrangements. The emergence of a group of very powerful tenants in this new market is the second argument. In the current rural reality of the field sites, these "supertenants" face many opportunities and few risks for their investments in commercial agriculture. This chapter's third argument is the critical role of local governments in the creation of this market for agricultural land. The local state has taken the lead in connecting supply and demand and thereby becomes an amplifying force in the commodification process.

The chapter is divided in four sections. It will begin with a section presenting empirical data on cases of land usage rights transfer as encountered during fieldwork in Anju District. Land transfer contracts collected in the field sites and interviews with officials, entrepreneurs, and villagers form the basis of this section. The second section will address the role of local governments for this emerging market. The first part of this section will explore the implementation of land transfer cooperatives as an example in which an intermediary organization for the transfer of farmland is created and the example of land transfer service centers, in which no such organization is established. The second part of this section focuses on an example of already planned initiatives in regard to land transfer in Qingdao that suggest even more involvement by the local state in this market in the near future. The third section will then present the available data on the general prevalence of the transfer of land usage rights in the other field sites for comparison. The final section will summarize the empirical findings in a theoretical model based on Heller's (1998) "Tragedy of the Anticommons" and Verdery's (2003) "Supertenants."

CONTRACT-BASED LAND TRANSFER IN RURAL PRACTICE

In this section the empirical cases of contract-based transfer of collective land usage rights encountered in Anju District will be discussed. Contract-based transfer of land usage rights differs considerably from small exchanges of land between family and friends. In fact, these latter exchanges should not be considered as being part of an emerging land market, as they are usually based on non-monetary reciprocity and have a short time frame. Contract-based transfers, in contrast, are larger in scale, have a longer time frame and are legally required to include some kind of (monetary) compensation.

The main basis for the presentation of contract-based land transfer here is the data collected in Anju District. Although fieldwork was also conducted elsewhere, the data from Anju is the most complete. The combined data from there allows drawing a clear and holistic image of several different instances of land transfer spread over four different townships. At a later point the data from Guizhou and Shandong will be used for comparison.

The focus of this presentation of contract-based land transfer is upon the interaction between the different actors and their respective bargaining power in regard to influencing the conditions of the transfers. In order to operationalize the power of market participants, three variables have been selected. These are the rental fees to be paid, the time frame of the contracts, and the sanctions for a breach of contract.

A few remarks regarding the comprehensiveness and structure of the collected material are necessary. Until recently the only popular and legally approved instrument for the transfer of large amounts of land usage rights in rural China have been individual contracts between one or several lessors and a tenant. The design of these contracts sometimes follows templates created at the township level, but occasionally non-standard contracts also appear in use. In Sichuan, copies of these contracts usually have been kept at township level governments, which made access to them easier for me. Copies of contracts based on newer initiatives for land transfer are not archived at the township level. In the case of the land transfer cooperatives, for example, the contracts are given to villagers and sent to higher-level authorities. Access to the contracts at these institutions through the cooperatives and the households locally and the relevant organs at district and prefecture level turned out to be much more difficult, so I was only occasionally able to get hold of such contracts. The following presentation of land transfers therefore largely excludes variants of land transfer based on newer policy initiatives— these will feature prominently in the next section.

Anju District has 21 towns and townships of which in this section the following four will be discussed in more detail: Anju Town (*Anju Zhen*), Yufeng Town (*Yufeng Zhen*), Majia Township (*Majia Xiang*), and Changli Township (*Changli Xiang*). The general characteristics of these locations are introduced in the appendix. The case selection is based on considerations of access to and comprehensiveness of the data. However, the underlying mechanisms and dynamics shown here may arguably withstand regional differences, even across provinces. A later section of the chapter with aggregated data on land transfer in other field sites as well as the cases presented in the introduction point in this direction.

Wherever possible the contracts were balanced with interviews and vice versa. In general, the descriptions and rental fees mentioned by the cadres during the interviews tend to be more in favor of the peasant households than the situation outlined in the contracts themselves.

Anju Town

Anju Town is a small town located within Anju District. According to its leading cadres about 10,398 mu of land were transferred in large-scale contract-based land transfer operations in 2009 (cf007). Tanghe Village in Anju Town is the site of several interesting cases of land transfers.

This village started early with agricultural commercialization. Village and township cadres proudly mentioned that already in the year 1989 the village had entered into the pomelos business. Being close to the National Road 318 has made it easy for them to sell these pomelos. In 2006, the first external investor rented roughly 45 mu of land, paying annual rental fees of about 600 RMB per mu to the villagers. In order for this transfer to happen, the village cadres had to do a lot of work convincing the villagers (*sixiang gongzuo*) of the benefits of this project (cf016).

The village cadres mentioned another land rental they were even more proud of. One former migrant worker had rented 20 mu of land to plant pineapple trees. He was paying 800 RMB per mu to the villagers and was giving them another 100 RMB after the harvest. Because of his success the village cadres made him a party member and also had him join the village committee (cf016). During the interviews in the following year in Tanghe, we discussed one case in which a commercial farmer was giving 800 jin of *Huanggu*[1] for each mu to the owners of the land usage rights. When asked about the amount a normal farmer could harvest if he would work the land by himself the answer was about 1,100 jin. From this amount, however, the costs for fertilizer, pesticides, and work still would have to be deducted (cf007). Employment in these newly formed agricultural enterprises usually seemed to be an option for the lessors, but the cadres mentioned certain requirements of age and skills that the peasants would have to meet (cf007).

In Tanghe Village I was also able to obtain a joint contract of several households of a natural village with another commercial agricultural enterprise.[2] Via this contract 36 households directly transferred their land usage rights to *Chunyang Agricultural Development Limited* for several use cases (cmm024).[3] The direct nature of the bargaining process was also mentioned during the interviews (cf007). This transfer in Tanghe happened already in 2003, years before tools like land transfer centers and land transfer cooperatives were devised and implemented in the countryside. This contract between a natural village and a company is interesting for a number of reasons. Not only does it include a short summary about the purpose of the transaction, but also very detailed articles on the rights and obligations of the two parties involved. The main motive for the transaction mentioned here is further development of the commercialization and marketization of agriculture as well as structural and economic adjustments. Ultimately this should translate into higher incomes and increased productivity. The contract emphasized the voluntary nature of the agreement—it stated that the villagers joined of their own free will. In later sections of the contract, the voluntary nature of the transaction is again frequently mentioned.

Chunyang Agricultural Development Limited is free to use the land for planting, raising animals, added labor services (in agriculture) and tourism. For these purposes, the company is also allowed to construct buildings on the farmland. The construction of buildings for tourism clearly is in opposition to national regulations for construction land. Given the comprehensive nature of the intended business of the company, the long time frame of 25 years of the transfer comes with little surprise. Every year the households renting out the land will receive the monetary equivalent of 888 jin *Huanggu* for each mu, calculated using the average market value for rice of that year between May and September. Altogether 35.64 mu of farmland has been rented to the company through this contract. The role of the households renting out the land is reduced to that of supervision. They have the right to check whether the company is using the land for illegal purposes, but no right to interfere with the production of the company in any way. Taxes and fees for the land still have to be paid by the peasants. The company, however, will receive any government subsidies for improving the quality of the land. The natural village has to provide water irrigation and electricity for the company, who in turn has to pay for these services.

There are also detailed regulations for an extension of the contract when the initial 25 years end. If the company has an interest in prolonging the contract, it must consult the villagers again. Under similar conditions (given that other competitors exist) *Chunyang Agricultural Development Limited* is to receive priority treatment in the selection of the future tenant. If the contract is not extended, the company is entitled to receive some compensation for its infrastructural investments. If the company has created constructions that interfere with the immediate agricultural usage of the land, it must consult with the villagers and either compensate the villagers or remove the buildings and restore the original condition of the land. The contract also includes a detailed list of penalties for breach of contract. In case the villagers fail to fulfill their part of the contract, they must compensate the company with double the amount of its incurred loss. If the company fails to pay the rental fee within the outlined time frame or fails in its other requirements, it must pay a penalty of 50 percent of the annual rental fee to the affected household. The household, in addition, then has the right to withdraw from the contract. Both parties must give way if the government intends to request the land (*zhengyong*).

Yufeng Town

One important variation of the land transfer in Yufeng Town has been land shareholding. As with all other forms of institutionalized land transfer there is considerable variation in terms of what this actually means in reality. A rental contract from Jitou Village in Yufeng Township of Anju

District provides insight into one instance of this type there (cmm026). In this case, the individual lessor of the land usage rights effectively becomes the employee of *Chenxin Modern Agriculture Development Limited,* a company from Suining City. During the interviews, it turned out that the company was founded by the local government and that, in addition to farming, it also subcontracted land of the villagers to external investors (cf014).[4] Like many other rental contracts this one starts with a purpose statement. The land rental is carried out in order to address the three main issues in agriculture: the scattered nature of traditional farming, the missing standardization necessary for a modern agriculture, and a lack of economies of scale. Moreover, it should contribute to Anju's model for agricultural modernization.

The contract covers not only land rental but constructs a complex framework for the economic relationship between the two parties. The household receives fruit and nut tree seedlings from the company, takes care of them according to regulations included in the contract and instructions of technical advisors of the company, and sells the resulting fruits back to company. The resulting profits are split, 80 percent for the farmer and 20 percent for the company. The contract commenced in October of 2007 and has a time frame of 22 years, ending in October of 2029.

The farmer operates under the directions of the company for the whole time frame of the contract and must cover all expenses for labor and agricultural inputs. The penalties for the households for breach of contract are harsh. For example, in case the household decides to sell to a third party and Chenxin finds out about this, all sales revenue has to be given to the company as compensation. There are also penalties in case the farming household does not follow the directions of the technical advisors of the company or steals the seedlings (Chenxin guarantees a survival rate of 80 percent of the seedlings and will return the following year to verify this). For any other breach of contract, all economic loss that the other side incurs must be compensated and a further compensation of 20 percent of the annual output value must be paid.

The options for terminating the contract seem similarly biased in favor of the company. Whereas the contract can easily be terminated if both parties agree to this or if the land has been "requested" by the government, the company has some additional options to terminate the contract. If, after three years, the profits from the tree business are not above what would be earned by growing grain, the company can ask the local government for a subsidy or can bargain for the end of the contract. If the continued operation has become unprofitable for the company or the company is bankrupt the contract may also end. The household does not enjoy similar rights. In addition to renting out their land to Chenxin and taking care of trees, the villagers could also start working for this company, the cadres claimed. By doing this work they could earn an additional 1,500–1,600 RMB (cf014). In the same interview, the cadres mentioned that the contracts with Chenxin usually were tied to the time frame of the land usage rights of the households (cf014). Variations of this contractual union between households and companies, which in effect turn the former into employees of the latter, are becoming increasingly popular in contemporary rural China (Zhang 2012; Zhang and Donaldson 2010). Yet, it is difficult to say whether and how the case in Jitou Village really represents land shareholding, especially since shares for land do not feature in the contract and were not mentioned in the interviews either.

Yufeng Town has also been the site of direct rental contracts between several individual households and companies. The contract between a household from village No. 6 and *Meining Enterprise Group Food Products Limited* from Anju provides insights into such arrangements (cmm027). Again, the contract begins with a purpose statement. Accordingly, this land rental arrangement should speed up the structural adjustment of agriculture, help to develop second and third sector industries, and contribute to the effort of turning Anju District into the "backyard garden" of Suining City.

More related to the actual agreement, the contract states that the land shall be used for the production of "yellow peaches" *(huangtao)*. The time frame of the contract is 15 years, until September 30, 2021. During that period, the household will receive an annual rental fee which is the equivalent of 320 kg conventional *Huanggu* for each mu of paddy fields, 253.6 kg for each mu of non-irrigated land, and 200 kg for each mu of hillside land. The monetary amount will be calculated using the national procurement price for this rice variation at the Suining market for the given year. The rental fee must be paid before the end of September for each year as a one-time payment. If the company needs labor services it should prioritize any application of the household renting out the land.

The contract also clearly lists the rights and obligations of both parties. Almost the only right of the lessor listed is to receive the rental fee on time. On the other hand, the household is not allowed to disrupt the companys' production process in any way. If harm to production or infrastructure has been inflicted, the household must compensate the company. The contract specifically states that the household must protect the assets of the company. When the contract runs out and the company wants to renew it, it is supposed to receive prioritization over other tenders. The only obligation for the company listed is that it should push for more government investment in the project in order to build up a local production base. The regulations for an early termination of the contract are similar to those presented in other contracts. The contract ends if both parties agree to terminate it, if the government requests the land, or if the company is unable to continue production. Again, there are no provisions for welfare hardships of the household renting out the land, e.g., the household does not have the right to terminate the rental contract for subsistence reasons.

During an interview that took place at a company specializing in pig husbandry in Yufeng in 2009, cadres proudly mentioned that the average income there in the last two years had risen by at least 1,500 RMB per capita, now being at 5,300–5,400 RMB. Twenty percent of the households would earn even more than 10,000 RMB per year. This huge boost in income was said to be completely related to several large animal husbandry and food processing enterprises which settled in Yufeng (cf012).

Majia Township

Majia is the site of a huge land rental agreement stretching over four natural villages and including 40 households and 51.6 mu (cmm030). Not only because of the number of villagers included in this contract is this an interesting case. It was the only contract encountered in the field sites that did not include a purpose statement of any kind. The contract states that the villagers discussed and agreed to rent out the land to *Xuantian Herding Agricultural Development Limited*, a company from Suining. The land is supposed to be used for creating a pig husbandry. The contract has a time frame of twenty years and is relatively favorable for the enterprise. Among other things it forbids the village to install another similar-sized breeding facility or other potentially harmful enterprises within a 3 km radius. The rental fee of 400 RMB per mu per year must be paid only once every five years. The fee is increased every five years by 8 percent as an adjustment for inflation. Furthermore, the village must construct a road to the main entrance of the breeding facility. In order to create one big land holding, villagers are not allowed to grow in the fields nearby or to disrupt the company in any other way. The village must compensate the company for any harm caused by villagers. If the village breaches the contract it must compensate the company for all investments taken plus an additional 200,000 RMB, or about ten years of all rental fees combined. In turn, if the land is not restored to its previous state when the contract ends, the company must pay the villagers a compensation of 200,000 RMB. If the company does not pay the rental fee on time this is considered breach of contract. In such a case, the villagers have the right to terminate the contract and seek an investigation into the responsibilities of the company. No financial compensation for such a case is mentioned. The contract is also interesting for some aspects it does not mention. For example, there is no provision to hire the villagers as workers for the new pig husbandry, as there had been in other contracts of a similar kind.

During the interviews in Majia, the leading township cadres mentioned that they had just started with the work on large-scale land transfer. One cadre linked this unsatisfying state, as seen from their perspective, to lacking financial support from higher levels:

Because of a situation in which the government does not hand out any subsidies for land transfer, transfer entirely relies on the local party committee, the local government and the villagers for completion. This is a thing I cannot understand at all (cf011).

Although the township government had established some land transfer cooperatives in the villages, the total amount of land transferred would still be very low. They estimated that the average annual rental fee in the villages of Majia in 2008 was between 300 and 400 RMB (cf013). In the following year, the same cadres mentioned that now 1,100 mu had been transferred within this township. The average price per mu would be 400 RMB for good quality land and 200 RMB for bad quality land. Most of the land was rented out to commercial farming households (*nongye dahu*). In addition, a limited amount of land shareholding also existed (cf011).

During the field trip to Majia in 2009, I was able to obtain a table ("Anju District Majia Township Land Transfer Situation Table") documenting almost all large-scale land transfer activities in this township (Majiaxiang Renmin Zhengfu 2009). It lists eight different large-scale transfer activities of which seven involve large individual tenants and one is a placeholder for land transfers to specialized households (*qitazhong yangzhi dahu*). The amount of transferred land lies between 50 mu for a university student research park and 50 mu for an environmental-friendly pig husbandry to 200 mu for specialized mushroom production. The households renting out the land received between 250 and 450 RMB per mu per year. The table showed the method of land transfer chosen as well as a considerable difference in rental fees between land rental and land shareholding. Pure cases of land rental consistently paid higher rental fees (400–450 RMB) than mixed forms of land rental and shareholding (250–300 RMB). The undated table lacked important details such as the time frame of the contracts and, in addition, it did not seem to represent the actual conditions in Majia. A report from 2009 already mentions 1,000 mu of rented land for mushroom production (Maweifa 2009). The case of land transfer involving *Xuantian Herding Agricultural Development Limited*, mentioned earlier, also did not appear on this table.

Changli Township

During the interviews in Dadong Village in Changli Township, the members of the local village committee introduced us to the land transfer in their village. In this village, high quality farmland is rare and hilly land dominates, therefore land transfer concentrates on land suitable for planting plum trees. The cadres stated that a major advantage of this project is that the work on these trees is not difficult, so elderly people could easily do it. Right now there would be about 50 mu of land usage rights transferred in this scheme. The annual rental fee was 600 jin of *Huanggu*. The village cadres also argued that the registration of all land transfers must take place at the village level and then needs to be reported to the higher levels of the administration (see cf021).

In Changli Township, I could also acquire a detailed table for all land transfers from 2008 (Changlixiang Renmin Zhengfu 2008). It lists the land transfer from households in two administrative villages to two specialized households (*nongye dahu*). While it does mention time frame, purpose, and amount of land involved in the transfer, it does not list the rental fee. The first specialized household rented 42.5 mu land for 20 years (starting in January 2007) from 11 households in one natural village. The intended purpose for the land listed was for Chinese medicine and raising chickens. The second rented 44.32 mu from 58 households in five natural villages for 30 years (again starting in January 2007). According to the table he was starting an animal husbandry enterprise. The time frame of the latter contract actually exceeded the time frame of the land usage rights of the villagers, legally a very problematic construction.

Summary

Contract-based land transfer in the townships of Anju as introduced above shows a certain pattern. Participating villagers are willing to accept rental agreements objectively biased against them. On average the annual rental fee in these contracts fell within a span of between 300 to 500 RMB per mu, with a few cases below and above that figure. This is ten to twenty times less than the profit (not revenue) agricultural investors will earn, as mentioned by local officials. Most of the contracts have a very long time frame, that of twenty years being much more likely than that of five years. Within this time frame the villagers have no option to get their land back and return to farming. The land is effectively gone. Furthermore, most contracts include numerous clauses to the disadvantage of the villagers and in favor of the new tenants. It appears that the intention of these clauses was to limit the risks for investors—for them it seems much easier to terminate the rental relationship. All these factors lead to the question of why villagers are engaging in this new rental market for land. In the final section of this chapter, this question will be picked up again.

The contract-based rental agreements presented in this section still stand out because most of them had been arranged before Beijing created a new set of tools to facilitate the commodification of land. The next section argues that these more or less isolated cases of land transfer may have just been the beginning and we now might witness a new boom of land transfer based upon the growing popularity of several new policy instruments.

LOCAL GOVERNMENTS AND NEW INSTRUMENTS
FOR LAND TRANSFER

In the interviews for this book the continued existence of informal exchanges of land between family members and fellow villagers (*sixia liuzhuan*) and the limited amount of formal transfer have been perceived by many cadres as a frustrating limitation for further development of a commercial agriculture. In most of these transfers, the amount of land exchanged is small, the time frame of the exchange short, and the compensation for the land rented out not a priority—it is rather the wish to have one's land worked that is most important here. Disputes between the land usage rights holders and sub-contractors are frequent and difficult to solve. This kind of traditional land rental may have had a stabilizing influence on smallholder agrarian production but in the eyes of local administrators is certainly not effective in pushing for more commercialized agrarian production.

As documented, the center has also grown increasingly critical toward smallholder farming and begun to transform the HRS framework to incorporate the legal basis for non-administrative market-like exchange of contracted collective land. This has been the starting point for the invention and implementation of several additional policy instruments to initiate and facilitate large-scale land transfer on the local level. These instruments may have considerable and lasting impact on the structure of agrarian production in the Chinese countryside.

Land transfer cooperatives (*tudi liuzhuan hezuoshe*), specialized cooperatives (*zhuanye hezuoshe*), land transfer service centers (*tudi liuzhuan fuwu zhongxin*), and land shareholdings (*tudi rugu*) are among the most popular of these instruments and all share three basic characteristics. First they are based upon the HRS. Accordingly, the conditions for the transfer of land outlined within this legal framework also apply to each of these instruments. This entails a standardized contract between the party with the land usage rights and the party interested in renting out the land, as in the cases introduced above. All of the core aspects of land transfer such as the compensation payment, the duration of the transfer and the rights of the sub-contractor must be added to this contract. The second shared characteristic of these new instruments is their explicit focus on long-term and large-scale transfers (*guimo liuzhuan*). Beyond the transfer itself the consolidation of plots into one bigger holding is another major goal. The third aspect in these new forms of land transfer is the pro-active role of local governments to facilitate every step of the land transfer process.

However, there are also important differences between these instruments. Land transfer cooperatives, specialized cooperatives, and land shareholdings establish an intermediary organizational body between the lessors and the tenants. Land transfer service centers, in turn, aim to facilitate the direct exchange between lessor and tenant. In the following section, land transfer cooperatives and land transfer service centers, two prominent examples of these new policy instruments, will be introduced.

Land Transfer Cooperatives

These cooperatives consist as a variety of the specialized cooperatives, as outlined by the law on the creation of specialized cooperatives in 2006 (Zhuxiling 2007a). However, while usually specialized cooperatives engage in agricultural production themselves, land transfer cooperatives (in addition to farming) are able to rent out the land usage rights rural households have entrusted it with to a third party.

While talking to officials from Anju District government, I was able the get a copy of village and township cadre coaching materials for the creation of a land transfer cooperative published by the Anju District Office for Agricultural Affairs in 2008 (Anjuqu Nongyebu 2008). In this material, we find two important types of information. First, it includes an opinionated statement on the current issues in agriculture and the role of land transfer, which may serve as an ideological guidance for lower level cadres. Second, it explains in detail the functions of a land transfer cooperative, the role and responsibilities of the local government (here: mostly at the township level) and how to implement the various steps needed to create such an organizational body.

The coaching materials describe land transfer cooperatives as organizations resting upon four main pillars. First, land transfer cooperatives are an intermediary organization, placed between households and tenants. Although it must report to the relevant organs at district level, it is registered as an enterprise and enjoys the status of a legal person. By definition its main purpose is to provide services in regard to the transfer of land usage rights. The second pillar consists of the rights and responsibilities of the members of the cooperative and the cooperative itself. The members entrust their land to the cooperative. The cooperative in turn either starts farming itself or rents out the land to a third party. To the best of its abilities it should thereby focus on encouraging entrepreneurial activities, promoting economic development, raising the technological standards, introducing economies of scale implemented by experts and advocating similar aspects of a modern agriculture. Third, the main institution for making decisions is the membership meetings. In addition, the cooperative has an executive director and a board of directors, a supervisory group, which includes a head of supervision and an accountant. All of these positions are elective. Fourth, the conduct of the cooperative should be based on a set of five main principles: 1. Transparency of the transfer in order to ensure the villagers a guaranteed benefit from the transfer, 2. Fairness in the consultations and voluntary membership of the villagers, who can decide to leave the cooperative whenever they wish to (and will get back their land in time), 3. Collective land owner-ship and (agricultural) land usage that are not subject to any change, 4. Land transfer activities which follow the regulations outlined in the LAL and the LCRL, and 5. Prioritization of tenants from households in the same village in which the collective is based.

The procedures for creating a land transfer cooperative are as follows: first, the land of all villagers with an interest in land transfer is examined and verified. Afterward, the villagers entrust their land at a fixed rate to the land transfer cooperative via an "entrust agreement." The available land is then publicly announced and a tenant is selected. The new tenant and the land transfer cooperative then sign a land rental contract, which includes all important information such as the name and location of the plot, its size, borders, rental fee, and payment, as well as rights and obligations.

The local government is envisioned to support and guide the creation of land transfer cooperatives. According to the coaching materials, it is the task of local cadres to convince the villagers of the benefits of such a cooperative. In all townships, organizations, and offices that support the creation of land transfer cooperatives should be established. Local cadres should also head the investigations into the potentially available land for the cooperative, going from house to house. Finally, local cadres should prepare the draft of the "Basic Agreement" (*caocheng*) based on templates provided by Anju District. This is the main legal document of the cooper-ative and should include statements concerning the reasons for creating a cooperative, the nature of the cooperative, conditions for joining the cooperative, rights and obligations of the members, the organizational structure, the mode of implementation, and similar aspects.

An incremental implementation of the land transfer cooperative is envisioned. The prepared Basic Agreement should be discussed at a gen-eral meeting of the village. Opinions and suggestions should be taken into account and the Basic Agreement changed accordingly. Then the preparation group should assemble again those households who have shown an interest in renting out land and ask them to complete an appli-cation to join the cooperative (*rushe shenqing shu*). The application should include all the important information such as the name, the amount of the household's land, the amount of land intended for contribution to the cooperative, and the number of household members. This information is then compiled into one file for the archive. Next, the village representa-tives and the preparatory group will examine the information from the households and verify the conditions of the land. Afterward, these villag-ers sign the "Entrust Land Usage Rights Agreement" (*tudi chengbaoquan weituo jingying xieyi shu*) and the cooperative hands out the "Cooperative Membership Certificates" (*sheyuan zheng*). Finally, a foundational meet-ing for the cooperative takes place. At this meeting the Basic Agreement is publicly approved and the election of the board of directors and its head as well as the supervision group and its head takes place.

After the households have entrusted their land to the cooperative, the cooperative will consult in a timely manner with an investor to set the rental fee and the time frame of the rental and, if suitable, a contract for the land rental will be set up. In order to stabilize the income of the former smallholders, the land rental fee can be set in accordance with rice yields at the national standard rate. The amount of rice is then multiplied by the annually fixed price and paid to the cooperative, which in turn will distribute the rental fee to households.

The setup of the land transfer cooperative in Tanghe Village in Anju Town provides insights into a typical instance of a land transfer cooperative. Here, the strong influence of the local state on the cooperative and its comprehensive, all-encompassing nature quickly became obvious. Government personnel was installed into key positions of the cooperative and the cooperative was loosely integrated into the official hierarchy and reporting system. It soon also became apparent that the label *land transfer cooperative* does not capture the full purpose of this organizational body in practice.

The declaration of interest to form a land transfer cooperative, signed by the villagers committee and addressed at the Office for Agricultural affairs at district level lists the preparatory work conducted as well as the new leadership selected for the cooperative-to-be (Tanghecun 2008a). As the director of the new cooperative the party secretary of Anju Township and as vice-directors the mayor of the township and the village party secretary were chosen.[5] The preparatory work for the formation of the new cooperative mentioned in the declaration falls within four categories. First, a number of households agreed to become the first group of members in the cooperative. Second, after proper investigations into the public opinion, a first draft of the Basic Agreement on the specifications of the financial and administrative system was produced. Third, a delegation of the cooperative members then signed this agreement to allow its implementation. Finally, in order to discuss the implementation of the cooperative structures, the members of the cooperative convened a working meeting. The results of this process were documented and sent to the appropriate administrative organizations for approval.

The Basic Agreement in Tanghe Village is a carefully set up document listing basic and advanced structural features of the land transfer cooperative (Tanghecun 2008b). Many articles cover in detail regulations for the organizational structure and the management of the finances.[6] Article 2 of the Basic Agreement specifies three main purposes of this organizational body: to provide land transfer services, to act as an intermediary legal person with the relevant administrative organs at the district level and, finally, to manage the land of the members of the cooperative for them. Important principles to be adhered to in this work are stated in the next article of the Basic Agreement. The most important of these are "managed by the people, supervision by the people, for the benefit of the people" (*minban, minguan, min shouyi*). The article further elaborates upon the fact that the cooperative should be of service to its members; that all members should benefit to the same degree; that the interaction should be characterized by fairness and voluntarism; and that members have the right to leave the cooperative if they wish to do so.

Articles 6 and 7 clarify the rights and purposes of the land transfer cooperative in more detail. The members entrust the cooperative with the management of the collective land and all other resources and assets brought into the cooperative, such as national subsidies and other legal funds. They further grant the right of possession, usage, and disciplinary action. The cooperative is allowed to begin commercial production on its land but also could rent out the land to a third party. A priority in the decision-making process should be that the chosen activities contribute to the economic strength (*jingji shili*), are high-tech and are specialized (e.g., cash crops). Furthermore, the cooperative should explore how it could contribute to more large-scale commercial and standardized agricultural production, which ultimately should raise the production effectiveness of the land. The Basic Agreement specifies the intention to explore the opportunities in added labor services, external investments, and cooperation with universities.

Article 8 points to the relationship of the land transfer cooperative with the local government. It states that the cooperative will receive (*jieshou*) guidance from the village party branch and the village committee, from the township government and relevant organs for agricultural affairs within the government at the district level in order to make the necessary adjustments and to help set free the productive forces.

Article 11 outlines the rights of the members of the collective. Among these rights are: to take part in a members meeting, to vote and have the right to get elected; to have priority over external parties if a member of the cooperative wishes to rent the cooperatives land; to accept job offers from the cooperative and to receive all services provided by the cooperative for its members; to receive a share of the surplus the cooperative produces plus interest for that portion of the member's land managed by the cooperative and to receive a wage for the work done for the cooperative; to consult the minutes for all previous meetings as well as the accounting report; to investigate the work of the cooperative, to criticize it and to make suggestions for the future; and finally, the right to withdraw from the cooperative in accordance with the basic guidelines.

However, members also have some obligations. These are detailed in Article 13. Among other points the members must comply with the Basic Agreement and all formal requirements; they must entrust the cooperative with their land usage rights in accordance with the regulations — either for direct management or shareholding; they must attend all of the cooperative's meetings and training sessions in order to ensure that the cooperative meets product and production standards; they must protect the interests and the property of the cooperative and not engage in activities that somehow could harm the interest of the cooperative in any way.

Articles 14 and 17 discuss the conditions that lead to or may lead to a situation in which a member forfeits his membership rights. The member is automatically expelled if the term of his land usage rights runs out, if he makes clear his intention to leave the cooperative, if he loses his civil rights or if the member happens to be a sub-organization or an enterprise[7] and goes bankrupt, or if the member is expelled by decision of the cooperative. A member may also be expelled upon the decision of the board of the directors, usually after it is shown that the member has failed to comply with the Basic Agreement or with other internal agreements, if he does not comply with the decisions of the representatives of the members or with the board of directors or does not perform membership tasks. Interestingly, one can also be expelled from the membership of the cooperative if the trainings given do not seem to have any impact upon the member (*jing jiaoyu wuxiao*).

Concerning land rental, even more relevant are situations in which members of the cooperative decide, for whatever reason, to revoke their membership and take back their land from the cooperative. Article 15 suggests that the process to leave the cooperative is straightforward and relatively easy. Three months before the end of the fiscal year the member must submit his written resignation. Within two months into the new fiscal year, which starts on January 1st, the land usage rights of the member and other investments or assets the member has brought in must be returned. Furthermore, the member will receive his share of the cooperative's profits, or, if the cooperative was operating at a loss, parts of the member's monetary assets can be deducted. Strangely, the land rental contracts, which are signed by the cooperative and the individual members, are not mentioned. In most cases, these rental contracts (as shown in the previous section) stretch over several years. This might make the process of returning the member's assets more difficult.

The Basic Agreement also pays great attention to the organizational structure of the cooperative. Many regulations aim to prevent potential conflicts of interest. For example, Article 33 prohibits direct relatives of the chairman of the board of directors to become members of the supervision group. And Article 34 highlights that the board of directors, the supervision group, and other management personal should not engage in business activities that compete with the cooperative.

The special character of and the difficulties in differentiating land transfer cooperatives from other cooperatives become evident in the articles meant to guide the financial structure of the cooperative. Article 40 lists all the cooperative's potential properties and sources of incomes. The primary asset is the land and the capital, which the members entrust the cooperative with. In addition however, the cooperative takes ownership of all village collective land that is not contracted out to farming households including farmland, wasteland, mountainous wasteland and unused slopes. Furthermore, it also gains ownership of other items owned by the village collective economic group such as fish pools, warehouses, and other physical assets. This article contains another interesting section. Among the list of the cooperative's incomes the income through land transfer also appears. The cooperative works the fields by itself or rents it out to another actor, either internally (to a member of the cooperative) or externally (to an investor). In return, the cooperative receives a rental fee from the subcontractor. What happens with these and other incomes of the cooperative? There is a huge section covering many articles (42–45, 47–49) on how to deal with the fiscal component of business operations. According to the Basic Agreement operational costs should be thoroughly checked and examined before being deducted from the revenues. The operational costs also include compensation for the board of directors and the executive director. The remaining profits are split up into four parts.

The first 10 percent of the profits go into a fiscal reserve, then 20 percent into a welfare fund (*gongyijin*), and 20 percent into a risk fund. The fiscal reserve funds will be used for investments to enlarge production as well as to balance (former) deficits, and the rest of the fund will be dispersed among the members based upon their contributions of land, shares, and labor. The welfare fund will be used for technical training and training for better cooperation. In addition, it should be used for cultural events, to help weaker members of the cooperative, and for (economic) self-help. The risk fund should help members to better deal with the effects of mismanagement and unfavorable market-trends. It can also be used to balance the cooperative's operational loss. What still remains of the profits is again split into two parts. Sixty percent will be distributed to the members in accordance with the key outlined above, which is based upon contributions of land, shares, and labor. The remaining 40 percent of the profits are paid into the accounts of the members and will be dispersed in the following year.

So how much rent do farmers receive in these land transfer cooperatives? Given the limited access to the actual rental contracts between villagers and the companies that exists, this question is difficult to answer. During the interviews, officials argued that the rental payments would be in line with those of other arrangements (as introduced in the previous section). Leading cadres from the Office for Agricultural Affairs, for example, put the number at 800 jin of *Huanggu* (cf020).

There are mixed signals concerning the prospects of the land transfer cooperatives for the future. Political prioritization may be an important factor here. For example, in the region of Qingdao the government financially encouraged the creation of land transfer cooperatives (see cf028), whereas township cadres in Anju complained about the lack of any financial support (cf011). However, political pressure to promote this land transfer mechanism also became visible during the interviews in Suining. The head of the Agricultural Commission (*shi nong wei*) indicated that they planned to establish 100 land transfer cooperatives in 2008, of which at the time of our interview (11.09.2008), 35 had been implemented (cf006). The work report for 2008 for the same Agricultural Commission lists a total of 59 new land transfer cooperatives within the city limits involving 7,967 households (translating into 24,030 members) and 22,085.5 mu land. According to the report, these cooperatives have attracted 74 large-scale enterprises. In January of 2010, *Renmin Ribao* published on its website a story about the achievements in Xiji County, which also belongs to Suining City, in creating new land transfer cooperatives. The emphasis on land transfer cooperatives here is supposedly rooted in the success of a new model: "Dragonhead enterprises as the subject, [promotion of] land rental transfer, peasants for local labor services" (*longtou qiye wei zhu, tudi zulin liuzhuan, nongmin jiudi wugong*). According to the article, the basic principles of the land transfer in Xiji consisted of a transfer according to the law, voluntarily in nature and with compensation (*yifa, ziyuan, youchang liuzhuan*). In total, 13,800 mu was transferred in this way to agricultural companies (Chen, He, and Zhou 2010).

In contrast to these reports on the successful introduction of land transfer cooperatives in the Suining area, in 2009 cadres of the Office for Agricultural Affairs in Anju toned down considerably their enthusiasm for this model in comparison to the previous year (cf009). They called the land transfer cooperatives one experiment among many to improve the transfer of farmland and added that, strictly speaking, these cooperatives would only serve as a variation of the already existing specialized cooperatives in agriculture. In the whole district, there would exist about 20 cooperatives and only 10 of them would perform well (cf009).[8] In the same interview the cadres complained that they had been given a target to create 20 cooperatives each year for the annual performance evaluation.

From this introduction to land transfer cooperatives and the example from Tanghe Village, four important findings regarding this variant of the commodification of farmland emerge. First, the main target for the creation of land transfer cooperatives is to put agricultural land to an assumed better use. Better, in this case, is defined in terms of output from the land in relation to resources invested. The underlying assumption is that the concentration of farmland, either in cooperative structures or in a rental arrangement, is always preferable to the existing smallholding arrangements. Second, just as with many other instruments designed to ease the transfer of farmland, new institutions outside of the formal ownership structures (e.g., the village collective) are created. Often the personnel of these new institutions are recruited from the ranks of village and township administration and the new cooperatives are (at least informally) integrated in the sphere of the administration. Third, great emphasis is placed upon the formal transparency of the whole process. The authors of the guidelines intended that the joining of land transfer cooperatives be as risk free for the farmers as possible. The profitability of these arrangements, in contrast, seems to be less important—given that the rental fees in land transfer cooperatives are similar to other rental agreements. Fourth, land transfer cooperatives are explicitly created to be an instrument for the modernization of the countryside. Language and goals in the Basic Agreement and other important documents leave no doubt that this serves as an instrument to create a modern and more efficient agriculture based upon economies of scale. Local governments can (and probably must to a certain degree) use these cooperatives to demonstrate their progressive nature, irrespective of the actual success of the cooperatives in practice.

Land Transfer Service Centers

Land transfer service centers are an institution of a very different kind than the just introduced land transfer cooperatives. At least in a formal sense the cooperatives are placed outside of formal government structures. The service centers, in contrast, are organizations installed by local governments within government structures at the county or district level.[9] They are accompanied by land transfer service stations (*tudi liuzhuan fuwu zhan*) at the township level. These service stations should provide services and information for land transfer to villagers while at the same time reporting cases of land transfer to the service center. Village level transfer service personnel assist the township stations in this system. They should help in all aspects of land transfer and transmit necessary information to the township service stations.

Officials from Xifeng provided me with a "handbook" (Xifengxian Renmin Zhengfu 2010) for the creation of land service centers, which provides interesting insights into the twofold purpose of this institution. On the one hand, the service center should carry out the administrative supervision of all land transfers in the county; on the other hand, it should itself facilitate land transfer as much as possible. The service centers have a physical presence in which information as well as various other services for land transfer are provided for both the contractors aiming to rent out their land and the investors aiming to rent in. Available land and rental prices must be publicly displayed on an electronic board. The handbook is quite specific in insisting that one of the main tasks of the personnel in these service centers is to frequently update this board and all other information provided. In order to carry out this task, they should compile the information provided by village level survey takers.

The handbook also outlines all the tasks and responsibilities of the director of such a land transfer center and thereby indirectly provides an idea about the purpose of this institution. The relevant central laws and regulations for the transfer of land usage rights, in particular the LCRL and the "Procedures for the management of the transfer of contracted usage rights for rural land" (Nongyebu 2005), are described as the legal basis for the work of the director and the land transfer center. The director has the obligation to oversee the work of the service center and should strengthen the supervision of all services in land transfer on the township and village level. Furthermore, the director has the responsibility to inspect the land transfer work on the ground, collect the necessary information, and publish it in a timely manner. Ultimately, it is his responsibility to mediate all conflicts that arise due to land transfer. Finally, the director should carry out regular research investigations to explore innovative and effective land transfer mechanisms, which would help in order to solve the *Three Rural Problems*. [10]

The handbook does not differentiate among the personnel of the land transfer center in any detail, with two notable exceptions. First, there is a position called "Conflict Mediation Officer" (*jiufen tiaojie yuan*). This official is responsible for the collection, registration, and mediation of conflicts emerging from the transfer of land. If the conflicts cannot be solved, this official pursues legal action. The second position is the "Archivist," who is supposed to collect basically all information relevant to the management of collective land in the countryside. This includes changes to the distribution of land usage rights (via death, birth, or permanent transfer), changes in the quality of land and all transfers of land. All of this information should be merged into a land transfer database. Cadres at the Qingdao Agricultural Commission argued in 2008 that these land transfer service centers reduce conflicts in land transfer because they encourage notarization (*gongzheng*), mediation (*zhongcai*), and information services (*xinxi fuwu*). They are seen as a necessary step to ease the transfer of land (see cf028).

The close connection between the land transfer service centers and the interests of the local state become obvious if one takes a closer look at the evaluation process for officials working in the township land transfer service stations, which are subordinate to the county level land transfer centers. As this author has earlier argued in a jointly written article, cadre performance evaluations should not be seen as an absolute standard that township cadres need to achieve or face punishment but more as an instrument to convey priorities from higher levels of the administration to lower echelons (Heberer and Trappel 2013). At the beginning of the evaluation guidelines (Xifengxian Tudi Liuzhuan Zhongxin 2009a) the goals to be achieved with this type of institution are cited: a better reporting of land transfer activities, more scale (*guimo*) land transfers and more cases of long-term land transfer. The contents of the evaluation are split into six sections. Performance in each section is measured, and reaching 90 or more points (out of 100) qualifies for a reward. There are deductions if the work falls short of certain standards. The first category, valued at up to 10 points, concerns the adherence to all relevant laws and regulations, the propogation (*xuanchuan*) of those laws to the general public, and the production of proper information material. The second consists of the proper management of local land transfers, including receiving representatives of both parties involved in the land transfer, and the formal registration and timely reporting to the county land transfer center. If done properly this qualifies for 20 points. The third category concerns the organization of fieldwork investigations in land transfer including the examination, registration, and provision of information and contracts for existing land transfer cases. The complete documentation of such investigations qualifies for another 20 points. Fourth, the proper collection of village level land transfer data and transmission to higher echelons qualifies for 15 points. The fifth category concerns filing a comprehensive and timely report about the land transfer conditions in a given township, worth another 20 points. The last section of the evaluation process consists of a statistical investigation into the amount of land already transferred, the supply situation for farmland, and other land resources. The resulting database should provide an account of all collective land and land transfer in the countryside. This segment of the evaluation is worth 15 points.

In contrast to Sichuan and Guizhou, land transfer service centers in the field sites in Shandong were placed at the administrative level of the township. An internal document collected in 2009 in Laixi outlines the seven main tasks of a land transfer service center in Xiagezhuang Town (Laixishi Renmin Zhengfu 2009b). In the order given, these are: to implement the LCRL and all other relevant laws from the center, the province, the prefecture and the township affecting contracted land and land transfer; to conduct necessary research on questions regarding contracted land and land transfer, land transfer policies, and other policy aspects; to receive the involved parties in land transfer applying for a registration of land transfer; to act as an intermediary party in the land transfer, putting on record the documentation of the transfer, guiding the process, and providing all intermediary land transfer services demanded; to investigate all incoming complaints dealing with aspects of collective land and land transfer; to create a database for all contracted land and land transfer, easing the management of statements made; to supervise and monitor all contracted land and land transfers for the CPC and the local government.

During fieldwork in 2009 it was possible for me to visit the land transfer center in Xiagezhuang Town.[11] Particularly interesting were two aspects during this visit: the large posters explaining to visitors the process and particularities of the land transfer system and the work of the land transfer service center and, secondly, an electronic board showing the available land in the surrounding villages and its renting conditions.

One poster depicted land transfer as a process divided into five steps. First, the party that wants to rent out the land applies to do so at the land transfer center. At the same time the party with an interest in renting land for farming activities also applies with the land transfer center. Second, an information liaison manager (*xinxi liange yuan*) at the center will then examine and register all applications. Third, this liaison officer provides the party interested in renting land with information regarding the available land and the party interested in renting out the land with information about the rental interest. The liaison officer will also suggest a meeting between the two parties. Fourth, representatives of the two parties meet and have trade talks. Fifth, upon reaching an agreement the two parties draft a contract and sign it. A Certification Officer (*hetong qianzheng yuan*) then certifies the contract.

Another poster describes the work of the land transfer service center in Xiagezhuang as a series of eight steps, displayed in a simple graph. According to these steps, the center must investigate the local conditions at the beginning of the process to create a database of available farmland for transfer. Afterward, land transfer in line with the planned future composition of local fields is planned. In the next step, the service center, in cooperation with the households, writes a formal draft of the land transfer intention. Thereafter, the center should search for and attract a suitable investor (the term used for the future tenant is *chanye dahu*, which could be translated approximately as "entrepreneurial household"). Then both parties should sign a land usage rights transfer contract. After this, the service center should continue to provide necessary follow-up services. A third poster provides a short rundown of the most important legal requirements and conditions of land transfer. At the core of this poster is the need for all land transfers to be conducted on the basis of a contract. It also explains how the service center assists and guides the two parties involved in managing all formalities.

Finally, located at the center of the main room of the land transfer service center in Xiagezhuang was a big electronic board announcing to all visitors the available land in the surrounding villages. Below the first row containing information on the name of the village and a date, the board was divided into eight vertical columns providing information on the name of the land usage rights holder, the amount of land to be transferred (in mu), the location in the village, the quality of the land, the suitable usage, the rental fee, the time frame, and remarks (this column being left blank for all accounts, see also the fourth photo in the photospread). On the day of our visit land was available in three villages. The average amount of land offered by each villager differed among the villages. In one village, three villagers offered between 10 and 12 mu of land for planting (*zhizhong*) for five years for an annual fee of between 300 and

330 RMB. In the second village, ten villagers offered between 2 and 8.5 mu, with an average of 5.08 mu. In the third village, seven villagers offered between 1.5 and 6 mu, with an average of 3.74 mu. All other conditions regarding time frame (five years), quality of the land, and rental fee (for the latter two villages between 300 and 320 RMB) were about the same in all villages. Differences in the amount of land transferred are most likely to have their origin in the differences in land endowments of these villages and do not show substantially different levels of land transfer endorsement.

During the visit at the land transfer center in Xiagezhuang, I was given a prepared contract for land transfer organized by the land transfer service center (cmm033). Although this was a blank contract, taking a closer look at it allows for identifying the local priorities in renting out land. As in most cases in Anju, introduced earlier, the contract included a short statement on the purpose of the contract. In this case, it was formulated in very general terms, referring only to the main national policies such as the HRS, which are stated as being the basis of any land transfer. Only in the last line is some local flavor added by stating that the land transfer service center will certify the contract and ensure that both parties adhere to it.

The contract does include blank boxes for the mode of transfer chosen[12], the time frame, the rental fee, the method of payment, and the quality and location of the land. The household renting out the land has the right to limit the land usage of the tenant to certain specified use cases, to receive a rental fee as detailed in the contract and to have the land returned after the end of the contract. The lessor in turn must transfer the land usage rights to the tenant and may not interfere in the tenant's business. The tenant has the right to operate on the land rented and receive the profits of the agricultural products. For this right, the tenant must pay the rental fee on time and may not change the land usage without authorization. In contrast to many other contracts, there is no regulation in this contract for who receives national and local subsidies for improving the land or agriculture. The contract may be changed or terminated under four distinct conditions: first, if both parties agree to such a change and neither national, collective, or individual interests are harmed; second, if important national policies change; third, if a breach of contract occurs which makes the continued operation of the contract impossible; fourth, if the tenant is unable to continue the operation.

It also includes a breach of contract clause. If the household renting out the land interferes with the production or, without authorization, modifies or terminates the contract, this is considered breach of contract and the household must compensate the tenant for all loss incurred. On the other hand, if the tenant does not pay the rental fee, lets the land lie idle, damages property on the land (especially irrigation infrastructure), does not comply with the national construction plan (e.g., uses the land for non-agricultural constructions), or does not adhere to the outlined usage this is also considered breach of contract and the tenant must compensate the lessor for all incurred loss. These regulations seem more favorable for the peasant households as compared to the ones encountered in Sichuan. However, the lack of a clear definition for what is to be considered an incurred loss may likely lead to legal disputes.

Four aspects of these land transfer centers are of particular interest. First, in contrast to the land transfer cooperatives the land transfer centers appear to be much more deeply integrated into the formal administration at the county level and below. The leadership in these organizations is bound by performance contracts just as all other leading cadres are. Here not only the creation but also the performance of the land transfer centers in certain fields is monitored, thus differing from the evaluation practice in regard to the land transfer cooperatives. Second, the majority of the tasks of land transfer centers and stations are envisioned to be temporary and supportive in nature. The land transfer centers are a wager on the private interest in a structured market for farmland, which would allow the local state to limit its role in the creation of a suitable framework for the commodification. Land transfer cooperatives, in contrast, are envisioned to step in and start agrarian production themselves if no suitable tenant has been found. Third, the creation of these land transfer centers also shows, just as in the land transfer cooperatives, that the existing institutions and organizations for village self-administration are not seen as being able to create the necessary dynamic in land transfer for a commercial agriculture. Fourth, these centers also exemplify again the importance of land transfer contracts in the HRS. Similar to the situation in the earlier large-scale transfers introduced in the first section of this chapter, these contracts have become the main tool for the commodification.

"Appropriate Scale" and the Future of Land Transfer

The two policy instruments introduced above should be treated as two variations of the same underlying theme: the local state is stepping up its game in land transfer. Although some of these new policy initiatives will prove unsuccessful, the strategic direction is unlikely to change. In the remaining parts of this section, more exemplary evidence of this new strategic direction from Qingdao will be discussed.

The recent "Suggestions of Qingdao Government on Speeding-up and Pushing Forward *Appropriate Scale Economies*[13] on Rural Land" (*Qingdaoshi renmin zhengfu guanyu jiakuai tuijin nongcun tudi shidu guimo jingying de yijian*) from 2011 summarizes Qingdao's strategy in regard to land transfer (Qingzhengzi 2011). This document puts prominent emphasis on the term "appropriate scale economies" (*shidu guimo jingying*), which appears to have become a cornerstone of the strategic planning in agriculture not only for Qingdao but also for most of China and already appears as early as in the No. 1 document of 2005. It refers to a strategy that integrates agricultural modernization in the overall aim of rural–urban integration and continued economic development. At the core of this strategy is the creation of new and innovative instances of economies of scale in agriculture leading to greater efficiency and productivity in agrarian production. These economies of scale should allow for more labor transition from farming to wage earning urban employment.

The document puts forward a number of goals, one of which stands out. Qingdao aims to increase the amount of appropriate scale economies from 15 percent of the farmland acreage in 2012 to 30 percent by 2015. This target is even more astonishing if one takes into account the four principles that should guide the quest to reach this target. First, the whole process should be based upon the basic rural economic system. This mainly refers to the continued existence of the HRS. Explicitly, the rights and benefits granted in the form of land usage rights should remain untouched. Second, the necessary land transfers should conform to the legal system (*yifa*), be of a voluntary nature (*ziyuan*, the peasants should by no means be forced to transfer their land), and must entail some kind of compensation (*youchang*). Third, the whole process should be guided by the government and driven by market demands. More specifically, the land should be distributed in accordance with market demands. Governments should enthusiastically foster and perfect markets for land usage rights. They should also ensure that the economic benefits from the lands are increased for land usage rights holders. Fourth, the whole process should take place in accordance with local conditions, e.g., the present progress of the transition of the rural labor force to non-agricultural employment and the development of social insurances. These principles are derived from central policy frameworks, as can be seen in chapter 3. The document frames the registration of land parcels and the handing out of certificates for land usage rights as a precondition for successful land transfer activities. Therefore, by the end of 2011 all registration work should be completed, including issuing the required documents.

The main intended forms of tenancy resulting from this kind of land transfer are listed: specialized households (*zhuanye dahu*), family farms (*jiating nongchang*), specialized cooperatives, land shareholding, land entrust systems, and Dragonhead enterprises. All of these new market participants should receive further government support. Specialized households are specifically listed as the currently most important method for improving the scale of operations. The document also encourages scientific households (*keji hu*) and cultivation experts (*zhongtian nengshou*) to be at the receiving end of land transfers. Family farms seem to be the expanded version of specialized households. The document states that specialized households should be encouraged to transform themselves into such family farms. Rather new are land entrust systems, in which villagers entrust their land usage rights to one actor, such as the village collective economic group or a cooperative, which are then able to make agricultural management decisions for the whole group or cooperative. This, for example, entails selecting the means of agricultural production or deciding on sales channels. Finally, Dragonhead enterprises should be further developed as an important part of agricultural commercialization.

One focus of this document is the pressure put on local governments to increase the amount of land transferred. For example, every district and prefectural city in the Qingdao area must install a service board showing supply and demand for land, which includes the available land reserve and available land transfer and entrust services. In 2011, the five cities within the Qingdao administrative region should select two to three sites and the three districts should each select one site for the location of permanent land transfer markets. Governments should guide the development of prices in this market to protect the interests of the peasants. For this purpose, governments at the city and district level should determine appropriate guiding prices for different kinds of land, based on quality and possible economic activities. The authors of the document want the whole land transfer process to be more standardized and transparent. Therefore, contracts are again described as the necessary foundation of all transfers. Furthermore, each and every case should be appropriately documented. Finally, the document insists that institutions to solve conflicts and to manage arbitrage cases be put in place.

Local governments should explore new approaches to land transfer, three of which are mentioned in the document: the entrust-representative system, land shareholding cooperatives and "land banks." Entrust-representative systems envision villagers signing an "entrust book" and allow the village collective to act on their behalf to arrange land transfers. This would imply even further institutionalization as compared to the present practice. It would also be the first model in which the existing village institutions would play a major role in land transfer. Land shareholding cooperatives seem to be a more advanced variation of the land transfer cooperatives discussed earlier. These cooperatives also have the option of either farming themselves or renting out the land to other actors. The most interesting innovation may be the "land banks" (*tudi yinhang*). According to the model outlined here, villagers deposit their land usage rights at these banks or other land entrust centers (*tudi xintuo zhongxin*) and get paid an annual interest.

There is an entire section dealing with government support for such adequate economies of scale. Four approaches in this supportive work are listed. The most obvious may be financial support. The city of Qingdao has prepared a special annual fund to be used for promotion of land transfer among villagers. There are also funds for land transfer cooperatives, funds for specialized households to become family farms and support for land transfer services on all levels of government including funding for subsidies, and awards for land transfer innovations. Policy projects are another important kind of support. All levels of government should set up support projects for the various variants of land transfer. Among the list's options for projects are land recovery projects, irrigation infrastructure projects, and agricultural research parks. Another kind of support mentioned is a "unified set" of policies. Within this category also falls the construction of supportive infrastructure on a portion of the farmland. In land transfers involving more than 100 mu and stretching over more than three years, about three percent of the farmland (but no more than 20 mu) can be used for construction purposes. The fourth aspect of support is a very interesting, different kind of financial support. In order to fund adequate economies of scale, experiments with mortgage-based credits are suggested that use land usage rights and rights to agricultural facilities as security. For now, this suggestion goes beyond the national legal framework. Finally, microcredit companies are noted as another alternative source of financing.

This strategic document concludes with a call for more local government guidance and especially for the need to eliminate all of the peasants' doubts regarding land transfers (*xiaochu nongmin qunzhong du tudiliuzhuan de yilü*). Clearly, Qingdao is increasing the pressure on lower level administrations to push and promote the modernization of agriculture. Policy experiments and new approaches to the transfer of farmland and other steps of agricultural commercialization are being greatly encouraged.

REGIONAL DISTRIBUTION AND TRENDS

The following section will present aggregated trends in land transfer in the field sites. Before entering this discussion, however, some remarks on the general demand for land transfer in China are necessary.

There are clear and important regional differences in potential demand and supply of farmland, and these differences certainly affect the demand for land transfer. Sun Zhaoxia, a scholar from Guizhou University argued, for example, that one should differentiate between three different zones in regard to the demand for farmland. First, there are those villages close to urban centers (*chengjiaoxing nongcun*) in which most of the discussion regarding land focuses on the creation of housing, commercial or industrial facilities. Most land transfer in these locations will occur out of more direct monetary profit interests (and usually does not involve agricultural production). Second are those villages between urban and very remote areas. Here most of the agrarian production takes place. Only in these so-called intermediate zone villages (*zhongjian didai nongcun*) is land transfer for agricultural purposes is really important. Third are the far away and remote villages (*bianyuan diqu nongcun*), fre-

quently located in poverty regions. Although subsistence farming continues to exist here, land is also frequently left behind because the villagers
migrate to urban areas in search of higher income (cf017). Zhang Hui,
another scholar present at the same interview, added that land transfer in
the peri-urban areas would also be less frequent because, even though
villagers would work in cities, they could easily return to their rural
homes and do the necessary farm work (cf017). These three categories of
villages outlined by Sun could be found in all field sites. Certainly population pressure, geographical conditions, and upcoming infrastructural
investments as well as other factors may have had an impact on the
individual categorization in the three provinces examined. In the handbook for the creation of land transfer cooperatives for local cadres published by the Office for Agricultural Affairs of Anju District in 2008 (Anjuqu Nongyebu 2008), the development in land transfer in the past is
described as following a certain pattern called "three more, three less"
(san duo, san shao). This means that there has been more land usage rights
transfers in quickly developing villages compared to economically stag-
nant villages; more land transfer in villages with high labor migration
rates compared to villages with little labor migration; and more land
transfer in villages with little per capita land as opposed to villages in
which villagers on average have bigger landholdings.

How important has the large-scale transfer of land usage rights in the
three field sites been? For Anju District the general conditions regarding
land transfer are outlined in the "Introduction to Rural Land Transfer
and Specialized Cooperative Organizations," published by the Anju District Office for Agricultural Affairs (Anjuqu Nongyebu 2009). According
to this document 152,100 mu land was transferred in Anju in 2009, which
is 23.3 percent of all farmland. This land transfer affects 55,680 or 28.3
percent of all households. It is organized as follows: land transferred
privately within the village (zhuanbao) accounts for 84,900 mu or 55.8
percent of all land transfers, rented-out land (chuzu) for 36,497 mu or 24
percent, land exchanged between two households (huhuan) for 1,510 mu
or 1 percent, land shareholding (rugu) for 12,206 mu or 8 percent, and
other methods for 16,998 mu or 11.2 percent. The document also sums up
all cases of large-scale land transfer. In total, land transfers involving 10
mu or more comprise 73,000 mu or 47.99 percent of all transfers. Whereby
land transfers involving 10–15 mu make up 32,400 mu, cases of 51–199
mu make up 6200 mu, cases of 200–499 mu make up 3,230 mu, cases of
500–999 mu amount to 6,950 mu and cases involving more than 1,000 mu
in total account for 24,220 mu. Most of the transferred land is used for
grain (87,600 mu), raising animals (28,440 mu) and fruit production
(20960 mu). Other uses involve the production of vegetables (7,080 mu),
flowers (5,000 mu), and medicine (3,000 mu).

In 2009, during a trip to Jinan, the capital of Shandong Province, I was
able to acquire the better part of an internal report (the appendix of the

report was missing) entitled "Research Report on the Issues in Land Usage Rights Transfer in this Province" (*Guanyu wosheng nongcun tudi chengbao jingyingquan liuzhuan wenti de diaoyan baogao*), published in 2009 by the Investigation and Research Office of the Shandong Province Government (Diaocha Yanjiu Shi 2009). The data for this report comes from a field investigation carried out in 2007 and statistical data from 2008. It describes land transfer work as a long-time priority of government work in the province and particularly highlights recent efforts to stabilize and improve the rural land usage rights system. Goals in this regard would be to create a "tangible market for land transfer" (*jianshe tudi liuzhuan youxing shichang*) and a "perfect system for the provision of land usage rights services" (*jianli jianquan tudi liuzhuan fuwu tixi*). The report speaks of clear trends in the field of land usage rights transfers. The transfers would become more pluralistic and more standardized, the modes of the transfer would become more diverse, and the effects of land transfer would become better over time. The report also claims that land transfer increased in speed, especially in more developed regions. According to statistics from 2008 the volume of transferred land has reached 5,486,000 mu in Shandong Province. This would imply an increase of 8 percent in area as compared to the previous year. The statistics also report that a total of 1.507 million households took part in land transfer activities in 2008. This would be an astonishing 27.6 percent more than in the year before. The report notes that the Qingdao region, to which the field site Laixi belongs, started in 2008 to provide subsidies to encourage further land usage rights transfers. In 2008, these subsidies amounted to 5 million RMB. Up until 2008, the transferred land in Qingdao constituted 441,000 mu, which is about 7 percent of all farmland and 1 percent above the provincial average. It involved 136,000 households, which is 11.68 percent of all households and 4 percent over the provincial average.

The report claims that peasants are the subjects in land usage rights transfers and, with the recent structural adjustments in agriculture and a new focus on effectiveness, specialized cooperatives, Dragonhead enterprises and specialized households bring a new force to these transfers. The report gives the example of Zaozhuang City, where in 2006 only 3,300 mu had been rented out to specialized cooperatives. In 2008, the amount had increased 14.2 times to 50,024 mu. All other variations of land usage rights in this city also reported a substantial growth.

Still, the newer economies of scale-oriented mechanisms for the transfer of farmland are complemented and contrasted by the continuing existence of a smaller and less formalized exchange of land between family members, friends, and neighbors. This type of transfer continues to be of importance in all field sites. It seems especially important in areas in which bigger commercial operations are not yet feasible. In Guizhou Province, this author encountered way less cases of large-scale land transfer than in Sichuan and Shandong. During an interview with several scholars in Guiyang, one of them argued in a similar direction:

> Usually plots between 1 and 3 mu will be given to relatives to farm, for example one's brother (*xiongdi*) or friend (*tang xiongdi*), and each year a small amount [of grain] is given in return. I have seen many cases in which no grain is given at all. After all these are still relatives and this is better than letting the land lie idle. In fact this does not take any serious form, it is only an oral contract. If you return from working in the cities the land will be returned to you, no matter what. So these are only short term cases of land transfer (cf001).

However, even in Guizhou Province contract-based land transfer is becoming an important trend. The research report by Hu Rong'en (2010) documents numerous instances of large-scale land transfer involving several different modes.

A TRAGEDY OF THE ANTICOMMONS AND THE RISE OF THE SUPERTENANTS

The emerging market for farmland has become an effective tool for reshaping agriculture and the countryside in general. The empirical data of the cases presented above, especially in regard to rental price, time frame and breach of contract clauses, suggest a weak position for the lessors and a strong one for the tenants. The continued existence of collective land usage rights does not seem to have a negative impact on the agrarian transition in China. More to the contrary, the present configuration of the market for farmland with its low rental fees even contributes to this transition and gives agricultural entrepreneurs the opportunity for low-risk investments in agriculture. Why did the commodification of farmland turn out this way?

The first puzzle to solve is the growing supply of farmland. If one accepts the assumption that most of these land transfers are not forced upon rural households, and the interviews (see, for example, cf025) and other available sources suggest this, then we have to assume that the smallholders' judgment on the value of the land has changed over the course of the last years and long-term rentals have become more feasible for a growing subsection of the rural population. Some potential reasons for this have been discussed in chapter 4. However, given the secure status of their land usage rights for the coming years, the smallholders could also decide to just let their land lie idle. The danger of unused or underused farmland in light of China's relatively little endowment of farmland and all its activities to recover wasteland seems absurd. Still, the tendency of some villagers to neglect farmland was mentioned by many cadres in the field sites, especially in regions with high labor migration rates (for example, by cf006). The official figure for idle farmland is somewhere between 10 to 15 percent (Ruan 2011). But there are no statistics that take into account the massive amount of underused land. Doing nothing or only very little with one's land has indeed become an important option for many rural households. The only emerging alternative to this status quo appears to be the land rental arrangements discussed in this chapter. Yet, in this rental market the former smallholders seem to have a very weak bargaining position. The rental fees are low, the time frame is long, and the penalties for breach of contract are harsh. Why are villagers willing to accept these terms?

The influence of competing property regimes appears to be a crucial factor of the explanation. The commodification of farmland via a rental system has been designed as a layer on top of an administrative land management still rooted in the previous socialist land administration. Administrative rights of local governments to determine usage and to change ownership of farmland compete with individualized and commodified usage rights of the villagers. This arrangement has a huge impact on the actual value of the land for the villagers.

Michael Heller (1998) provides an interesting theoretic perspective to conceptualize the effects of collective ownership of farmland in China upon the willingness of farmers to accept sub-par contracts. Heller wondered why, after the economic transition in Russia in the early 1990s, kiosks[14] flourished while the storefronts right behind them remained empty. His explanation was neither corruption nor legal limitations for conducting business or even unclear property rights for these stores. For him, the fragmented nature of the property rights was to blame. In the same store, different actors had clearly defined rights to sell the property, to receive the sales revenue, to lease the store, to receive the lease revenue, to determine the use, and to occupy the store (see table in Heller 1998, 638). All of these actors could block other actors, who also have some rights, from engaging with the store in a more meaningful way. Heller chose to call this configuration a *tragedy of the anticommons.*

In contrast to the tragedy of the commons,[15] in which access to common pool resources is not limited by individual property rights and overuse of the resource in question is the consequence, in a tragedy of the anticommons underuse is a common result (Heller 1998, 639). The configuration of farmland in collective China shows considerable similarities to these Russian storefronts. In a similar manner, many "owners" have some rights on the same piece of land. The county level has the right to determine the usage of the land and receives the majority of the sales revenue if is sold as construction land, for example, to real estate investors. Higher levels of the administration as well as the township level will also profit from these transactions to some degree. The township level may even have an agenda of its own to (illegally) transform farmland to non-agricultural use.[16] The village collective, the formal owner of the land, has the least effective rights to the land but may nevertheless have plans to consolidate the land into more efficient holdings via cooperative organizations or mediation. The individual villagers have the right to farm, lease and receive the lease revenue. They do not have the right to change the usage of the land or to sell it to external actors. Villagers may block anyone who wants to farm on their land or intends to take it away and Beijing continues to strengthen these rights as documented earlier. Local governments in turn may block any transformation of the land usage away from farming initiated by the land usage rights holders. Ironically, as Heller notes for Russia, improving the legal protection of each of these conflicting rights under the conditions of a tragedy of the anticommons leads to even less effective use (Heller 1998, 631).

How can this tragedy of the anticommons for collective farmland in China be overcome? Heller's answer to the anticommons in Russia, inspired by his firm appreciation of a Western property rights perspective, is that fragmented property rights need to be unified into usable private property rights bundles. The Chinese government, however, seems less concerned with the question of how to maximize welfare for individual land usage rights holders, especially if this would involve any move toward a full privatization of land. This author argues that the Chinese central and local government have discovered the anticommons as a very useful tool to promote the transformation of agriculture, a usage that Heller could not anticipate from the Russian case. This argument is based upon the observation that many important policy tools for structural reform in agriculture take advantage of the current situation.

In order to make use of the anticommons, the Chinese state has created specific avenues to replace frustrated owners of usage rights with those individuals and organizations it deems better suited to achieve its goal of a modern, profitable, and efficient agriculture. For local cadres, considerable benefits correlate with this new policy direction as discussed in chapter 5. Villagers in the field sites, in turn, seemed willing to accept the commodification of their farmland via these instruments because this was one of the few options to profit at least to some degree from their limited property rights. During an interview session with several peasants, they concurred with this analysis (cf014).

The situation outlined in a report on the development of land transfer in Anju (Anjuqu Nongyebu 2009) may serve as another example to show the great interest local governments have in the continuation of the commodification of farmland via the rental system. The report mentions the case of Tucheng Village in Sanjia Town. Not unlike many other villages in Anju most of the labor force had left the village, leaving behind children and grandparents. Farming had become very inefficient and despite the good quality of the land productivity has been low. In May of 2006, one commercial farmer rented 185 mu from the villagers and in his first spring harvest already produced an output worth 160,000 RMB. This project alone increased the annual income of the villagers on an average by 300 RMB. It is these success stories the local governments are after. For them, underused land is the real problem for rural China and its agriculture. This had been a major argument in all locations (see, for example, cf022). In the view of the cadres, the only way to address this issue is to further ease the transfer of farmland to more competent operators, hence these cadres are willing to step in as an intermediary party, lowering transaction costs and providing transparency for all other actors involved. The goal is not to give the peasants the best value for their land but rather to improve the structure of production by any means. The implicit argument here is that villagers will profit more when their land is rented out to commercial farmers (through rental fees and wage labor), who not only know how to use far more advanced production technologies but also have the necessary connections for procurement. In other words, it is much easier to help create several large agricultural companies to take hold in a location than to raise the level of smallholder production to sustained profitability.

The new tenants in this emerging market for farmland are in a very advantageous position. They can cherry pick the best rental conditions from an abundant selection of available farmland. In most villages, they will also be able to select from a variety of cheap labor for their enterprise. As shown in the previous chapter, local governments and individual cadres depend upon enterprises and the support they provide for their operations. Because of this commercial tenants can count on substantial support from the local state. Compared to ordinary farming households government subsidies and loans are much easier to attain for them. The local government also prepares the rental contracts in most cases and ensures very competitive rates for the rent. Katherine Verdery has identified seemingly similar powerful tenants in Transylvania and coined the term *supertenant* for them. She explains:

> Their peculiar situation arose from the *rentier* society decollectivization had created: instead of many tenants seeking land from a few large owners, we have many owners and few tenants. I call them *supertenants* to indicate that even though they rented means of production belonging to others, their social situation was superior to that of their lessors. (Verdery 2003, 195)

While in her Romanian case study it was primarily the "wealth in terms of the expertise and connections necessary to make a go [in] farming" which enabled supertenants "to find value in land and bring it to fruition" (Verdery 2003, 312), in the Chinese case we have to add superior financial resources and political support to the mix. The preference for a certain group of tenants becomes not only implicitly evident via the configuration of the rental system, it is also explicitly mentioned in numerous policy documents, among them the "Suggestions of Qingdao Government on Speeding-up and Pushing Forward Appropriate Scale

Economies on Rural Land" (Qingzhengzi 2011) discussed earlier in this chapter or in various No. 1 documents in recent years.

An interesting question for further research would be how sustainable this dominant position of the tenants is. Institutional changes that introduce unified property rights bundles and put an end to the tragedy of the anticommons in collective land would greatly disrupt the current mode of commodification of farmland. Any changes to the commodification, however, would affect the overarching goals of agricultural modernization and rural–urban integration (at least in the way they are conceptualized now). These are two core goals for the Communist Party in China, used by the Party-State to legitimize itself. It seems, therefore, very unlikely that, if the current political system continues to exist in China, there will be changes to management of farmland in the near future.

There might be an additional reason for why Beijing has chosen this approach to the agrarian transition. The only feasible alternatives to a market based on the HRS would either be the privatization of collective farmland or its nationalization. Irrespective of ideological problems that such a move may create, it would push rural China into a stage of institutional transition with many uncertainties and potential risks for social stability. As noted in the first chapter, many scholars have argued against privatization because of the centrifugal forces for society that they assume to be attached to this move. Given the current narrative of land grab in the Chinese countryside centered on corrupt behavior of local governments, nationalization would also be very controversial.

One could argue that stability has become another major pillar of legitimacy the regime rests on[17] and that this currently is more important to Beijing than all the potential benefits of stepping up the transformation of the countryside through changes of the property regime. Looking at the past achievements in creating a market for agricultural land, such changes also do not seem to be a pressing issue.

SUMMARY

This chapter has dealt with the main questions raised in the introduction and provides a conceptualization of the commodification of farmland in China based upon the empirical data from the field sites. It shows how a layer of market-like transactions for land usage rights has been installed on top of a still existing socialist property regime. The first section of the chapter introduces the main characteristics of contract-based transfer of farmland in four townships in Anju. This section shows that many transfer contracts are framed to the disadvantage of the villagers holding land usage rights. The rental fees appear low, while the contracts have a long time frame and include unbalanced (and perhaps unfair) breach of contract clauses.

These transfers are in many ways only the first step toward a commodification. Beijing, still unsatisfied with the speed of the process, continues to twist the institutional framework and several new policy initiatives for land transfers have emerged. This development was the focus of the second section. The local practice of two of these initiatives, land transfer cooperatives and land transfer centers, was introduced in more detail. This section also discussed how these initiatives relate to the general strategy of "appropriate scale economies." Overall the great interest and involvement of the local state in the commodification of land was shown. The subsequent section presented the available data on the general prevalence of this type of land transfer in the field sites. Although an upward trend in the development of land transfer is clearly evident, Guizhou still lags behind the dynamic of the developments in Shandong and Sichuan.

The final section summed up the findings in a theoretical model for the commodification of farmland in China. It argued that, via the present framing of farmland into a usage rights system and the ongoing competition between various property regimes in the countryside, a tragedy of the anticommons in farmland has emerged. The farmland anticommons lead to an underuse of precious agricultural land because several actors share rights to the same resource and can exclude each other from more profitable use. Instead of trying to end this anticommons, for example, via the strengthening of property rights bundles for villagers, the Chinese central and local state are currently using it to push through structural changes in agriculture. A new type of agricultural tenant plays a crucial role in this process. These tenants have skills and resources to invest and are now taking advantage of the anticommons for making low-risk investments in commercial agriculture. In line with their dominant position in the Chinese countryside, these tenants are referred to as supertenants.

NOTES

1. A rice variety, which was sold in Anju for approximately 0.9 RMB per jin or half a kg in 2009.

2. Note that in China one administrative village (*xingzhengcun*) administers several natural villages (*zirancun*) or hamlets.

3. For a list of all contracts please refer to the appendix. The contracts have been given an indicator composed of "cmm", short for collected material, and a number (e.g., cmm001, cmm002, etc.) for easier reference.

4. However, there might also be a potential confusion of names here. In the interviews, the cadres speak of an enterprise called *Chenxing Agricultural Investment Company* (*Chenxing Nongye Touzi Gongsi*). It is possible but highly unlikely that the company of the contract and the company in the interviews are two separate organizations with similar sounding names.

5. Formal regulations actually prohibit more than one vice director. In addition to the director and the vice director, there is also a chief executive who manages the day-to-day business of the cooperative.

6. A Basic Agreement is set up for each cooperative individually and the parts following refer only to the Basic Agreement of Tanghe Village.

7. There are group memberships for other cooperative and even commercial organizations envisioned.

8. All of them located in Sanjia Town and Ximei Town.

9. For example in Suining, which had a land transfer service center at Anju District (see cf027).

10. On the Three Rural Problems, see the literature review and chapter 3.

11. The visit has been documented by taking numerous pictures for later analysis.

12. In reference to the modes outlined in the "Procedures for the Management of the Transfer of Contracted Usage Rights for Rural Land" (Nongyebu 2005) summarized in chapter 3.

13. The translation of *shidu guimo jingying* is tricky. The term could also imply moderate or proper scale economies.

14. Little stores on the sidewalks offering various consumer goods, from cigarettes and alcohol to toiletries.

15. Bromley (see chapter 2) would argue that Heller confuses common property with open access.

16. Many cases of illegal transformation of farmland into industrial parks or housing land have turned out to be very profitable—the coherence of the local community and the conscience of its leadership then being the important factors in deciding whether only a few or many benefited from this change. For the latter case, places such as Chen Village described by Chan et al. (2009) or Huaxi Village (Watts 2011) come to mind. As Chen (2004) pointed out, regional variances may be an important factor in how property rights work in China.

17. Peter Sandby-Thomas (2011), for example, argues that stability is a third main pillar of the legitimacy of the Party-State in China, next to economic development and nationalism.

SEVEN
Conclusion

The idea for this book was rooted in the realization of the puzzling nature of China's most recent transformation toward an increasingly commercial and industrialized agrarian production. In China, this transformation is taking place while the underlying collective nature of farmland ownership remains intact. Classical theories of agrarian transition suggest the importance of a commodification of farmland as one of the cornerstones of this process. China, it appears, managed to allow the emergence of a market for farmland in the absence of private ownership and with a set of institutions firmly rooted in its socialist past. This makes China's transition an interesting deviant case in international and historical comparison. Based upon this observation the core interest of the research presented here became the question of how this organization of farmland into collective ownership structures has affected the nature of the Chinese agrarian transition.

In the first part of this conclusion a synthesis of the empirical findings will be presented, structured by the three independent variables, property institutions, peasant differentiation, rural politics, and the dependent variable commodification of farmland. The presentation of the rural politics variable has been split into two sections, one looking at the role of the political center in Beijing and one covering the findings regarding the role of the local state for the agrarian transition. The second part of the conclusion puts the findings of this book in perspective to the ongoing debate about the nature and the future of Chinese agriculture.

SYNTHESIS OF FINDINGS

The Changing Nature of the HRS

Based upon a thorough investigation of legal documents, secondary literature and newspaper reporting, the book argues that Beijing has transformed the HRS from a system of egalitarian land distribution into an instrument for the modernization of agriculture. This book has identified three themes in the reforms of land administration that followed the introduction of the HRS. First, there have been considerable efforts to stabilize and improve the legal framework of the HRS. In consequence, the reform of agriculture in China is happening through the HRS and not despite of it. Second, a strong emphasis has been put on the goal of protecting the remaining farmland and recovering lost land for agriculture. Still, land loss appears to be an unresolved issue and a major threat for agriculture. Third and finally, the purpose of the HRS has been transformed from serving as the basis of a smallholder-centered agriculture to becoming a means for more and flexible access to farmland for commercial farming entities. Beijing wants to establish a "perfect market" for the transfer of land usage rights. All of these reforms have greatly affected the nature of the later commodification of farmland and the agrarian transition in China in general. In the following section, these three themes in land administration and the respective arguments of the book will be presented in more detail.

The first theme in land administration has been the continuing effort to install the HRS as the main point of reference for agricultural land usage and the strengthening of the villagers' rights to access land for farming through this system. In 1986, the first LAL established a legal framework for the new HRS. In the years that followed, the framework was constantly improved and new aspects were added. This early version of the LAL included regulations regarding the transfer of land, its usage and the registration of land usage rights contracts. The No. 11 Document of 1993, which initiated the move away from the frequent redistributions of land in the villages, is interesting also for what it is not. Many arguments presented in this policy document could actually be used to justify a privatization of collective land. However, with the No. 11 Document the Chinese central leadership has chosen to take a different and almost opposite path. Instead of privatization, the collective ownership of farmland and the HRS have been reinforced. The HRS is explicitly mentioned as being the basis of Chinese agriculture.

Three additional reforms serve as examples to highlight the importance the stabilization of the HRS has had for the center. While the "Opinion Regarding the Work to Complete in Agriculture and the Countryside in the Year 2001" called for bold structural changes in Chinese agriculture, it also emphasized that all of these changes needed to take place in accordance with the HRS. In 2002, the LCRL further improved the legal framework of the HRS and, for example, specifies the conditions under which contracted land is returned to the collective. Finally, albeit most of the 2007 Property Law concerns urban areas, there are several articles that also affect collective land. Most important among them is perhaps Article 126, which may prolong the villagers land usage rights contracts indefinitely.

The second major theme in rural land administration has been the intention to protect farmland for later agricultural usage. The weak institutional basis in collective ownership turned out to be a major disruptive influence for smallholder agriculture. Local governments could change the status of land and thereby transform collective land into state-owned construction land. The enormous profitability of this process, also related to the ridiculously low compensation for the former collective owner and the household holding the land usage rights (the latter still based upon the 1982 "Regulation for Land Requisitioning for National Construction [Projects]") has turned the transformation of farmland into construction land into one of the major risks for the future of Chinese agriculture.

Already in 1986, the LAL mentions the introduction of land usage master plans that were supposed to guide all land conversions and help to economize land usage. This seems to have produced insufficient results as the State Council published in 1994 the "Basic Regulations for the Protection of Farmland." With this document the center aimed to further clarify the regulations regarding the change of land usage, the monitoring of land usage, thereby improving the protection of farmland from conversion into construction land. In 2004, the State Council published the "Decision of the State Council to Deepen the Reform of a Strict Land Administration," which is notable in two regards. First, it is more or less an interesting admission that previous initiatives to protect arable land in China have not produced the intended outcomes. Second, in light of this admission the policy calls for the "strictest administration and control of the usage of farmland possible." In 2008, the "Decisions of Central Committee of the CPC Regarding Several Big Issues in Pushing Forward the Reform and Development of the Countryside" then introduced the concept of a so-called Red Line, which is a minimum of 1.8 billion mu of arable land in China, which should be protected by all means.

The third theme in the HRS reforms concerns efforts to make access to farmland more flexible for a commercializing agriculture. Already the 1988 Revision of the LAL legalized renting out land usage rights. This effectively was the starting point for the commodification of farmland for future agricultural use. Another important step was the No. 11 Document of 1993, which fixed land usage rights for 30 years. Before this reform, cadres had the right to redistribute farmland, officially taking into account changing household compositions among the villagers. In the aftermath of this policy, collective farmland lost much of its collective character and became an individualized asset for households, at least from the villagers' point of view. The 1993 AL reinforced this process with regulations that suggest that a former contractor should receive preferential treatment if land is redistributed (because the time frame of the contract has ended) and that the contractor's family would receive his land usage rights in case he or she dies. This individualization of access to land must be seen in light of the new efficiency debate in agriculture. Documents such as the 2001 Opinion mentioned earlier made clear that Beijing did not see the smallholders themselves being able to provide the much-needed impetus for structural change in rural China and that new actors in agriculture with flexible access to farmland would be necessary for the creation of commercial agriculture. Long-term fixed individualized land usage rights could provide a much better basis for a market-based exchange than the previous administratively redistributed access to farmland.

The 2002 LCRL then provided an improved institutional basis of land transfer activities and included clearer regulations and limitations. The LCRL defined four modes of land transfer (subcontracting, lease, exchange, and transfer) and left room for experiments with other modes of transfer. The LCRL also outlines core principles for any land transfer activities and introduces additional requirements for the transfer of land usage rights to village external groups. In 2005, the Ministry of Agriculture published the "Procedures for the Management of the Transfer of Contracted Usage Rights for Rural Land" that were intended to add further momentum to the development of a market for land transfer and to refine the process. The document also explains in detail the contents of the various modes of land transfer and lays out if and how they are affecting the HRS.

The 2008 "Decisions of Central Committee of the CPC Regarding Several Big Issues in Pushing Forward the Reform and Development of the Countryside" is the latest step forward for the commodification of farmland in China. Although the importance of the HRS to protect the interests of the farmers and to stop land loss is noted here, the current distribution of farmland is seen as being unsuitable for the creation of a modern agriculture. Therefore, the 2008 Decisions call for the "creation of a 'perfect market' for the transfer of land usage rights" (*jianli jianquan tudi chengbao jingyingquan liuzhuan shichang*). There is a huge difference in tone and content between the original basis of the HRS and the 2008 Decisions.

Rural Politics: Fading-Out Smallholding

The book argues that a negative view on smallholding has taken hold at the political center. In an environment of rapid economic growth and a huge and growing income gap between rural and urban areas, agrarian efficiency and raising rural incomes have become the main concerns in Beijing's reform initiatives. Smallholding is seen as being unable to contribute much to either of these goals. This negative view on smallholding is increasingly reflected in structural reform policies. Since at least 2001 several official documents have openly advocated fading out smallholding in China. In the following section, the rise of the efficiency paradigm to fame, as documented in the book, will be summarized.

There have been at least three waves in rethinking efficiency in agriculture. The No. 11 Document in 1993, which is most famous for prolonging the land usage right contracts to thirty years, is also one of the first legal signs that the center envisioned a change in the structure of agriculture. This document already justifies the changes made to the HRS with regard to shortcomings in productivity and decreasing investments in agriculture. In other words, the central government legitimizes its move away from the system of egalitarian redistribution with concerns over the efficiency of land usage. The document also advocates the rearrangement of land into bigger holdings in order to create economies of scale.

The breakthrough for a structural reform in agriculture, however, came with the "Opinion Regarding the Work to Complete in Agriculture and the Countryside in the Year 2001" (Zhonggong Zhongyang Guowuyuan 2001). This document firmly establishes the role of the efficiency paradigm as an important cornerstone in Chinese agricultural policies. It argues that structural inefficiencies were the major reason for the low-income levels of the rural population. Instead of catching up with urban areas, rural regions were falling further behind. The 2001 Opinion argues that the only way out of this mess and thereby the only way to maintain rural stability would be to conduct a thorough structural reform of agriculture that puts emphasis upon the quality and the efficiency of agriculture. The key argument in the 2001 Opinion is that "if 900 million peasants do not change their ways of earning a living, peasant prosperity will never take off, and the modernization of the countryside will be difficult to realize." Not the peasants but rather a new set of actors should drive the transformation of agriculture. The 2001 Opinion lists in particular the role of Dragonhead enterprises to provide a link between local producers and the market.

The 2008 "Decisions of Central Committee of the CPC Regarding Several Big Issues in Pushing Forward the Reform and Development of the Countryside" (Zhongfa 2008a) reemphasize this vision. The new agriculture should be defined by high yields, high quality, high levels of efficiency in the production process, the protection of environmental resources, more security for the producers, the use of scientific methods and modern equipment, and the integration of food production and processing. In this vision, almost no part of agriculture remains untouched. Structural reform, including more and bigger Dragonheads, is seen as the key to raising rural incomes and narrowing the rural-urban income gap.

New operations of scale should be installed wherever the proper conditions exist. Similar arguments consistently have appeared in all of the No. 1 documents of the State Council and the Standing Committee of the CPC since 2006. Although the program to create a *New Socialist Countryside* introduced with the 2006 No. 1 Document included many aspects beyond agriculture, agricultural upgrading was among its top priorities. The No. 1 documents integrated many aspects of a structural reform outlined previously. For example, it also called for further promotion of the transfer of land usage rights.

Through these policy changes the center emerges as a major promoter of an agrarian transition in China. This becomes even more evident if the scope of the investigation is broadened to include other changes in rural politics.

Local Government Support for the Agrarian Transition

The book argues that the local state in China has become a staunch proponent of agrarian transition. It further argues that the almost unconditional support for a structural transformation of agriculture, the implementation of related policies of the center, and the creation of additional local initiatives are related to the great political, economic, and moral pressure these local governments are under. Promoting agrarian transition appears to help leading local cadres to take some of the pressure from their shoulders. The pro-active role in agrarian transition also affects the position of the local state toward the commodification of land. In many locations, local cadres have become the main architects of a market for farmland.

In line with much of the secondary literature the fieldwork has shown that there is a huge mismatch between the tasks local governments at the township and county level have to provide, for example, in public service delivery and infrastructure construction, and the funding they have at their disposal. Revenues had been mediocre and local governments especially complained about their limited tax revenue. Financial difficulties certainly have contributed to the spread of many "creative" funding mechanisms and the great dependence of local governments on land sales. Political pressure arises from the goal of local officials to rise within the nomenclature system and the importance of performing well within an internal monitoring and evaluation system in order to achieve this. Only cadres who have received the best evaluation ratings have good chances to advance. There is, perhaps, a third kind of pressure for local cadres, which may have received too little attention in the discussion so far. This is the moral pressure on local governments and originates from three different sources: a carefully constructed narrative by the center in Beijing to put the blame for corruption in the political system on the local state, reports about clashes between the local state and the village population that increasingly undermine the legitimacy of the local state in many locations, and the moral pressure many cadres feel because they see themselves as the responsible body to bring about positive changes for the countryside.

The findings presented suggest that agrarian transition and the implementation of respective policies of the political center offer local governments and the officials within them an almost magical way to address all three of these pressures at the same time, although perhaps to varying degrees. Somewhat surprisingly, tax effects and other institutionalized forms of new income linked to a successful agrarian transition appear to be limited (at least from a short-term perspective). However, new local companies replacing the smallholders provide local governments with additional funding sources in addition to those of the official channels. The payoff in the political arena might be more important. Central policies regarding agrarian transition have been tightly integrated into the official monitoring and evaluation system for local governments. The evaluation system in Anju, for example, put high priority on GDP growth, investments and attraction of investors, average peasant income, government revenue, and fixed investments/assets—all related to an agrarian transition. In order to get the best evaluation results and to improve their career prospects, these cadres had almost no choice but to pursue the structural transformation of agriculture. The moral and ideological opportunities related to agrarian transition seem especially rich for local officials. For example, the mission to create higher rural incomes is used to legitimize their preference for commercial agricultural enterprises over smallholders. The interviews also suggest that the center's agrarian transition rhetoric allows local officials to neglect the previous dominant food security paradigm and more or less openly argue against the value of grain production.

The embracing of the agrarian transition by local governments is a crucial factor influencing the nature of the commodification of farmland. Local governments have emerged as a catalytic factor in creating markets for farmland for continued agricultural usage. This is also done to attract new commercial actors in agriculture. Among these actors Dragonhead enterprises seem especially interesting for local cadres, as they are administratively connected to considerable financial support and political reward.

Peasant Differentiation and the Devaluation of Farmland

The research design has characterized peasant differentiation, the process in which smallholders diversify their livelihood strategies, as one of the core processes of an agrarian transition. On the one hand, smallholders who give up farming and take on wage labor provide the necessary labor force for an emerging industrialized agriculture (and of course industry in general). On the other hand, the land of these former smallholders may become the basis of larger landholdings.

The findings presented in this book suggest that the differentiation of the peasantry in China indeed has become an important factor for the commodification of farmland and the transformation of agriculture. A growing need for more monetary income and the huge differences in income opportunities between smallholding and other occupations appears to be a major driving force in peasant differentiation. Since the economic reforms in China in the early 1980s many public services that did not exist earlier or traditionally had been provided for free to the rural population became costly paid-for services—education and health care perhaps being the prime examples of this development.

Smallholding in China seems to struggle to provide the income necessary to fully participate in modern society and the gap between the monetary income needed and the income possible in smallholding appears to even increase over time. The resulting frustration of the rural population with smallholding fuels two developments of crucial importance for the commodification of farmland. First, given huge and growing income differences between income from urban wage labor and smallholding, the continuation of the rural-urban mass migration in China seems very likely. The general attractiveness of urban life for the younger generation in the countryside may be an additional factor in this development. Higher migration rates imply even higher rates of idle or underused land (in the present system of fixed land usage rights). The second aspect is a devaluation of farmland for ordinary rural households. If the land is not the primary source of income for the household, it loses its economic importance. This rationale, described in detail by Verdery (2003) for Transylvania, appears to also exist in contemporary rural China. In consequence, villagers have become more open-minded in regard to rental arrangement for rural land as it is a relatively secure option to receive at least some financial income from the land usage rights. In the remaining parts of this section, the underlying argument of an existing frustration in smallholding will be explored in more depth.

In the face of growing monetary income needs one would assume that smallholders would as a first means aim to professionalize their production and become commercial farmers. Indeed, the emergence of family-based commercial farming entities such as specialized households (*nongye dahu*) and family-farms (*jiating nongchang*) is an important trend in the countryside. Another trend is the integration of farmers into commercial operations on a contractual basis, as described by Zhang (2012) and Huang (2011). Even more frequently seen, however, are households that withdraw their primary labor force from agriculture. Five major reasons for the frustration of smallholders that may prevent them from becoming commercial farmers have been discussed in this book.

First, the distribution and the quality of the land available for small-holders was a major influence in the decision made by farmers in the field sites to engage in commercial agriculture. Especially in Sichuan the land available per capita was sparse and fragmented. Statistics for the field sites show that the land available for farming has shrunk considerably since the beginning of the economic reforms. The efforts of the central and the local governments to reclaim lost farmland do not appear to be geared to the needs of smaller farming entities. The structure and direction of the subsidies for agrarian production are the second reason for smallholder frustration. Secondary literature clearly shows an upward trend in subsidies for agrarian production but notes that most of this support is directed to already economically successful households and enterprises. The findings from the field sites seem to confirm this picture. The subsidies paid to smallholders do not increase the profitability or competitiveness of small- and sub-scale farming entities. Commercial farmers, able to invest in greenhouses or livestock farming, are likely to receive much higher rates of financial support. The third reason for smallholder frustration arises from the dependence upon chemical inputs for agrarian production in China. Fertilizers, herbicides, and pesticides are the nuts and bolts of Chinese agriculture. Given the small amount of farmland available in China these chemicals are needed for the intensive farming practiced. The costs for them, however, have increased tremendously in recent years and seem to negate all positive effects of the increase in subsidies for agriculture. Fourth, smallholders still have great difficulties in getting the capital needed for a commercial agrarian production. This difficulty has been widely noted in the literature presented in chapter 4. Finally, many of the remaining smallholders are part of an older generation lacking the necessary skills and motivation to move from subsistence farming to commercial operations of scale. Given the scare resources of local governments adequate official support for this transformation for the peasantry is questionable.

Many if not all of the factors listed above could be considered political in nature. The lack of funding, the lack of affordable inputs, and the quality of the land are also the consequence of government action or the lack of it. Chapter 3 documents that the profitability of family farming in China since its return in the early 1980s was subject to political decisions from the very first days of its existence. In parts of the mainstream literature, the return to family farming in the early 1980s is presented as the trigger for enormous economic growth and rising incomes in the countryside. The book has taken a closer look at this claim and argues that the center may have had different and perhaps more important motives in embracing family farming than economic efficiency. Although output and diversity of agricultural production had increased in most locations after the land was given back to households to farm, the increases in economic growth and rural incomes were also linked to two factors *not* directly connected to the restructuring of agriculture into smallholding. First, in the beginning Beijing was willing to support the new family-based farming with very favorable terms of trade through the procurement system. The unsustainable nature of this model only became apparent when the center changed its procurement policy in 1985. This had a considerable negative impact upon the income of smallholders and their ability to make a living in agriculture. Later changes in market prices and the inflation in 1986 reinforced these effects. Smallholding never fully recovered from these changes. Second, job opportunities outside of agriculture may have been more important for rising incomes in the countryside than structural changes in agriculture. It must be noted that the continuation of the peasant differentiation in China should not be seen as proof that smallholder farming in general is less productive than larger commercial agricultural enterprises but rather that the conditions for it have been particularly bad.

The Commodification of Farmland and the Tragedy of the Anticommons

The commodification of farmland in China is based upon a rental system. Villagers, the owners of temporary exclusive land usage rights, rent out these rights in exchange for monetary compensation. The conditions of the transfer are fixed in rental contracts. Sometimes the new lessors are also made the offer to work for their tenants, but this is rarely included in the written contracts. The contract-based transfer of land is legally binding and thereby arguably different from former informal types of exchange of the land usage rights between family and friends. In addition, these contract-based exchanges of land are increasingly embedded in varying policy frameworks provided for the transfer.

While the existence of such rental markets has been suggested by the analysis of the legal framework and secondary literature, research on the nature of these institutions in rural practice has been very limited so far. One main finding presented in this book has been that there are strong asymmetric power relationships between lessors and tenants in this new rental market. As indicators for relative power three different aspects of the rental contracts have been selected for closer examination: the rental fee, the time frame of the contracts, and the penalties for a breach of contract. Examining rental contracts from four townships in Anju District it is argued that the rental fees are relatively modest, most of them between 300 and 500 RMB/mu/year. These rates are not related to revenue or profit created on the fields (which is many times higher) and are fixed for the whole time frame of the contract (with some adjustment for inflation). Many rental contracts examined have long time frames and expire with the original 30 years of the land usage rights. The breach of contract clauses in the rental contracts also tend to favor the entrepreneurial tenants considerably.

A second major finding in regard to the commodification of the farmland is the growing importance of the local state as an intermediary actor in bringing together lessors and tenants in the rental market and thereby in facilitating the exchange. A set of policy tools for this purpose has been implemented in all field sites. These instruments share several features: they are based upon the legal framework of the HRS, aim for long-term and large-scale land transfer, and envision a pro-active role by the local government. The analysis in this book has been focused on two of these instruments, the land transfer cooperatives and the land transfer service centers, which provide interesting examples because they are based on two different conceptions of the role of the local state for local development.

Land transfer cooperatives employ a cooperative model for the transfer of farmland. Villagers enter the cooperative with their land (or parts of it). The cooperative then consolidates the land of several households into one holding and either rents out the land to external investors or starts farming by itself. The main purpose for their creation is to make better use of the villagers' farmland by any means. Therefore the cooperative should start farming by itself if there are no suitable external investors. The existence of these cooperatives shows that policy makers still believe in collective-type organizations (or at least support them, if necessary) and distrust the existing structures and actors in their ability to create the necessary momentum for land transfer. The cooperatives are created in a way that builds on strong local government support. Finally, the cooperatives are based upon the narrative that smallholding is an inefficient form of agricultural production and even reinforce this narrative.

In contrast to the land transfer cooperatives, the land transfer service centers embody a different understanding of the role local governments in the transformation of agriculture. At the core of this approach is the belief that the new Chinese agriculture should be based upon private enterprises and an (almost) private land market. The service centers have been constructed only to facilitate the exchange between two parties and little more. The idea of providing a service runs very strong in this policy tool. Goals for the performance of these land transfer service centers are integrated into the performance contracts of leading cadres. Not only is the existence of these centers checked (as is the case with the land transfer cooperatives) but also the amount of land transferred, the services provided and similar aspects. These service centers have been created within the administration and are formally independent of the community and investors they are intended to assist—in contrast to the cooperative model presented above.

Policy instruments such as the just introduced land transfer cooperatives and the land transfer service centers are part of a larger strategy to create economies of scale in agriculture and crucially depend on local government action. To provide more evidence for this hypothesis the newly published strategy of the Qingdao City government to create "economies of appropriate scale" was discussed. This strategy calls for even more land transfer, an increase in the transparency of the transfers in order to counter any reservations the rural population still might hold, and an increase in the pressure on local governments to bring about agrarian modernization and in this regard also to allow new innovative policy experiments that provide alternative and perhaps improved ways to transfer farmland.

How to conceptualize these findings of the commodification of farmland in China in light of the empirical data presented earlier? I argue that the emerging market for collective farmland is based upon a *tragedy of the anticommons*. This term, introduced by Michael Heller (1998), is an interesting play on the well-known *tragedy of the commons*. A tragedy of the commons describes when a resource is overused because everyone aims to maximize profits and no effective means for exclusion exists. A tragedy of the anticommons, in contrast, comes into existence if there are several actors that hold conflicting exclusive rights to the same property and are able to block each other. The tragedy of the anticommons is a tragedy of underuse. It is argued in this book that for the management of farmland in China various property regimes and ultimately various actors compete for influence upon the same farmland. This is the result of a very unique configuration of farmland management via the HRS. In effect, a layer of tradable land usage rights has been installed on top of a socialist property management system. Administrative, owner, and user rights now compete with each other. Local governments (mostly at the county level) manage the very profitable market for construction land and are the only actor with the power to transform the usage of farmland. Their rights to do this supersede the rights of the village collective and the individual land usage rights holders to exclude other parties from using the farmland for agricultural purposes. The current rental market for farmland is a product of this constellation.

The empirical findings suggest that smallholders engage in this market because farming in many parts of the countryside has become a frustrating experience. The traditional perspective on the value of land as discussed in the second chapter appears to continuously lose importance for a growing subset of the rural population. In the absence of private ownership (and the option to sell the land), the rental market for farmland is the second best option to profit, at least to some degree, from one's land usage rights. The central government in Beijing and local administrations are well aware of this tragedy of the anticommons, as their strategies for agricultural modernization envision the transfer of unused or underused land to commercial operations of scale. Several new policy instruments have been designed to provide additional incentives for villagers and investors to participate in this transfer and to ease the process.

The conditions in the rental market and the focus of agricultural subsidies show a strong bias toward the new tenants. There are interesting similarities to other post-socialist countries. Katherine Verdery has reported on a tenancy market in Romania in which many villagers had small pockets of land they could not or did not want to farm anymore and commercial tenants who would use this situation to their benefit. These tenants were able to dictate very favorable terms for them in tenancy agreements. She chose to refer to this group of tenants as "supertenants." This term and its meaning seem to fit the conditions in the present Chinese countryside very well.

THE NATURE OF CHINESE AGRICULTURE

How does the research presented here relate to the existing debate on the nature of Chinese agriculture and its future? My findings suggest that there are at least three potential misconceptions in this debate. The first misconception is that collective land and the HRS have an important protective function of sorts for rural households. The second misconception is the assumption of a healthy smallholding agriculture in China that only needs protection from negative external influences in order to prosper. The third misconception is that the restructuring of agriculture toward larger commercial operations is a natural process in an increasingly market-oriented society.

Especially among Chinese scholars the connotation exists that the collective ownership of farmland is a powerful protective instrument for the rural population. There are several different angles to this protective argument. As noted previously, the prominent Chinese scholar of rural affairs Wen Tiejun (2006) has, for example, described collective land usage rights as a type of "social protection" (*shehui baozhang*) for Chinese farmers. Irrespective of faltering urban employment opportunities or villagers' financial difficulties—their land usage rights and thereby their means to make a living cannot be taken from them. Zhang and Donaldson (2008; 2010) highlight a different kind of protection. Because of the collective nature of farmland it provides protection against enclosure, a real threat in many other transitory nations. There should be considerable skepticism about both sides of this protective claim.

Qin Hui (2003; 2007) has already pointed to several weaknesses of the argument that collective land usage rights are a form of efficient social protection. For example, how does having access to farmland back in one's village help against sickness, age, or unemployment in the short-run? Requirements in terms of the preparation of the land and physical labor in agriculture exist which seriously impact the social protective functions of land usage rights. Leaving out these limitations for a moment, there may even be another new and disruptive change in this regard. In the advent of long-term land rental contracts without any option for early termination, there is little left in regard to any social protective functions of land usage rights. Still, the theme of the social protective function of farmland is running strong among a subset of scholars in China, particularly in the New Rural Reconstruction movement, and also gets mentioned frequently by local officials.

The more interesting protective argument is the one made by Zhang and Donaldson. They argue that the collective nature of the farmland should be seen as an effective means of protection against enclosure of smallholder land by big commercial and capitalist enterprises. Rightfully they point out that legal regulations in place prohibit any change in ownership. Underlying this view is the assumption of an inherent profitability of one's land usage rights—if not in a commercial sense then at least to secure the subsistence needs of households. They do not consider the fact that farmers would want to leave farming and their land behind because they are threatened in their survival. Earlier studies on agrarian transition, for example the previously cited classical works of Brenner and Polanyi, have noted that the failure of smallholders to survive under the conditions of capitalist competition has been a powerful driver for the transfer of farmland to new groups. This kind of transfer is characterized not by brute force but by economic pressure. This is exactly what appears to take place in many locations in China, including the field sites. The legal protection included within the collective ownership framework provides little protection against this.

Dysfunctional smallholding seems to be more common than the rising numbers for rural income and economic growth suggest. In many locations, only a move to cash crops will produce sustainable incomes in smallholding. This step demands not only capital, political support, and necessary skills—it also needs a risk-taking farming population. Many of the younger generation, however, have already left the countryside because urban or wage employment provides a better living with fewer risks, a factor which is not adequatley considered by authors such as Philip Huang (2011) arguing for "new-age farms" in China. The frustration of smallholders with farming is based upon structural and political conditions that are very unlikely to change soon.

The third possible misconception is the idea that the present transformation of Chinese agriculture is a natural development that reflects the influence of an expanding market economy in China. This view negates the influence of the state and its agents upon the central and local level for the transformation of Chinese agriculture. In China, a very interesting dichotomy exists between the large increases in rural subsidies and a strong pro-peasant rhetoric by the Hu/Wen administration on the one hand, which are used by many Chinese scholars and cadres as evidence that the Chinese central state now has taken on the plight of smallholding villagers and, on the other hand, the effects of structural reform policies on the ground. Although indeed there have been several improvements for the rural population in recent years, smallholding or family-based farming certainly does not enjoy preferential treatment by local and central officials. The unfavorable terms of trade and the low procurement prices since the mid-1980s, the high costs for agricultural chemicals and machinery, the new financial burden in education and health care for villagers, the difficulties of farm households in acquiring capital for production in comparison with the support given to larger commercial investors, all these factors speak volumes. In the current economic and political context, the efficiency of smallholding does not really matter in the market. State agencies have already begun to phase out smallholding in favor of new commercial operations. The frustration of the peasantry, the agenda of the state, and the interest of commercial actors create a special dynamic for the transformation of agriculture in China. At the core of this process is the transfer of farmland to commercial farmers, the commodification of farmland.

Appendix: Data Collection and Field Sites

The excellent online databases Wanfang and Beidafabao (accessed via *crossasia.org*) were used to obtain national and local policy documents. Given the nature of the Chinese political system, laws in specific policy fields are frequently supplemented by documents that carry in their title "notice" (*tongzhi*), "opinion" (*yijian*), or "regulation" (*tiaoli*) (for more details on naming conventions of official documents see Zhongbanfa [1996]). In the past, access to these documents from abroad was difficult, online databases such as the aforementioned Wanfang greatly ease the process now.

Still, many interesting reform initiatives and policy experiments in China are well hidden within the formal documentation system. Major Chinese newspapers such as the *Renmin Ribao* and magazines such as *Caijing*, however, report on these experiments on a regular basis. Therefore, the author has put into place a system that automatically screens these sources' online articles for relevant news.

Additional empirical data for this book was collected in fieldwork between 2008 and 2010. As part of two joint projects by the China Center for Global Governance and Development in Beijing, Tübingen University and Duisburg-Essen University, the author of this book took part in three field trips to rural China. The projects were funded by the DFG (Deutsche Forschungsgesellschaft, German Research Association) and the BMBF (Bundesministerium für Bildung und Forschung, German Federal Ministry of Education and Research). Although the field sites were ultimately chosen in cooperation with the Chinese partner institution, the choice of the province and the degree of local economic development had been jointly planned beforehand. The main research objective of both projects was to improve our understanding of the role of local cadres for policy implementation. We chose to focus on a policy called *Building a New Socialist Countryside* (*Shehui zhuyi xin nongcun jianshe*, XNCJS), which at the time was among the top priorities of local cadres.

The selection of field sites for the case study brings with it some limitations. Although the field sites were also chosen to reflect differences in regional classification and economic development, the primary goal was to find out more about cadre behavior in the context of XNCJS. It is safe to assume that the Chinese partner institution would not have selected locations with known serious issues in their policy implementation work. Therefore, a small false-positive selection bias may exist.[1] Furthermore, given the sheer size of China, large proportions of the country did not enter this research. Especially more remote locations, far from any highway and the main grain production areas were not part of this study. The book may therefore present results that have less authority in these regions, although one may argue that the effects of the processes described here may only have been delayed for these regions for now.

The field sites for the first two years included a coastal region, Laixi, a county-level city (*xianji shi*) belonging to the vice-provincial city of Qingdao in Shandong Province and Anju, a recent county-turned-district (*qu*) under the administration of the prefectural city Suining, in the Western province of Sichuan. Both locations qualify as average or slightly above average economically developed in comparison with the surrounding areas. In the first two years, the focus of the fieldwork was almost equally split between the county-level administration and lower levels (township and village level). Semi-structured interviews with a major focus on the *New Socialist Countryside* policy were conducted with officials on these levels of the local government. A subset of the questions dealt with land transfer and new types of agrarian production. The data gathered in this regard in the first two years of fieldwork was especially rich and forms the empirical basis of the later analysis on the commodification of farmland in rural China.

In 2010, Guizhou Province was chosen as a new focus for the research project. Two counties were selected for further investigation, Meitan County and Xifeng County. During this investigation, more emphasis was put on interviews with administrators at the county level. Although several trips to lower levels of the administration were made, the data gathered, especially in regard to land transfer, lacks in detail compared to the previous two years. The data from Guizhou is therefore mainly used for comparison.

The questions on land transfer and new forms of agrarian production were not seen as sensitive or problematic, as, for example, those dealing with rural finances and the results of cadre evaluation. On several occasions local cadres started to introduce land transfer projects or Dragonhead enterprises as personal pet-projects—independent of any previous inquiry. The changes in agriculture and the end of smallholding were viewed favorably by a large majority of administrators. Discontent among the local population with these developments seemed limited. Yet, given the form and organization of the field trips, it was difficult to speak with villagers independently. In most cases, we entered the townships and villages in vehicles of higher-level administrators, who had informed everyone about our arrival. Most interviews were conducted with one representative of our Beijing partner institute present. Furthermore, a local student had been hired to document the interviews. These students used a recording machine for the interviews and produced a transcribed version in Chinese. The usage of the recording machine never came up as a problematic issue.

It must be noted that in all four locations a high number of villagers had left for urban locations as migrant workers. The agricultural labor force appeared overly feminized and elderly. All locations were rather well-connected with nearby urban centers, the two counties in Guizhou less so than the locations in Shandong and Sichuan. In the following section, the most important socio-economic data on the four field sites will be presented.

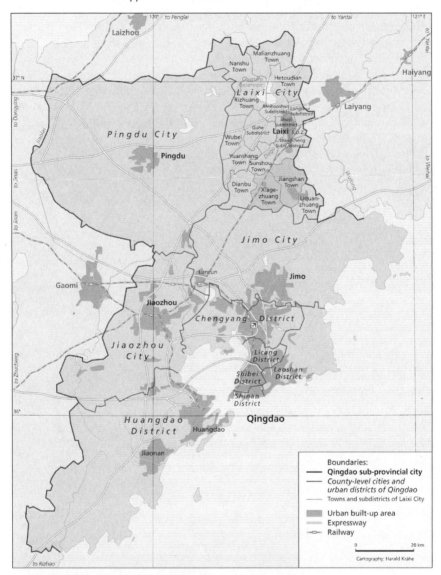

Qingdao. Reproduced with permission from Harald Krähe.

Laixi

The county-level city of Laixi administers eleven towns and four subdistricts (*jiedao*), a provincial level economic development park (*shengji jingji kaifa qu*), and 862 administrative villages (Laixishi Renmin Zhengfu 2009c). The administrative region covers an area of 1,568 sq km (Shandong Provinicial Statistics Bureau 2010, 729). In 2008, cadres reported that the average rural income in 2007 was 7,159 RMB, 14.4 percent more than the year before—representing then the highest year-to-year increase in the last ten years. They also mentioned that since 2002 income had increased by 3,214 RMB and therefore had almost doubled in five years (see cf022). In 2011, the average rural income in Laixi rose to 12,048 RMB, representing an 18.66 percent year-to-year increase (Qingdaoshi Laixishi Tongjiju 2012). The same source stated that the total population in Laixi was 736,323 in 2011. Laixi is well known for its agriculture and about one-third of all peanuts produced in China originate here (cf024). Fieldwork was mainly conducted in two towns, Xiagezhuang and Jiangshan.

Xiagezhuang Town (*Xiagezhuang Zhen*) has 54 administrative villages and a population of 33,000 or 10,300 households in 2008. In total, the agricultural land amounts for 89,000 mu, which translates into 2.7 mu per capita on average (this is double the national average of 1.3 mu). A major part of the local economy consisted of horticulture in greenhouses, with more than 1,400 existing in 2008. Other important branches are animal husbandry and food processing, with the *Jiulong* Group as a major actor and model for further expansion (Xiagezhuangzhen Renmin Zhengfu 2008).[2] Jiangshan Town (*Jiangshan Zhen*) spreads over 122 sq km and 57 administrative villages. It has a population of 66,000 in 13,000 households. According to the Party Committee the average rural income in 2007 was 7,618 RMB (Jiangshanzhen Dangwei 2008). A data sheet gathered in 2009 showed an average rural income of 7,759 RMB for 2007 and 8,597 RMB, an increase of 10.8 percent, for 2008 (Jiangshanzhen Dangwei 2009).

Suining. *Reproduced with permission from Harald Krähe.*

Anju

Anju District is one of the newest county-turned-district in all of China. It spans over 1,258 sq km and had 810,000 inhabitants in 2009, of which 706,000 had a rural resident registration. Anju belongs to the administration of the prefectural city of Suining, which is located halfway between Chengdu and Chongqing. These two regions have recently been granted the status of special developmental zones for rural-urban integration. Cadres in Anju occasionally mentioned land transfer initiatives in one of these two locations as an inspiration for their own work. All parts of the Suining administrative region, including Anju, have a very bad land per capita rate (0.925 mu) and high rates of labor migration (see Anjuqu Nongyebu 2009). The average income in 2007 was 3,568 RMB

(Suiningshi Tongjiju 2008, 7). Anju District has 21 towns and townships of which the following four were visited: Yufeng Town (*Yufeng Zhen*), Anju Town (*Anju Zhen*), Changli Township (*Changli Xiang*), and Majia Township (*Majia Xiang*).

Yufeng Town is located in the west of Anju District. According to the website of the local government it had 23 administrative villages and a population of 31,575 in 8,735 households in 2011, of which 8,783 had left the town as labor migrants. The town has 31,460 mu of farmland (Yufengzhen Renmin Zhengfu 2012). In interviews, local cadres mentioned that the average income in 2009 was between 5,300–5,400 RMB (cf012). The website claims that in 2011 the average income was 6,420 RMB. Anju Town has 41 administrative villages and 7 districts (*shequ*). The population stands at 74000, farmland at more than 42,700 mu. In 2007, the GDP was 420 million RMB, the average income reached 3,415 RMB (cf018). Majia Township is located halfway between Anju District and Suining City (both are 35 km away), at the border of Sichuan and Chongqing. According to the township leadership it has a population of about 20,000, of which 9,000 have already left as migrant workers. The remaining population is mostly very old or very young, sick and/or female in their composition. The average rural income in 2008 was about 3,800 RMB, but cadres expected for 2009 an income of up to 4,200 RMB (cf011). Changli Township is spread over 25 administrative villages. The township, like the whole district, is famous for a local variety of pears ("Golden Pears," *huangjin li*), of which it had already 14,000 mu planted in 2008 and was aiming for another 1,500 mu by the end of 2009 (cf036). During the interviews in 2009, the township head estimated a population of 27,000 for the township. The average income for the whole township in 2008 was just above 2,300 RMB (cf027). Changli was the poorest township of all field sites visited.

Guizhou. *Reproduced with permission from Harald Krähe.*

Meitan

Meitan County, a stretch of 1,864 sq km of land, is 70 km from the prefectural city Zunyi and 220 km from the provincial capital Guiyang. It has a population of 480,000 spread over 9 towns, 6 townships and 131 villages (Meitanxian Renmin Zhengfu 2010). In 2009, the average rural income was 5,594 RMB (Zunyishi Tongjiju 2010, 404). In 1987, Meitan was selected as one of 14 experimental zones[3] for the newly established HRS. In December of 1987, 369 villages in 47 towns and townships were chosen for the implementation of a modified version of the HRS that did not allow for any adjustments to the distribution of land based on changes in the composition of households (in other words, redistributions based on births and deaths were not allowed anymore), which later became national policy. In 1998, Meitan was selected as the first county in China in which land usage rights were granted for fifty years (instead of the usual 30 years) (Meitan Dangxiao 2010). As mentioned earlier, most interviews in Meitan (and Xifeng for that matter) took place at the county level, with the exception of some field trips to villages and local enterprises.

Xifeng

Xifeng County spreads over 1,036.5 sq km. In 2009, it had a population of 250,400, of which 218,100 (87.1 percent) had a rural household registration (see Guiyangshi tongjiju 2010, 418). Agricultural land stood at 228,300 mu, the per capita land ratio therefore is 1.05 mu.[4] Local documents show a considerable economic dynamic in Xifeng. In 2008, the average rural income was 3,802, which was a 19.3-percent increase from the year before. In 2009, the income was 4,343 RMB, a 14.2-percent increase (Guiyangshi tongjiju 2010, 419). The county is famous for its many historic sites related to the *Long March* and heavily invests in promoting "red" tourism to these locations.

List of all interviews mentioned

Identifier	Date	Location	Rank of Cadre(s)
cf001	September 3, 2010	Xifeng	Township
cf004	September 17, 2008	Anju	District
cf006	September 11, 2008	Suining	City
cf007	September 4, 2009	Anju	Township, Village
cf008	September 8, 2009	Anju	District
cf009	September 8, 2009	Anju	District
cf010	September 8, 2009	Anju	District
cf011	September 7, 2009	Anju	Township
cf012	September 7, 2009	Anju	Township
cf013	September 16, 2008	Anju	Township
cf014	September 16, 2008	Anju	Village, Township,

			villager delegation
cf015	September 19, 2008	Suining	City
cf016	September 11, 2008	Anju	Township/ Village
cf017	September 10, 2010	Guiyang	various scholars from Guiyang
cf018	September 12, 2008	Anju	Township, Village
cf019	September 10, 2009	Suining	City
cf020	September 17, 2008	Anju	District
cf021	September 4, 2009	Anju	Township, Village
cf022	September 4, 2008	Laixi	County
cf023	September 4, 2008	Laixi	County
cf024	September 4, 2008	Laixi	County
cf025	August 21, 2009	Laixi	County
cf026	September 1, 2008	Laixi	County, Township, Village
cf027	September 4, 2009	Anju	Township
cf028	September 8, 2008	Qingdao	Vice-Provincial
cf029	September 17, 2008	Anju	County
cf030	September 2, 2010	Xifeng	County
cf031	September 11, 2009	Chengdu	Sichuan Academy of Social Science
cf033	August 31, 2008	Laixi	County
cf036	September 11, 2008	Anju	Township, Village

List of all rental contracts mentioned

Identifier	Date Issued	Location	Lessor	Tenant
cmm024	March 12, 2003	Anju Town, Tanghe Village	Village Group No. 3	Chunyang Agricultural Development Limited
cmm026	October 10, 2007	Yufeng Town, Jitou Village	one household	Chenxin Modern Agriculture Development Limited
cmm027	September 29, 2006	Yufeng Town, Village No. 6, Village Group No. 5	one household	Meining Enterprise Group Food Products Limited
cmm030	August 2, 2008	Majia Town	40 villagers in four natural villages	Xuantian Herding Agricultural Development Limited
cmm033	not yet issued	Xiagez-huang Town	empty	empty

NOTES

1. However, the various issues in policy implementation, including a huge funding gap for the work of rural administrators, suggests that our field sites were not exceptionally well equipped with resources and higher-level support.

2. The *Jiulong* Group is a major agricultural company in Laixi, specializing in meat processing. It now processes about 200,000 chickens per day for many national and even some well-known international customers. The company has emerged out of clan structures and provides good housing, education, and many other benefits for the original villagers. Although in 2008 the company party secretary proudly argued that farming households were tightly integrated into the production (e.g., they raised the chickens on behalf of the company), in 2009, he complained about the unreliability of this model (and farmers) and pointed out that the company would move away from these structures.

3. Meitan was the only county in Guizhou Province.

4. The Guiyang yearbook lists 15,220 hectares of agricultural land (15 mu equals 1 hectare). The per capita rate is calculated using the resulting number and dividing it by all rural residents.

Bibliography

AFP. 2012. "Nearly Half China Farmers 'Suffer Land Grabs.'" *AFP*, February 7. Accessed February 29, 2012. http://www.google.com/hostednews/afp/article/ALeqM5h-rLJET4ZgujQMlrTl_isJaErNLQ?docId=CNG.9a22c95cb0e7b0a49350a92381891d4c.2
21.

Ahlers, Anna L. 2014. *Rural Policy Implementation in Contemporary China: New Socialist Countryside*. New York: Routledge.

Ahlers, Anna L. and Gunter Schubert. 2009. "'Building a New Socialist Countryside'–Only a Political Slogan?" *The Journal of Current Chinese Affairs* 38(4):35–62.

Ahlers, Anna L. and Gunter Schubert. 2013. "Strategic Modelling: 'Building a New Socialist Countryside' in Three Chinese Counties." *The China Quarterly* 216:1–19.

Ahmad, Ethisham. 2008. "Taxation Reforms and the Sequencing of Intergovernmental Reforms in China: Preconditions for a Xiaokang Society." In *Public Finance in China: Reform and Growth for a Harmonious Society*, edited by Jiwei Lou and Shuilin Wang, 95–126. Washington, D.C,: World Bank Publications.

Akram-Lodhi, A Haroon. 2004. "Are 'Landlords Taking Back the Land'? An Essay on the Agrarian Transition in Vietnam." *The European Journal of Development Research* 16(4):757–789.

Akram-Lodhi, A Haroon. 2005. "Vietnam's Agriculture: Processes of Rich Peasant Accumulation and Mechanisms of Social Differentiation." *Journal of Agrarian Change* 5(1):73–116.

Akram-Lodhi, A Haroon. 2007. "Land, Markets and Neoliberal Enclosure: An Agrarian Political Economy Perspective." *Third World Quarterly* 28(8):1437–1456.

Alpermann, Björn. 2010. *China's Cotton Industry: Economic Transformation and State Capacity*. London and New York: Routledge.

Amnesty International. 2012. *Standing Their Ground: Thousands Face Violent Eviction in China*. London: Amnesty International.

Anjuqu Nongyebu. 2008. "Nongcun Tudi Liuzhuan Hezuoshe (Fudao Cunliao)" 农村土地流转合作社 (辅导村料) [Rural Land Transfer Cooperatives (Village Coaching Materials)]. Anjuqu Nongyebu 安居区农业部 [Office for Agricultural Affairs, Anju District].

Anjuqu Nongyebu. 2009. "Guanyu nongcun tudi liuzhuan ji nongmin zhuanye hezuo zuzhi jieshao" 关于农村土地流转及农民专业合作组织介绍 [Introduction to Rural Land Transfer and Specialized Cooperative Organizations]. Anjuqu Nongyebu 安居区农业部 [Office for Agricultural Affairs Anju District].

Ash, Robert F. 1988. "The Evolution of Agricultural Policy." *The China Quarterly* 116:529–555.

Assies, Willem. 2009. "Land Tenure, Land Law and Development: Some Thoughts on Recent Debates." *Journal of Peasant Studies* 36(3):573–589.

Banaji, Jarius. 1976. "Summary of Selected Parts of Kautsky's: The Agrarian Question." *Economy and Society* 5(1):1–49.

Bardach, Eugene. 1977. *The Implementation Game: What Happens after a Bill Becomes a Law*. Cambridge, MA: MIT.

Bates, Robert H. 1984. *Markets and States in Tropical Africa: The Political Basis of Agricultural Policies*. Berkeley: University of California Press.

Baum, Richard and Alexei Shevchenko. 1999. "The "State of the State." In *The Paradox of Reform in China,* edited by Merle Goldman and Roderick MacFarquhar, 333–360. Cambridge, Massachusetts and London, England: Harvard University Press.

Bernstein, Henry. 2006. "Once Were / Still Are Peasants? Farming in a Globalising 'South.'" *New Political Economy* 11(3):399–406.

Bernstein, Henry. 2010. "Rural Livelihoods and Agrarian Change: Bringing Class Back in." In *Rural Transformations and Development: China in Context,* edited by Norman Long, Jingzhong Ye, and Yuhuan Wang, 79–109. Cheltenham, UK and Northhampton, USA: Edward Elgar Publishing Ltd.

Berry, Albert. 2011. "The Case for Redistributional Land Reform in Developing Countries." *Development and Change* 42(2):637–648.

Blanchard, Ben. 2012. "China Says Rebel Village was Right to Complain." *Reuters,* November 3. Accessed November 3, 2012. http://www.reuters.com/article/2011/12/31/us-china-village-report-idUSTRE7BU03K20111231.

Blumenthal, David and William Hsiao. 2005. "Privatization and Its Discontents: The Evolving Chinese Health Care System." *The New England Journal of Medicine* 353(11):1165–1170.

Borras Jr., Saturnino M. 2009. "Agrarian Change and Peasant Studies: Changes, Continuities and Challenges—An Introduction." *Journal of Peasant Studies* 36(1):5–31.

Bramall, Chris. 2004. "Chinese Land Reform in Long-Run Perspective and in the Wider East Asian Context." *Journal of Agrarian Change* 4(1–2):107–141.

Brandt, Loren, Scott Rozelle, and Matthew A Turner. 2004. "Local Government Behavior and Property Right Formation in Rural China." *Journal of Institutional and Theoretical Economics* 160(4):627–662.

Brandt, Loren et al. 2002. "Land Rights in Rural China: Facts, Fictions and Issues." *The China Journal* 47:67–97.

Branigan, Tania. 2011. "China's Rural Poor Left Stranded as Urbanites Race Ahead." *The Guardian,* October 3. Accessed November 29, 2011. http://www.guardian.co.uk/world/2011/oct/03/china-rural-poor-left-stranded.

Brenner, Robert. 1985a. "Agrarian Class Structure and Economic Development in Pre-Industrial Europe." In *The Brenner Debate,* edited by T. H. Aston, and C. H. E. Philpin, 10–63. Cambridge, UK: Cambridge University Press.

Brenner, Robert. 1985b. "The Agrarian Roots of European Capitalism." In *The Brenner Debate,* edited by T. H. Aston, and C. H. E. Philpin, 213–327. Cambridge, UK: Cambridge University Press.

Bromley, Daniel W. 1991. *Environment and Economy: Property Rights and Public Policy.* Oxford, UK ; Cambridge, USA: Blackwell.

Buckley, Chris. 2011. "Heavy Metals Pollute a Tenth of China's Farmland-Report." *Reuters,* November 6. Accessed November 13, 2011. http://www.reuters.com/article/2011/11/07/us-china-pollution-agriculture-idUSTRE7A60DO20111107.

Byres, Terence J. 1996. *Capitalism from Above and Capitalism from Below.* New York: Palgrave Macmillian.

Byres, Terence J. 2009. "The Landlord Class, Peasant Differentiation, Class Struggle and the Transition to Capitalism: England, France and Prussia Compared." *The Journal of Peasant Studies* 36(1):33–54.

Cai, Hongbin and Daniel Treisman. 2006. "Did Government Decentralization Cause China's Economic Miracle?" *World Politics* 58(4):505–535.

Cai, Jiming. 2011. "'Tudi fubai' de zhidu fenxi - difang zhengfu kao tudi shengcai、jucai" 土地腐败"的制度分析地方政府靠土地生财、聚财 [Analysis of the "land corruption" system: local governments rely on land to make money and become rich]. *Renmin Wang,* December 10. Accessed November 19, 2011. http://politics.people.com.cn/GB/1026/15873220.html.

Cai, Yongjun, and Xingyu Fu. 2010. "Liaoning Zhuangheshi shichang yin 'qianren xiagui shijian' cizhi huopi" 辽宁庄河市市长因"千人下跪事件"辞职获批 [Resignation of mayor of Zhuanghe City in Liaoning because of the "Thousand People Kneel

Down Incident" has been approved]. *Xinhua Wang*, April 29. Accessed April 22, 2011. http://news.xinhuanet.com/local/2010-04/29/c_1263833.htm.

Cai, Yongshun. 2003. "Collective Ownership or Cadres' Ownership? The Non-agricultural Use of Farmland in China." *The China Quarterly* 175:662–680.

Chan, Anita, Richard Madsen, and Jonathan Unger. 2009. *Chen Village: Revolution to Globalization*. Berkeley: University of California Press.

Chan, Kam Wing and Ying Hu. 2003. "Urbanization in China in the 1990s: New Definition, Different Series, and Revised Trends." *The China Review* 3(2):49–71.

Chang, Hong. 2011a. "Chengxiang yitihua gaige zuida kunnan shi shiye shidi nongmin de shehui baozhang" 城乡一体化改革最大困难是事业失地农民的社会保障 [Social protection for peasants without land and employment is the biggest difficulty of the rural–urban integration reform]. *Renmin Wang*, March 14. Accessed November 18, 2011. http://politics.people.com.cn/GB/1026/14141506.html.

Chang, Hong. 2011b. "Tudi xinyong hezuoshe shi tudi chengbao jingyingquan liuzhuan zhidu de chuangxin" 土地信用合作社是土地承包经营权流转制度的创新 [Land credit cooperatives are an institutional innovation for the transfer of land usage rights]. *Renmin Wang*, March 14. Accessed April 18, 2011. http://politics.people.com.cn/GB/1026/14141513.html.

Changlixiang Renmin Zhengfu. 2008. "Anjuqu Changlixiang nongcun tudi liuzhuan beian biao" 安居区常理乡农村土地流转备案表 [Table of Land Transfer Cases in Changli Township, Anju District]. Changlixiang Renmin Zhengfu 常理乡人民政府 [People's Government of Changli Township].

Changwu Weiyuanhui. 1982. "Guojia jianshe yong tudi tiaoli" 国家建设用土地条例 [Regulation for Land Requisitioning for National Construction]. Quanguo Renda Changwu Weiyuanhui 全国人大常务委员会 [Standing Committee of National People's Congress].

Changwu Weiyuanhui. 1986. "Zhonghua Renmin Gongheguo Tudi Guanlifa" 中国人民共和国土地管理法 [Land Administration Law of the People's Republic of China]. Quanguo Renda Changwu Weiyuanhui 全国人大常务委员会 [Standing Committee of National People's Congress].

Changwu Weiyuanhui. 1988. "Zhonghua Renmin Gongheguo Tudi Guanlifa (1988 Xiuzheng)" 中华人民共和国土地管理法(1988修正) [Land Administration Law of the People's Republic of China (1998 Amendment)]. Quanguo Renmin Daibiao Dahui Changwu Weiyuanhui 全国人民代表大会常务委员会 [Standing Committee of National People's Congress].

Changwu Weiyuanhui. 2004. "Zhonghua Renmin Gongheguo Tudi Guanlifa (2004 Xiuzheng)" 中华人民共和国土地管理法 (2004修正) [Land Administration Law of the People's Republic of China (2004 Amendment)]. Quanguo Renda Changweihui 全国人大常委会 [Standing Committee of National People's Congress].

Chen, Chih-jou Jay. 2004. *Transforming Rural China: How Local Institutions Shape Property Rights in China*. London and New York: RoutledgeCurzon.

Chen, Gang. 2011. "32 hu nongmin shouci lingdao "chanquanzheng" kaichuang Shanxi nongcun chanquan zhidu gaige xianhe" 32户农民首次领到"产权证"开创陕西农村产权制度改革先河 [32 peasant households receive the first "Property Rights Certificates" and thereby initiate the beginning of Shaanxi [Province] property rights system reform]. *Renmin Wang*, March 22. Accessed April 20, 2011. http://politics.people.com.cn/GB/14562/14208253.html.

Chen, Qi. 2010. "Woguo nongcun tudi liuzhuan de moshi bijiao [Contrasting different modes of land transfer in China]" 我国农村土地流转的模式比较 [Contrasting different modes of land transfer in China]. *Xuexi yu Shijian* 学习与实践 [Study and Practice] 10:126–130.

Chen, Xiaoning, Yonghong He, and Zhizhong Zhou. 2010. "Suining Xiji chuangxin tudi liuzhuan fangshi cu xiandai nongye fazhan" 遂宁西吉创新新土地流转方式促现代农业发展 [The innovative mode of land transfer in Xiji County in Suining encourages the modernization of agriculture]. *Renmin Wang*, January 8. Accessed May 1, 2011. http://politics.people.com.cn/GB/1026/10733608.html.

Cheng, Yuk-Shing and Shu-Ki Tsang. 1995. "Agricultural Land Reform in a Mixed System: The Chinese Experience of 1984–1994." *China Information* 10(3–4):44–74.

Christiansen, Flemming. 2009. "Food Security, Urbanization and Social Stability in China." *Journal of Agrarian Change* 9(4):548–575.

Christiansen, Flemming. 2010. "Building Livelihoods: How Chinese Peasants Deal with State Regulation of Opportunity and Risk." In *Rural Transformations and Development—China in Context: The Everyday Lives of Policies and People,* edited by Norman Long, Jingzhong Ye, and Yuhuan Wang, 133–151. Cheltenham, UK: Edward Elgar Publishing Limited.

Collier, Paul. 2008. "Politics of Hunger." *Foreign Affairs* 87(6):67–79.

Commons, John R. 1968. *Legal Foundations of Capitalism.* New York: Macmillian.

Cui, Zhiyuan. 2011. "Partial Intimations of the Coming Whole: The Chongqing Experiment in Light of the Theories of Henry George, James Meade, and Antonio Gramsci." *Modern China* 37(6):646–660.

Das, Raju. 2005. "Rural Society, the State and Social Capital in Eastern India: A Critical Investigation." *Journal of Peasant Studies* 32(1):48–87.

Day, Alexander. 2008. "The End of the Peasant? New Rural Reconstruction in China." *Boundary 2* 35(2):49–73.

Deininger, Klaus and Songqing Jin. 2009. "Securing Property Rights in Transition: Lessons from Implementation of China's Rural Land Contracting Law." *Journal of Economic Behavior & Organization* 70(1–2):22–38.

Demsetz, Harold. 1967. "Toward a Theory of Property Rights." *The American Economic Review* 57(2):347–359.

Diaocha Yanjiu Shi. 2009. "Guanyu wosheng nongcun tudi chengbao jingyingquan liuzhuan wenti de diaoyan baogao" 关于我省农村土地承包经营权流转问题的调研报告 [Provincial Research Report on Issues in Land Usage Rights Transfer]. Shandongsheng Renmin Zhengfu Diaocha Yanjiu Shi 山东省人民政府调查研究室 [Investigation and Research Office of Shandong Province Government].

Du, Runsheng. 1989. *Many People, Little Land: China's Rural Economic Reform.* Beijing: Foreign Languages Press.

Edin, Maria. 2003. "State Capacity and Local Agent Control in China: CCP Cadre Management from a Township Perspective." *The China Quarterly* 173:35–52.

Ellis, Frank. 2006. "Agrarian Change and Rising Vulnerability in Rural Sub-Saharan Africa." *New Political Economy* 11(3):387–397.

Fewsmith, Joseph. 1994. *Dilemmas of Reform in China: Political Conflict and Economic Debate.* Armonk, USA: Sharpe.

Friedmann, Harriet. 1980. "Household Production and the National Economy: Concepts for the Analysis of Agrarian Formations." Journal of Peasant Studies 7(2):158–84.

Fung, Brian. 2012. "Wukan Revisited: No, China's Village Experiment in Democracy Isn't Over." *The Atlantic,* September 23. Accessed October 6, 2012. http://www.theatlantic.com/international/archive/2012/09/wukan-revisited-no-chinas-village-experiment-in-democracy-isnt-over/262734/.

Gao, Jie. 2010. "Hitting the Target but Missing the Point: The Rise of Non-Mission-Based Targets in Performance Measurement of Chinese Local Governments." *Administration & Society* 42(1):56S–76S.

Gao, Liangzhi. 2008. "Zhongguo nongmin you caichan ma?" 中国农民有财产吗? [Do Chinese peasants have property?]. *Yanhuang Chunqiu* 炎黄春秋 [Chronicles of History] 9:4–12.

George, Alexander L and Andrew Bennett. 2005. *Case Studies and Theory Development in the Social Sciences.* Cambridge, Massachusetts and London, England: MIT Press.

Göbel, Christian. 2012. "Government Propaganda and the Organization of Rural China." In *Organizing Rural China: Rural China Organizing,* edited by Ane Bislev and Stig Thogersen, 51–68. Plymouth, UK: Lexington Books.

Guiyangshi tongjiju. 2010. *Guiyangshi Tongji Nianjian* 贵阳市统计年鉴 [Guiyang Statistical Yearbook]. Guiyang: China Statistics Press.

Guo, Xiaolin. 2001. "Land Expropriation and Rural Conflicts in China." *The China Quarterly* 166:422–439.

Guofa. 2004. "Guowuyuan guanyu shenhua gaige yange tudi guanli de jueding" 国务院关于深化改革严格土地管理的决定 [Decision of the State Council to Deepen the Reform of a Strict Land Administration]. No. 28. Zhonghua Renmin Gongheguo Guowuyuan 中华人民共和国国务院 [State Council of the People's Republic of China].

Guowuyuan. 1994. "Jiben Nongtian Baohu Tiaoli" 基本农田保护条例 [Basic regulations for the protection of farmland]. No. 162. Zhonghua Renmin Gongheguo Guowuyuan 中华人民共和国国务院 [State Council of the People's Republic of China].

Guowuyuan. 1999. "Zhonghua Renmin Gongheguo Tudi Guanlifa shishi tiaoli " 中华人民共和国土地管理法实施条例 [Regulation for the Implementation of the Land Administration Law of the People's Republic of China]. No. 256. Zhonghua Renmin Gongheguo Guowuyuan 中华人民共和国国务院 [State Council of the People's Republic of China].

Hall, Peter A. and Rosemary C. R. Taylor. 1996. "Political Science and the Three New Institutionalisms." *Political Studies* 44(5):936–957.

Hannum, Emily and Peggy Kong. 2007. *Educational Resources and Impediments in Rural Gansu, China*. Working Paper Series on China. No. 3 [2007]. Washington, DC: The World Bank.

Harrell, Stevan. 1996. "Introduction: Civilizing Projects and the Reaction to Them." In *Cultural Encounters on China's Ethnic Frontiers*, edited by Stevan Harrell, 3–36. Seattle and London: University of Washington Press.

Hart, Gillian. 1989. "Agrarian Change in the Context of State Patronage." In *Agrarian Transformations*, edited by Gillian Hart, Andrew Turton, and Benjamin White, 31–49. Berkeley and London: University of California Press.

Hartford, Kathleen. 1985. "Socialist Agriculture is Dead: Long Live Socialist Agriculture! Organizational Transformation in Rural China." In *The Political Economy of Reform in Post-Mao China*, edited by Elizabeth J. Perry and Christine Wong, 31–61. Cambridge (Massachusetts) and London: Harvard University Press.

He, Baogang and Stig Thogersen. 2010. "Giving the People a Voice? Experiments with Consultative Authoritarian Institutions in China." *Journal of Contemporary China* 19(66):675–692.

He, Shenjing and Desheng Xue. 2014. "Identity Building and Communal Resistance Against Landgrabs in Wukan Village, China." *Current Anthropology* 55(S9):S126–S137.

Heberer, Thomas. 1996. *The Power of the Fait Accompli: The Peasantry as the Motive Force of Change in the People's Republic of China*. Occasional Papers. Trier: Universität Trier, Zentrum für Ostasien-Pazifik-Studien.

Heberer, Thomas. 2003. *Private Entrepreneurs in China and Vietnam: Social and Political Functioning of Strategic Groups*. Leiden and Boston: Brill.

Heberer, Thomas and René Trappel. 2013. "Evaluation Processes, Local Cadres' Behaviour and Local Development Processes." *Journal of Contemporary China* 22(84):1048–1066.

Heller, Michael. 1998. "The Tragedy of the Anticommons: Property in the Transition from Marx to Markets." *Harvard Law Review* 111(3):621–688.

Hillman, Ben. 2010. "Factions and Spoils: Examining Political Behavior within the Local State in China." *The China Journal* 64:1–18.

Ho, Peter. 2001. "Who Owns China's Land? Policies, Property Rights and Deliberate Institutional Ambiguity." *The China Quarterly* 166:394–421.

Ho, Peter. 2005. *Institutions in Transition: Land Ownership, Property Rights, and Social Conflict in China*. Oxford, UK: Oxford University Press.

Ho, Samuel P. S. and George C. S. Lin. 2003. "Emerging Land Markets in Rural and Urban China: Policies and Practices." *The China Quarterly* 175:681–707.

Ho, Samuel P. S. and George C. S. Lin. 2004. "Converting Land to Nonagricultural Use in China's Coastal Provinces: Evidence from Jiangsu." *Modern China* 30(1):81–112.

Hohfeld, Wesley Newcomb. 1913. "Some Fundamental Legal Conceptions as Applied in Judicial Reasoning." *Yale Law Journal* 23(1):16–59.

Hohfeld, Wesley Newcomb. 1917. "Fundamental Legal Conceptions as Applied in Judicial Reasoning." *Yale Law Journal* 26(8):710–770.

Hood, Christopher. 2006. "Gaming in Targetworld: The Targets Approach to Managing British Public Services." *Public Administration Review* 66(4):515–521.

Hsing, Youtien. 2010. *The Great Urban Transformation: Politics of Land and Property in China*. Oxford, UK: Oxford University Press.

Hu, Rong'en. 2010. *Liudong De Tudi: Guizhou Tongren Diqu Tudi Liuzhuan Diaocha* 流动的土地：贵州同仁地区土地流转调查 [Mobile land: Investigation into the land transfer in the Tongren Region, Guizhou Province]. Beijing: Peking University Press.

Huang, Philip C. C. 2011. "China's New-Age Small Farms and Their Vertical Integration: Agribusiness or Co-ops?" *Modern China* 37(2):107–134.

Huang, Philip C. C., Gao Yuan, and Yusheng Peng. 2012. "Capitalization without Proletarianization in China's Agricultural Development." *Modern China* 38(2):139–173.

Jacoby, Hanan G., Guo Li, and Scott Rozelle. 2002. "Hazards of Expropriation: Tenure Insecurity and Investment in Rural China." *The American Economic Review* 92(5):1420–447.

Jiangshanzhen Dangwei. 2008. "Guanyu xin nongcun jianshe qingkuang huibao" 关于新农村建设情况汇报 [Report on the situation of Building a New Countryside]. Jiangshanzhen Dangwei 姜山镇党委 [Party Committee of Jiangshan Town].

Jiangshanzhen Dangwei. 2009. "Jiangshanzhen jinjinian jingji zhibiao wancheng qingkuang ji qita you guan shuzi" 姜山镇近几年经济指标完成情况及其他有关数字 [Target achievements and other related data for the situation in Jiangshan Town in recent years]. Jiangshanzhen Dangwei 姜山镇党委 [Party Committee of Jiangshan Town].

Jin, Zhu. 2011a. "Huge Tracts of Arable Land Neglected." *China Daily*, August 8. Accessed September 3, 2011. http://www.chinadaily.com.cn/china/2011-08/08/content_13065766.htm.

Jin, Zhu. 2011b. "Protection of Farmland to Be Reviewed." *China Daily*, August 4. Accessed September 1, 2011. http://www.chinadaily.com.cn/china/2011-08/04/content_13045824.htm.

Jinan Ribao. 2011. "Guowuyuan yunniang xiufa guifan jiti tudi zhengshou buchang" 国务院酝酿修法规范集体土地征收补偿 [The State Council takes a look at overhauling the compensation for the requisitioning of collective land]. *Renmin Wang*, April 11. Accessed November 13, 2012. http://politics.people.com.cn/GB/1027/14357068.html.

Jinghua Shibao. 2011. "Guojia tudi fuzhong jiancha Gan Zangchun: Wo guo jiang gaige zhengdi buchang anzhi zhidu" 国家土地副总检察甘藏春：我国将改革征地补偿安置制度 [Deputy Inspector for Land Supervision Gan Zangchun: The national system for the compensation and resettlement of expropriated land will be reformed]. November 7. Accessed November 13, 2011. http://finance.people.com.cn/GB/16149815.html.

Jingji Cankao Bao. 2012. "Woguo duodi caizheng shouru zengshu mingxian xiajiang" 我国多地财政收入增速明显下降 [The financial income of administrations in many locations is increasingly clear in decline]. *Jingji Cankao Bao*, April 17. Accessed May 14, 2012. http://www.cnwest88.com/2012/xibusx_0417/117591.html.

Johnston, Deborah and Hester Le Roux. 2007. "Leaving the Household Out of Family Labour? The Implications for the Size–Efficiency Debate." *The European Journal of Development Economics* 19(3):355–371.

Kautsky, Karl. 1899. *Die Agrarfrage: Eine Uebersicht über die Tendenzen der modernen Landwirtschaft und die Agrarpolitik der Sozialpolitik*. Stuttgart: I. H. W. Dietz.

Kelliher, Daniel. 1992. *Peasant Power in China: The Era of Rural Reform, 1979–1989*. New Haven and London: Yale University Press.

Kipnis, Andrew B. 1995. "Within and Against Peasantness: Backwardness and Filiality in Rural China." *Comparative Studies in Society and History* 37(1):110–135.

Kipnis, Andrew B. 2006. "Suzhi: A Keyword Approach." *The China Quarterly* 186:295–313.

Kipnis, Andrew B. 2008. "Audit Cultures: Neoliberal Governmentality, Socialist Legacy, or Technologies of Governing?" *American Ethnologist* 35(2):275–289.

Klein, Jakob A. 2013. "Everyday Approaches to Food Safety in Kunming." *The China Quarterly* 214:376–393.

Kong, Sherry Tao and Jonathan Unger. 2013. "Egalitarian Redistributions of Agricultural Land in China through Community Consensus: Findings from Two Surveys." *The China Journal* 69:1–19.

Kostka, Genia and William Hobbs. 2012. "Local Energy Efficiency Policy Implementation in China: Bridging the Gap between National Priorities and Local Interests." *The China Quarterly* 211:765–785.

Kung, James Kai-sing. 1997. "Farmers' Preferences Regarding Ownership and Land Tenure in Post-Mao China: Unexpected Evidence from Eight Counties." *The China Journal* 38:33–63.

Kung, James Kai-sing. 2000. "Common Property Rights and Land Reallocations in Rural China: Evidence from a Village Survey." *World Development* 28(4):701–719.

Kung, James Kai-sing. 2002. "Off-Farm Labor Markets and the Emergence of Land Rental Markets in Rural China." *Journal of Comparative Economics* 30(2):395–414.

Laixishi Renmin Zhengfu. 2009a. "Guanyu xiandai nongye ji shehuizhuyi xin nongcun jianshe kaohe jiangli de yijian" 关于现代农业及社会主义新农村建设考核奖励的意见 [Notice Regarding Evaluation Encouragement and Rewards for the Creation of a Modern Agriculture and the New Socialist Countryside]. Laixishi Renmin Zhengfu 莱西市人民政府 [People's Government of Laixi City].

Laixishi Renmin Zhengfu. 2009b. "Xiagezhuangzhen tudi liuzhuan fuwu zhongxin zhuyao zhize" 夏格庄镇土地流转服务中心主要职责 [Priority Responsibilities of the Land Transfer Service Center in Xiagezhuang Town]. Laixishi Renmin Zhengfu 莱西市人民政府 [People's Government of Laixi City].

Laixishi Renmin Zhengfu. 2009c. "Laixishi xin nongcun jianshe 'wuhua' gongcheng qingkuang huibao" 莱西新农村建设"五化"工程情况回报 [Report on the Situation Regarding Laixi's "Wuhua" Project as Part of Building a New Countryside]. Laixishi Renmin Zhengfu 莱西市人民政府 [People's Government of Laixi City].

Larson, Christina. 2011. "Where the River Ends." *Foreign Policy*, June 2. Accessed November 10, 2011. http://www.foreignpolicy.com/articles/2011/06/02/where_the_river_ends.

de la Rupelle, Maëlys et al. 2009. "Land Rights Insecurity and Temporary Migration in Rural China." *IZA Discussion Paper* 4668:1–47.

Lasseter, Tom. 2011. "In Rebellious Wukan, China, a Raresight: No Authorities." *McClatchy Newspapers*, December 15. Accessed December 25, 2011. http://www.mcclatchydc.com/2011/12/15/133208/in-rebellious-wukan-china-a-rare.html.

Le Mons Walker, Kathy. 2006. "'Gangster Capitalism' and Peasant Protest in China: The Last Twenty Years." *The Journal of Peasant Studies* 33(1):1–33.

Li, Changping. 2003. "The Crisis in the Countryside." In *One China, Many Paths*, edited by Chaohua Wang, 198–218. London and New York: Verso.

Li, Lianjiang. 2004. "Political Trust in Rural China." *Modern China* 30(2):228–258.

Li, Linda Chelan and Wen Wang. 2014. "Pursuing Equity in Education: Conflicting Views and Shifting Strategies." *Journal of Contemporary Asia* 44(2):279–297.

Li, Ling, Qiulin Chen, and Dillon Powers. 2012. "Chinese Healthcare Reform: A Shift toward Social Development." *Modern China* 38(6):630–645.

Li, Tania Murray. 2007. *The Will to Improve: Governmentality, Development, and the Practice of Politics*. Durham and London: Duke University Press.

Lin, George C. S. 2007. "Reproducing Spaces of Chinese Urbanisation: New City-Based and Land-Centred Urban Transformation." *Urban Studies* 44(9):1827–1855.

Lin, Wanlong and Christine Wong. 2012. "Are Beijing's Equalization Policies Reaching the Poor? An Analysis of Direct Subsidies under the 'Three Rurals' (*Sannong*)." *The China Journal* 67:23–46.

Lingohr-Wolf, Susanne. 2011. *Industrialisation and Rural Livelihoods in China: Agricultural Processing in Sichuan*. London and New York: Routledge.

Liu, Jun. 2011. "Guotu ziyuan bu: dui suoyou sunhui tudi jinxing fuken" 国土资源部：对所有损毁土地进行复垦 [Ministry of Land and Natural Resources: All Ruined Land Should Be Restored for Cultivation]. *Renmin Wang*, March 29. Accessed April 28, 2011. http://politics.people.com.cn/GB/1027/14266022.html.

Liu, Liangqun and Rachel Murphy. 2006. "Lineage Networks, Land Conflicts and Rural Migration in Late Socialist China." *Journal of Peasant Studies* 33(4):612–645.

Liu, Yia-Ling. 2012. "From Predator to Debtor: The Soft Budget Constraint and Semi-Planned Administration in Rural China." *Modern China* 38(3):308–345.

Liu, Yuan, Keqin Rao, and Willam C. Hsiao. 2003. "Medical Expenditure and Rural Impoverishment in China." *Journal of Health, Population and Nutrition* 21(3):216–222.

Liu, Yunyun. 2011. "Sichuan fawen tuijin nongcun tudi zhengzhi, yanjin qiangpo nongmin zhu gaolou" 四川发文推进农村土地整治严禁强迫农民住高楼 [Sichuan Publishes Fix for Rural Land, Strictly Prohibits Villagers to Lve in [too] tall buildings]. *Renmin Wang*, April 13. Accessed April 28, 2011. http://politics.people.com.cn/GB/14562/14377715.html.

Lora-Wainwright, Anna. 2011. "'If You Can Walk and Eat, You Don't Go to Hospital': The Quest for Healthcare in Rural Sichuan." In *China's Changing Welfare Mix: Local perspectives*, edited by Beatriz Carrillo, and Jane Duckett, 104–125. New York: Routledge.

Majiaxiang Renmin Zhengfu. 2009. "Anjuqu Majiaxiang tudi liuzhuan qingkuang jibiao" 安居区马家乡土地流转情况计表 [Anju District Majia Township Land Transfer Situation Table]. Majiaxiang Renmin Zhengfu 马家乡人民政府 [People's Government Majia Township].

Maweifa. 2009. "2009 Niandu Gongzuo Yaodian" 2009 年度工作要点 [Year 2009 Key Work Points]. Zhonggong Anjuqu Majiaxiang Weiyuanhui、Anjuqu Majiaxiang Renmin Zhengfu 中共安居区马家乡委员会、安居区马家乡人民政府 [Party Committee of the Communist Party of China of Majia Township, Anju District and People's Government of Majia Township, Anju District].

Meitan Dangxiao. 2010. "Meitan jingyan: Zhongguo tudi zhidu jianshe de yizuo fengbei" 湄潭经验:中国土地制度建设的座丰碑 [Meitan Experience: A Monument in the Construction of the Chinese Land Institutions]. Meitan Dangxiao 湄潭党校 [Meitan Party School].

Meitanxian Renmin Zhengfu. 2010. "Meitanxian shehui zhuyi xin nongcun jianshe qingkuang jianjie" 湄潭县社会主义新农村建设请看简介 [Brief Introduction to the Situation Regarding Building a New Socialist Countryside in Meitan County]. Meitanxian Renmin Zhengfu 湄潭县人民政府 [People's Government of Meitan County].

McMichael, Philip. 2008. "Peasants Make Their Own History, But Not Just as They Please...." *Journal of Agrarian Change* 8(2–3):205–228.

Moore, Malcolm. 2011a. "Chinese Police Besiege Town and Cut of Food Supplies in Bid to Quell Riots." *The Telegraph*, December 12. Accessed December 12, 2011. http://www.telegraph.co.uk/news/worldnews/asia/china/8951638/Chinese-police-besiege-town-and-cut-of-food-supplies-in-bid-to-quell-riots.html.

Moore, Malcolm. 2011b. "Over 20 Million Kindergarten-age Children Living without Their Parents in China." *The Telegraph*, November 21. Accessed November 28, 2011. http://www.telegraph.co.uk/news/worldnews/asia/china/8904412/Over-20-million-kindergarten-age-children-living-without-their-parents-in-China.html.

Moore, Malcolm. 2012. "Chinese Setting Themselves on Fire to Protest Against Forced Evictions." *The Telegraph*, October 11. Accessed October 11, 2012. http://

www.telegraph.co.uk/news/worldnews/asia/china/9599098/Chinese-setting-them-selves-on-fire-to-protest-against-forced-evictions.html.

Mulgan, Aurelia George. 2000. *The Politics of Agriculture in Japan*. London and New York: Routledge.

Mullan, Katrina, Pauline Grosjean, and Andreas Kontoleon. 2011. "Land Tenure Arrangements and Rural–Urban Migration in China." *World Development* 39(1):123–133.

Murphy, Rachel. 2004. "Turning Peasants into Modern Chinese Citizens: 'Population Quality' Discourse, Demographic Transition and Primary Education." *The China Quarterly* 177:1–20.

National Bureau of Statistics of China. 1995. *Zhongguo Tongji Nianjian 1995* 中国统计年鉴1995 [China Statistical Yearbook 1995]. Beijing: China Statistics Press.

National Bureau of Statistics of China. 2010. *Zhongguo Tongji Nianjian 2010* 中国统计年鉴2010 [China Statistical Yearbook 2010]. Beijing: China Statistics Press.

Ngai, Pun and Huilin Lu. 2010. "Unfinished Proletarianization: Self, Anger, and Class Action among the Second Generation of Peasant-Workers in Present-Day China." *Modern China* 36(5):493–519.

Nolan, Peter and Suzanne Paine. 1987. "Towards an Appraisal of the Impact of Rural Reform in China, 1978-1985." In *The Re-Emergence of the Chinese Peasantry: Aspects of Rural Decollectivisation*, edited by Ashwani Saith, 81–104. London, New York and Sydney: Croom Helm.

Nongyebu. 2005. "Nongcun tudi chengbao jingyingquan liuzhuan guanli banfa" 农村土地承包经营权流转管理办法 [Procedures for the Management of the Transfer of Contracted Usage Rights for Rural Land]. Zhonghua Renmin Gongheguo Nongye-bu 中华人民共和国农业部 [Ministry of Agriculture of the People's Republic of China].

O'Brien, Kevin J. and Lianjiang Li. 1999. "Selective Policy Implementation in Rural China." *Comparative Politics* 31(2):167–186.

Oi, Jean C. 1993. "Reform and Urban Bias in China." *Journal of Development Studies* 29(4):129–148.

Ong, Lynette H. 2011. "Greasing the Wheels of Development: Rural Credit in China." In *Politics and Markets in Rural China*, edited by Björn Alpermann, 48–68. London: Routledge.

O'Brien, Kevin J. and Lianjiang Li. 2006. *Rightful Resistence in Rural China*. Cambridge: Cambridge University Press.

Park, Choong-Hwan. 2014. "Nonjiale Tourism and Contested Space in Rural China." *Modern China* 40(5):519–548.

Ping, Yew Chiew. 2011. "Explaining Land Use Change in a Guangdong County: The Supply Side of the Story." *The China Quarterly* 207:626–648.

Polanyi, Karl. 1997. *The Great Transformation*. Frankfurt: Suhrkamp.

Power, Michael. 2003. "Evaluating the Audit Explosion." *Law & Policy* 25(3).

Qin, Hui. 2003. "Dividing the Big Family Assets: On Liberty and Justice." In *One China, Many Paths*, edited by Chaohua Wang, 129–159. London and New York: Verso.

Qin, Hui. 2007. "Nongmin diquan liulun" 农民地权六论 [Six theses on peasant's land rights]. *Shehui Kexue Lunyun* 社会科学论坛 [Social Science Forum] 5:122–146.

Qingdaoshi Laixishi Tongjiju. 2012. "Qingdaoshi Laixishi 2011 nian guomin jingji he shehui fazhan tongji gongbao" 青岛市莱西市2011年国民经济和社会发展统计公报 [2011 Citizens' Statistical Report of Qingdao and Laixi City on Economic and Social Development]. April 19. Accessed April 25, 2012. http://www.tjcn.org/tjgb/201204/24371.html.

Qingdaoshi Tongjiju. 1992. *Qingdaoshi Tongji Nianjian* 青岛市统计年鉴 [Qingdao Statistical Yearbook]. Qingdao: China Statistics Press.

Qingdaoshi Tongjiju. 2011. *Qingdaoshi Tongji Nianjian* 青岛市统计年鉴 [Qingdao Statistical Yearbook]. Qingdao: China Statistics Press.

Qingzhengzi. 2011. "Qingdaoshi renmin zhengfu guanyu jiakuai tuijin nongcun tudi shidu guimo jingying de yijian" 青岛市人民政府关于加快推进农村土地适度规模经

营的意见 [Suggestions of Qingdao Government on Speeding-up and Pushing Forward Appropriate Scale Economies for Rural Land]. Qingdaoshi Renmin Zhengfu 青岛市人民政府 [People's Government of Qingdao City].

Quanguo Renmin Daibiaohui. 1982. "Zhongguo Renmin Gongheguo Xianfa" 中国人民共和国宪法 [Constitution of the People's Republic of China]. Quanguo Renmin Daibiaohui 全国人民代表会 [National People's Congress].

Quanguo Renmin Daibiaohui. 1988. "Zhonghua Renmin Gongheguo Xianfa Xiuzhengtiao" 中华人民共和国宪法修正条 [Revision of the Constitution of the People's Republic of China]. Quanguo Renmin Daibiao Dahui 全国人民代表大会 [National People's Congress].

Ramzy, Austin. 2010. "What China's Labor Unrest Means for Its Future." *Time Magazine*, June 28. Accessed July 10, 2011. http://www.time.com/time/magazine/article/0,9171,1997298,00.html.

Rozelle, Scott. 1996. "Stagnation without Equity: Patterns of Growth and Inequality in China's Rural Economy." *The China Journal* 35:63–92.

Rozelle, Scott, Jikun Huang, and Keijiro Otsuka. 2005. "The Engines of a Viable Agriculture: Advances in Biotechnology, Market Accessibility and Land Rentals in Rural China." *The China Journal* 53:81–111.

Ruan, Yulin. 2011. "Guotubu: Zhongguo weilai yongdi xingshi gengjia yanjun" 国土部：中国未来用地形势势更加严峻 [Ministry of Land: Land Usage Situation in China Will Be Even More Severe in the Future]. *Renmin Wang*, June 25. Accessed July 12, 2011. http://politics.people.com.cn/GB/1027/14996712.html.

Saich, Tony. 2007. "China in 2006: Focus on Social Development." *Asian Survey* 47(1):32–43.

Sandy-Thomas, Peter. 2011. *Legimtimating the Chinese Communist Party since Tiananmen: A Critical Analysis of the Stability Discourse*. Abingdon, UK: Routledge.

Sargeson, Sally. 2012. "Villains, Victims and Aspiring Proprietors: Framing 'Land-losing Villagers' in China's Strategies of Accumulation." *Journal of Contemporary China* 21(77):757–777.

Scharpf, Fritz W. 2000. *Interaktionsformen: Akteurszentrierter Institutionalismus in der Politikforschung*. Wiesbaden: VS Verlag für Sozialwissenschaften.

Schubert, Gunter and Anna L. Ahlers. 2011. "Constructing a New Socialist Countryside and Beyond: An Analytical Framework for Studying Policy Implementation and Political Stability in Contemporary China." *Journal of Chinese Political Science* 16(1):19-46.

Schubert, Gunter and Anna L Ahlers. 2012. "County and Township Cadres as a Strategic Group: "Building a New Socialist Countryside" in Three Provinces." *The China Journal* 67:67–86.

Scott, James C. 1998. *Seeing Like a State: How Certain Schemes to Improve the Human Condition Have Failed*. New Haven and London: Yale University Press.

Selden, Mark. 1998. "Household, Cooperative, and State in the Remaking of China's Countryside.'" In *Cooperative and Collective in China's Rural Development: Between State and Private Interests*, edited by Eduard B. Vermeer, Frank N. Pieke, and Woei Lien Chong, 17-45. Armonk, New York and London, England: M. E. Sharpe.

Shandong Provinicial Statistics Bureau. 2010. *Shandong Statistical Yearbook*. China Statistics Press.

Shao, Jing'an et al. 2007. "Farmers' Responses to Land Transfer Under the Household Responsibility System in Chongqing (China): A Case Study." *Journal of Land Use Science* 2(2):79–102.

Sicular, Terry. 1995. "Redefining State, Plan and Market: China's Reforms in Agricultural Commerce." *The China Quarterly* 144:1020–1046.

Skinner, G. William. 1978. "Vegetable Supply and Marketing in Chinese Cities." *The China Quarterly* 76:733–793.

Skinner, Mark W., Richard G. Kuhn, and Alun E. Joseph. 2001. "Agricultural Land Protection in China: A Case Study of Local Governance in Zhejiang Province." *Land Use Policy* 18(4):329–340.

Smil, Vaclav. 1981. "China's Food: Availablity, Requirements, Composition, Prospects." *Food Policy* 6(2):67–77.

Smith, Graeme. 2009. "Political Machinations in a Rural County." *The China Journal* 62:29–59.

Smith, Graeme. 2010. "The Hollow State: Rural Governance in China." *The China Quarterly* 203:601–618.

Smith, Graeme. 2011. "Franchising the State: Farmers, Agricultural Technicians, and the Marketization of Agricultural Services." In *Politics and Markets in Rural China*, edited by Björn Alpermann, 69–86. London: Routledge.

Smyth, Russell. 1998. "Property Rights in China's Economic Reforms." *Communist and Post-Communist Studies* 31(3):235–248.

Steinmo, Sven. 2010. "Historical Institutionalism." In *Approaches and Methodologies in the Social Sciences: A Pluralist Perspective*, edited by Donatella Della Porta, and Michael Keating, 118–138. Cambridge, UK: Cambridge University Press.

Suiningshi Tongjiju. 2008. *Suiningshi Tongji Nianjian* 遂宁市统计年鉴 [Suining Statistical Yearbook]. Suining: Suiningshi Tongjiju.

Szelenyi, Ivan. 2011. "Third Ways." *Modern China* 37(6):672–683.

Tanghecun. 2008a. "Guanyu chengli Anjuzhen Tanghecun nongcun tudi liuzhuan hezuoshe de qingshi" 关于成立安居镇唐河村农村土地流转合作社的轻视 [Application for the Creation of a Land Transfer Cooperative in Tanghe Village in Anju Town]. Tanghecun 唐河村 [Tanghe Village].

Tanghecun. 2008b. "Suiningshi Anjuqu Anjuzhen Tanghecun tudi liuzhuan hezuoshe caocheng" 遂宁市安居区安居镇唐河村土地流转合作社草程 [Basic Agreement of the Land Transfer Cooperative of Tanghe Village in Anju Town, Anju District, Suining City]. Tanghecun 唐河村 [Tanghe Village].

Tao, Ran and Zhigang Xu. 2007. "Urbanization, Rural Land System and Social Security for Migrants in China." *Journal of Development Studies* 43(7):1301–1320.

Thelen, Kathleen. 1999. "Historical Institutionalism in Comparative Politics." *Annual Review of Political Science* 2(1):369–404.

Tian, John Q. 2007. "Challenge, Governance Reform and Disharmony in Rural Society." In *China's Post-Reform Economy: Achieving Harmony, Sustaining Growth*, edited by Richard Sanders and Chen Yang, 44–68. New York: Routledge.

Tsai, Lily Lee. 2002. "Cadres, Temple and Lineage Institutions, and Governance in Rural China." *The China Journal* 48:1–27.

Unger, Jonathan. 2002a. "Poverty, Credit and Microcredit in Rural China." *Development Bulletin* 57:23–26.

Unger, Jonathan. 2002b. *The Transformation of Rural China.* Armonk, NY: M. E. Sharpe.

Vendryes, Thomas. 2010. "Land Rights in Rural China since 1978: Reforms, Successes, and Shortcomings." *China Perspectives* 4:87–99.

Verdery, Katherine. 2003. *The Vanishing Hectare: Property and Value in Postsocialist Transylvania.* Ithaca and London: Cornell University Press.

Verdery, Katherine. 2004. "The Obilgations of Ownership: Restoring Rights to Land in Postsocialist Transylvania." In *Property in Question: Value Transformation in the Gobal Economy*, edited by Katherine Verdery and Caroline Humphrey, 139–159. London: Bloomsbury Academic.

Waldron, Scott, Colin Brown, and John Longworth. 2006. "State Sector Reform and Agriculture in China." *The China Quarterly* 186:277–294.

Wang, Hua-shu and Henk Moll. 2010. "Education Financing of Rural Households in China." *Journal of Family and Economic Issues* 31(3):353.

Wang, Hui, Ran Tao, and Juer Tong. 2009. "Trading Land Development Rights under a Planned Land Use System: The 'Zhejiang Model.'" *China & World Economy* 17(1):66–82.

Wang, Qian. 2011. "Illegal Land Use Gives Year-end GDP Boost." *China Daily*, October 26. Accessed October 26, 2011. http://www.chinadaily.com.cn/china/2011-10/26/content_13977191.htm.

Wang, Qian and Anfei Guo. 2011. "Drive to Play Golf Puts Pressure on Land." *China Daily*, July 13. Accessed October 2, 2011. http://www.chinadaily.com.cn/china/2011-07/13/content_12889206.htm.

Wang, Qian and Jing Li. 2011. "Groundwater Gets Worse, Land Agency Says." *China Daily*, October 21. Accessed November 6, 2011. http://www.chinadaily.com.cn/china/2011-10/21/content_13944892.htm.

Wang, Xiaqi and Fu'ning Zhong. 2008. "Tudi xisuihua yu nongyongdi liuzhuan shichang" 土地细碎化与农用地流转市场 [Land fragmentation and the land transfer market]. *Zhongguo Nongcun Guancha* 中国农村观察 [China Rural Survey] 82(4):29–34.

Wang, Yanchun. 2011. "Zhongguo nongfahang hangchang Zheng Hui jianyi tansuo nongcun tudi liuzhuan jingyingquan diya daikuan" 中国农发行行长郑晖建议探索农村土地流转经营权抵押贷款 [President Zheng Hui of the Chinese Agricultural Development Bank suggests to explore the use of rural land transfer rights for mortgage loans]. *Caijing Wang*, March 8. Accessed November 18, 2011. http://www.caijing.com.cn/2011-03-08/110659985.html.

Watson, Andrew. 1983. "Agriculture Looks for 'Shoes that Fit': The Production Responsibility System and Its Implications." *World Development* 11(8):705–730.

Watts, Jonathan. 2011. "Huaxi: the Village that Towers above China." October 6. Accessed November 6, 2011. http://www.guardian.co.uk/world/2011/oct/06/huaxi-village-tower-china.

Wegren, Stephen. 1998. *Agriculture and the State in Soviet and Post-Soviet Russia*. Pittsburgh: University of Pittsburgh Press.

Weishengbu. 2009. "Zhongguo weisheng fuwu diaocha yanjiu" 中国卫生服务调查研究 [An Analysis Report of National Health Services Survey in China]. Weishengbu Tongji Xinxi Zhongxin 卫生部统计信息中心 [Center for Health Statistics and Information, Ministry of Health].

Wen, Tiejun. 2006. "Nongmin shehui baozhang yu tudi zhidu gaige" 农民社会保障与土地制度改革 [Social protection for peasants and the reform of the land institutions]. *Xuexi Yuekan* 学习月刊 [Study Monthly] 10:20–22.

Whiting, Susan H. 2001. *Power and Wealth in Rural China: The Political Economy of Institutional Change*. New York: Cambridge University Press.

Whiting, Susan H. 2004. "The Cadre Evaluation System at the Grass Roots: The Paradox of Party Rule." In *Diversity and National Integration in the Post-Deng Era*, edited by Barry J. Naughton, and Dali L. Yang, 101–119. Cambridge: Cambridge University Press.

Wong, Christine. 2009. "Rebuilding Government for the 21st Century: Can China Incrementally Reform the Public Sector?" *The China Quarterly* 200:929–952.

Wong, Edward. 2011. "Yangtze Rains Bring Drought Relief, and Floods." *The New York Times*, June 7. Accessed November 10, 2011. http://www.nytimes.com/2011/06/08/world/asia/08drought.html.

Wood, Ellen Meiksins. 2002. *The Origin of Capitalism: A Longer View*. London and New York: Verso.

Xiagezhuangzhen Renmin Zhengfu. 2008. "Xiagezhuangzhen xin nongcun jianshe gongzuo qingkuang" 夏格庄镇新农村建设工作情况 [Situation Regarding Building a New Countryside in Xiagezhuang Town]. Xiagezhuangzhen Renmin Zhengfu 夏格庄镇人民政府 [People's Government of Xiagezhuang Town].

Xifa. 2009. "Guanyu 2009 niandu zhen (jiedao) ji dangzheng zhengzhi mubiao jixiao kaohe de yijian" 关于2009年度镇（街道）及党政正职目标绩效考核的意见 [Opinion Regarding the 2009 Annual Target Achievement Evaluation for Government and Party Officials at Township (and Subdistrict) Level]. No. 5. Zhongong Laixi Shiwei Laixishi Renmin Zhengfu 中共莱西市委莱西市人民政府 [Municipal Party Committee of Laixi City and People's Government of Laixi City].

Xifengxian Renmin Zhengfu. 2010. "Unnamed collection of regulations regarding the creation of Land Transfer Service Centers" Xifengxian Renmin Zhengfu 息烽县人民政府 [People's Government Xifeng County].

Xifengxian Tudi Liuzhuan Zhongxin. 2009a. "Xifengxian nongcun tudi chengbao jingyingquan liuzhuan gongzuo kaohe banfa" 息烽县农村土地承包经营权流转工作考
核办法 [Xifeng County Regulations for the Evaluation of the Work in Land Usage
Rights Transfer]. Xifengxian Tudi Liuzhuan Zhongxin 息烽县土地流转中心 [Xifeng
County Land Transfer Center].

Xifengxian Tudi Liuzhuan Zhongxin. 2009b. "Xifengxian nongcun tudi liuzhuan xinx-
iyuan kaohe banfa" 息烽县农村土地流转信息员考核办法 [Xifeng County Guide-
lines for the Evaluation of Land Transfer Information Officers]. Xifengxian Tudi
Liuzhuan Zhongxin 息烽县土地流转中心 [Xifeng County Land Transfer Center].

Xinhua. 2008a. "Chronology of the CPC's Decision on Rural Reform, Development."
China.org.cn, August 20. Accessed May 7, 2012. http://www.china.org.cn/govern-
ment/central_government/2008-10/20/content_16640072.htm.

Xinhua. 2008b. *"Zhonggong zhongyang guanyu tuijin nongcun gaige fazhan ruogan zhongda wenti de jueding"* 中共中央关于推进村改革发展若干重大问题的决定 [Decisions of
the Central Committee of the Chinese Communist Party on a Number of Important
Questions Regarding Pushing Forward the Reform and Development of the Coun-
tryside]. *Renmin Wang,* October 20. Accessed May 7, 2012. http://poli-
tics.people.com.cn/GB/1026/8194300.html.

Xinhua. 2009. "Arable Land Fears Halt Reforestation Drive." *China Daily,* June 23.
Accessed September 13, 2012. http://www.chinadaily.com.cn/china/2009-06/23/con-
tent_8314969.htm.

Xinhua. 2010. "Shrinking Arable Land Threatens Grain Security." *China Daily,* October
18. Accessed October 18, 2010. http://www.chinadaily.com.cn/china/2010-10/18/
content_11423618.

Xinhua. 2011a. "China Enhances Protection of Farmers' Land." *China Daily,* November
10. Accessed November 19, 2011. http://www.chinadaily.com.cn/china/2011-11/10/
content_14068070.htm.

Xinhua. 2011b. "China Has 7.3 Million Hectares of Reserve Land." *China Daily,* July 5.
Accessed July 11, 2012. http://www.chinadaily.com.cn/china/2011-07/05/con-
tent_12832929.htm.

Xinhua. 2011c. "China Says 'Relocation First' in Requisitioning Farmers' Land." *China
Daily,* July 14. Accessed July 17, 2011. http://www.chinadaily.com.cn/china/2011-07/
14/content_12903071.htm.

Xinhua. 2011d. "Clampdown on Illegal Land Seizures." *China Daily,* July 20. Accessed
September 5, 2011. http://www.chinadaily.com.cn/china/2011-07/20/con-
tent_12947184.htm.

Xinhua. 2011e. "Hu Jintao: shifen zhenxi he heli liyong mei yi cun tudi, cujin jingji
shehui fazhan yu tudi liyong xiang xietiao" 胡锦涛：十分珍惜合理利用每一寸土
地；促进经济社会发展与土地利用相协调 [Hu Jintao: Fully treasure and only prop-
erly use every inch of land; going forward with bringing social and economic development and land usage in balance]. *Renmin Wang,* August 24.

Xu, Jiang, Anthony Yeh, and Fulong Wu. 2009. "Land Commodification: New Land
Development and Politics in China since the Late 1990s." *International Journal of
Urban and Regional Research* 33(4):890–913.

Yan, Jie. 2011. "Demolitions Cause Most Social Unrest." *China Daily,* June 27. Accessed
July 21, 2011. http://europe.chinadaily.com.cn/china/2011-06/27/con-
tent_12780846.htm.

Yan, Jinming. 2009. "Woguo zhengdi zhidu de yanbian yu gaige mubiao he gaige
lujing de xuanze" 我国征地制度的演变与改革目标和改革路径的选择 [Transforma-
tion and reform targets of the national land requisitioning system as well as [future
alternative] directions of reform]. *Jingji lilun yu jingji guanli* 经济理论与经济管理
[Economic Theory and Business Management] 1:39–43.

Yan, Yunxiang. 2012. "Food Safety and Social Risk in Contemporary China." *The Journal of Asian Studies* 71(3):705–729.

Yang, Dali L. 1996. *Calamity and Reform in China: State, Rural Society, and Institutional
Change Since the Great Leap Famine.* Stanford: Stanford University Press.

Yang, Huayun. 2011a. "Zhong nong ban: jiti tudi zhengshou buchang you nongmin he zhengfu xieshang" 中农办：集体土地征收补偿由农民和政府协商 [Central Office of Rural Affairs: Fixing compensation for requested collective land through consultations between peasants and government]. *Renmin Wang,* January 21. Accessed April 28, 2011. http://finance.people.com.cn/GB/13853330.html.

Yang, Wanli. 2011b. "Pesticides Bring a Silent Spring." *China Daily,* October 19. Accessed October 20, 2011. http://www.chinadaily.com.cn/2011-10/19/content_13929526.htm.

Yeh, Anthony Gar-on. 2005. "The Dual Land Market and Urban Development in China." In *Emerging Land and Housing Markets in China,* edited by Chengri Ding and Yan Song, 39–58. Cambridge, MA: Lincoln Institute of Land Policy.

Yep, Ray. 2013. "Containing Land Grabs: A Misguided Response to Rural Conflicts Over Land." *Journal of Contemporary China* 22(80):273–291.

Yu, Wusheng and Hans G. Jensen. 2010. "China's Agricultural Policy Transition: Impacts of Recent Reforms and Future Scenarios." *Journal of Agricultural Economics* 61(2):343–368.

Yufengzhen Renmin Zhengfu. 2012. "Yufengzhen jiben qingkuang jianjie" 玉丰镇基本情况简介 [Brief introduction to the basic conditions of Yufeng Town]. *Webpage of the People's Government of Yufeng Town,* October 24. Accessed February 6, 2013. http://www.yfzzf.com/Article/ShowArticle.asp?ArticleID=29.

Yuan, Cheng. 2010. *Zhidu Bianqian Guocheng Zhong Nongmin Tudi Quanli Baohu Yanjiu* 制度变迁过程中农民土地权利保护研究 [Research on the process of institutional changes in regard to the protection of peasants' rights to farmland]. Beijing: Zhongguo shehui kexue chubanshe.

Zhang, Forrest Qian. 2012. "The Political Economy of Contract Farming in China's Agrarian Transition." *Journal of Agrarian Change* 12(4):460–483.

Zhang, Forrest Qian, Qingguo Ma, and Xu Xu. 2004. "Development of Land Rental Markets in Rural Zhejiang: Growth of Off-Farm Jobs and Institution Building." *The China Quarterly* 180:1050–1072.

Zhang, Forrest Qian and John A. Donaldson. 2008. "The Rise of Agrarian Capitalism with Chinese Characteristics: Agricultural Modernization, Agribusiness and Collective Land Rights." *The China Journal* 60:25–47.

Zhang, Forrest Qian and John A. Donaldson. 2010. "From Peasants to Farmers: Peasant Differentiation, Labor Regimes, and Land-Rights Institutions in China's Agrarian Transition." *Politics & Society* 38(4):458–489.

Zhang, Shengnan. 2008. "Woguo nongcun gaige zhong tudi liuzhuan moshi tansuo" 我国农村改革中土地流转模式探索 [Investigation into the different modes of land transfer in the Chinese rural reform efforts]. *Guotu Ziyuan* 国土资源 [Land and Resources] 10:26–29.

Zhao, Pan. 2010. "Qiantan nongcun jiceng fubai jiqi fangkong duice" 浅谈农村基层腐败及其防空对策 [Brief discussion of corruption at the grassroots level in the countryside and countermeasures]. *Fazhi yu Shehui* 法制与社会 [Legal System and Society]:221, 231.

Zhao, Shukai. 2007. "The Debt Chaos of Township Governments." *Chinese Sociology & Anthropology* 39(2):36–44.

Zhe, Xiaoye and Yingying Chen. 2011. "Xiangmuzhi de fenji yunzao jizhi he zhili luoji" 项目制的分级运作机制和治理逻辑 [The operating classification mechanism and administrative logic of the project-based system]. *Zhongguo Shehui Kexue* 中国社会科学 [Social Science in China] 4:126–148.

Zheng, Jinran. 2011. "Courts Want Humane Approach in Demolitions." *China Daily,* September 10. Accessed December 13, 2011. http://www.chinadaily.com.cn/china/2011-09/10/content_13663289.htm.

Zhong, Yang. 2003. *Local Government and Politics in China: Challenges from Below.* Armonk, NY: M. E. Sharpe.

Zhongbanfa. 1996. "Zhonggong Zhongyang Bangongting guanyu yinfa《Zhongguo Gongchandang jiguan gongwen chuli tiaoli》de tongzhi" 中共中央办公厅关于印发

《中国共产党机关公文处理条例》的通知 [Notice of the General Office of the Central Committee of the Communist Party of China regarding the publication of 《Regulations for Organizations of the Communist Party of China regarding the handling of official documents》]. No. 14. Zhonggong Zhongyang Bangongting 中共中央办公厅 [General Office of the Central Committee of the Communist Party of China].

Zhongbanfa. 1997. "Zhonggong Zhongyang Bangongting、Guowuyuan Bangongting guanyu jin yibu wending he wanshan nongcun tudi chengbao guanxi de tongzhi" 中共中央办公厅、国务院办公厅关于进一步稳定和完善农村土地承包关系的通知 [Notice of the General Office of the Central Committee of the Communist Party of China and the General Office of the State Council Regarding Efforts to Stabilize and Perfect the Rural Land Contracting System One Step Further]. No. 16. Zhonggong Zhongyang Bangongting、Guowuyuan Bangongting 中共中央办公厅、国务院办公厅 [General Office of the Central Committee of the Communist Party of China and General Office of the State Council].

Zhongfa. 1993. "Zhonggong Zhongyang、Guowuyuan guanyu dangqian nongye he nongcun jingji fazhan de ruogan zhengce cuoshi" 中共中央、国务院关于当前农业和农村经济发展的若干政策措施 [A Number of Policy Measures by the Central Committee of the Chinese Communist Party of China and the State Council to Economically Develop the Present Agriculture and Villages]. No. 11. Zhonggong Zhongyang, Guowuyuan 中共中央, 国务院 [Central Comittee of the Communist Party of China and the State Council].

Zhongfa. 2005. "Zhonggong Zhongyang、Guowuyuan guanyu tuijin shehui zhuyi xin nongcun jianshe de ruogan yijian" 中共中央、国务院关于进一步加强农村工作提高农业综合生产能力若干政策的意见 [Several Suggestions of the Central Committee of the Communist Party of China and the State Council on Pushing Forward the Building of a New Socialist Countryside]. No. 1. Zhonggong Zhongyang、Guowuyuan 中共中央、国务院 [Central Committee of the Communist Party of China and State Council].

Zhongfa. 2008a. "Zhonggong Zhongyang guanyu tuijin nongcun gaige fazhan ruogan zhongda wenti de jueding" 中共中央关于推进农村改革发展若干重大问题的决定 [Decision of the Central Committee of the Communist Party of China on Several Big Issues on Promoting the Reform and Development of Rural Areas]. No. 16. Zhonggong Zhongyang 中共中央 [Central Committee of the Communist Party of China].

Zhongfa. 2008b. "Zhonggong Zhongyang、Guowuyuan guanyu 2009 nian cujin nongye wending fazhan nongmin chixu zengshou de ruogan yijian" 中共中央、国务院2009年促进农业稳定发展农民持续增收的若干意见 [Several Suggestions of the Central Committee of the CCP and the State Council on Accelerating Stable Development of Agriculture and Increasing Peasant Incomes in 2009]. Zhonggong Zhongyang、Guowuyuan 中共中央、国务院 [Central Committee of the Communist Party of China and the State Council].

Zhonggong Zhongyang, Guowuyuan. 2001. "Zhonggong Zhongyang、Guowuyuan guanyu zuohao 2001 nian nongye he nongcun gongzuo de yijian" 中共中央、国务院关于做好2001年农业和农村工作的意见 [Opinion of the Central Committee of the Communist Party of China and the State Council Regarding the Work to Complete in Agriculture and the Countryside in the Year 2001]. Zhonggong Zhongyang, Guowuyuan 中共中央, 国务院 [Central Committee of the Communist Party of China and the State Council].

Zhou, Kate Xiao. 1996. *How the Farmers Changed China: Power of the People*. Boulder, CO: Westview Press.

Zhou, Xueguang. 2010. "The Institutional Logic of Collusion among Local Governments in China." *Modern China* 36(1):47–78.

Zhou, Xueguang. 2012. "The Road to Collective Debt in Rural China: Bureaucracies, Social Institutions, and Public Goods Provision." *Modern China* 38(3):271–307.

Zhu, Ling and Zhongyi Jiang. 1993. "From Brigade to Village Community: The Land Tenure System and Rural Development in China." *Cambridge Journal of Economics* 17(4):441–461.

Zhuxiling. 1987. "Zhonghua Renmin Gongheguo Cunmin Weiyuanhui Zuzhifa" 中华人民共和国村民委员组织法 [Organic Law of the Villagers Committees of the People's Republic of China]. No. 59. Quanguo Renmin Daibiao Dahui Changwu Weiyuanhui 全国人民代表大会常务委员会 [Standing Committee of National People's Congress].

Zhuxiling. 1993. "Zhonghua Renmin Gongheguo Nongyefa" 中华人民共和国农业法 [Agriculture Law of the People's Republic of China]. No. 6 [1993]. Quanguo Renmin Daibiao Dahui Changwu Weiyuanhui 全国人民代表大会常务委员会 [Standing Committee of National People's Congress].

Zhuxiling. 1998. "Zhonghua Renmin Gongheguo Cunmin Weiyuanhui Zuzhifa" 中华人民共和国村民委员会组织法 [Organic Law of the Villagers Committees of the People's Republic of China]. No. 9. Quanguo Renda Changweihui 全国人大常委会 [Standing Committee of National People's Congress].

Zhuxiling. 2003. "Zhonghua Renmin Gongheguo Nongcun Tudi Chengbaofa" 中华人民共和国农村土地承包法 [Law on Contracting Rural Land of the People's Republic of China]. No. 73. Quanguo Renda Changweihui 全国人大常委会 [Standing Committee of National People's Congress].

Zhuxiling. 2007a. "Zhonghua Renmin Gongheguo Nongmin Zhuanye Hezuoshe Fa" 中华人民共和国农民专业合作法 [Peasants' Specialized Cooperatives Law of the People's Republic of China]. No. 57. Quanguo Renmin Daibiaohui 全国人民代表会 [National People's Congress].

Zhuxiling. 2007b. "Zhonghua Renmin Gongheguo Wuquanfa" 中华人民共和国物权法 [Property Law of the People's Republic of China]. No. 62. Quanguo Renmin Daibiao Dahui 全国人民代表大会 [National People's Congress].

Zmolek, Mike. 2004. "Debating Agrarian Capitalism: A Rejoinder to Albritton." *Journal of Peasant Studies* 31(2):276–305.

Zunyishi Tongjiju. 2010. *Zunyishi Tonji Nianjian* 遵义统计年鉴 [Zunyi City Statistical Yearbook]. Zunyi: China Statistics Press.

Zweig, David. 1989. "Struggling Over Land in China: Peasant Resistance after Collectivization, 1966–1986." In *Everyday Forms of Peasant Resistance,* edited by Forrest D. Colburn, New York: M. E. Sharpe.

Index

About the Author

René Trappel is lecturer at the Institute of Chinese Studies at Albert Ludwigs University of Freiburg. His main research interests include comparative politics, rural China, political economy, and local governance.